AN AREA OF DARKNESS

V. S. NAIPAUL

An Area of Darkness

Vintage Books
A Division of Random House
New York

First Vintage Books Edition, March 1981
Copyright © 1964 by V.S. Naipaul
All rights reserved under International and
Pan-American Copyright Conventions. Published in
the United States by Random House, Inc., New York.
Originally published by Andre Deutsch Limited,
London, in September 1964.

Library of Congress Cataloging in Publication Data
Naipaul, V.S. (Vidiadhar Surajprasad), 1932-
An area of darkness.
Originally published: London: A. Deutsch, 1964.
1. India—Description and travel—1947-
2. Naipaul, V.S. (Vidiadhar Surajprasad), 1932-
3. India—Social life and customs. I. Titlc.
DS414.N23 1981   954   80-6132
ISBN 0-394-74673-2   AACR2

Manufactured in the United States of America

To
FRANCIS WYNDHAM

CONTENTS

AN AREA OF DARKNESS

Traveller's Prelude: A Little Paperwork

As soon as our quarantine flag came down and the last of the barefooted, blue-uniformed policemen of the Bombay Port Health Authority had left the ship, Coelho the Goan came aboard and, luring me with a long beckoning finger into the saloon, whispered, 'You have any cheej?'

Coelho had been sent by the travel agency to help me through the customs. He was tall and thin and shabby and nervous, and I imagined he was speaking of some type of contraband. He was. He required cheese. It was a delicacy in India. Imports were restricted, and the Indians had not yet learned how to make cheese, just as they had not yet learned how to bleach newsprint. But I couldn't help Coelho. The cheese on this Greek freighter was not good. Throughout the three-week journey from Alexandria I had been complaining about it to the impassive chief steward, and I didn't feel I could ask him now for some to take ashore.

'All right, all right,' Coelho said, not believing me and not willing to waste time listening to excuses. He left the saloon and began prowling lightfootedly down a corridor, assessing the names above doors.

I went down to my cabin. I opened a new bottle of Scotch and took a sip. Then I opened a bottle of Metaxas and took a sip of that. These were the two bottles of spirits I was hoping to take into prohibition-dry Bombay, and this was the precaution my friend in the Indian Tourist Department had advised: full bottles would be confiscated.

Coelho and I met later in the dining room. He had lost a little of his nervousness. He was carrying a very large Greek doll, its folk costume gaudy against his own shabby trousers and shirt, its rosy cheeks and unblinking blue eyes serene beside the restlessly melancholy of his long thin face. He saw my opened bottles and nervousness returned to him.

'Open. But why?'

'Isn't that the law?'

'Hide them.'

'The Metaxas is too tall to hide.'

'Put it flat.'

'I don't trust the cork. But don't they allow you to take in two bottles?'

'I don't know, I don't know. Just hold this dolly for me. Carry it in your hand. Say souvenir. You have your Tourist Introduction Card? Good. Very valuable document. With a document like that they wouldn't search you. Why don't you hide the bottles?'

He clapped his hands and at once a barefooted man, stunted and bony, appeared and began to take our suitcases away. He had been waiting, unseen, unheard, ever since Coelho came aboard. Carrying only the doll and the bag containing the bottles, we climbed down into the launch. Coelho's man stowed away the suitcases. Then he squatted on the floor, as though to squeeze himself into the smallest possible space, as though to apologise for his presence, even at the exposed stern, in the launch in which his master was travelling. The master, only occasionally glancing at the doll in my lap, stared ahead, his face full of foreboding.

For me the East had begun weeks before. Even in Greece I had felt Europe falling away. There was the East in the food, the emphasis on sweets, some of which I knew from my childhood; in the posters for Indian films with the actress Nargis, a favourite, I was told, of Greek audiences; in the instantaneous friendships, the invitations to meals and homes. Greece was a preparation for Egypt: Alexandria at sunset, a wide shining arc in the winter sea; beyond the breakwaters, a glimpse through fine rain of the ex-king's white yacht; the ship's engine cut off; then abruptly, as at a signal, a roar from the quay, shouting and quarrelling and jabbering from men in grubby jibbahs who in an instant overran the already crowded ship and kept on running through it. And it was clear that here, and not in Greece, the East began: in this chaos of uneconomical movement, the self-stimulated din, the sudden feeling of insecurity, the conviction that all men were not brothers and that luggage was in danger.

Here was to be learned the importance of the guide, the man who knew local customs, the fixer to whom badly printed illiterate forms held no mysteries. 'Write here,' my guide said in the customs house, aswirl with porters and guides and officials and idlers and policemen and travellers and a Greek refugee whispering in my ear, 'Let me warn you. They are stealing tonight.' 'Write here. One Kodak.' He, the guide, indicated the dotted line marked *date*. 'And here,' pointing to *signature*, 'write no gold, ornaments or precious stones.' I objected. He said, 'Write.' He pronounced it like an Arabic word. He was tall, grave, Hollywood-sinister; he wore a fez and lightly tapped his thigh with a cane. I wrote. And it worked. 'And now,' he said, exchanging the fez marked *Travel Agent* for one marked *Hotel X*, 'let us go to the hotel.'

Thereafter, feature by feature, the East, known only from books, had continued to reveal itself; and each recognition was a discovery, as much as it had been a revelation to see the jibbah, a garment made almost mythical by countless photographs and descriptions, on the backs of real people. In the faded hotel, full, one felt, of memories of the Raj, there was a foreshadowing of the caste system. The old French waiter only served; he had his runners, sad-eyed silent Negroes in fezzes and cummerbunds, who fetched and cleared away. In the lobby there were innumerable Negro pages, picturesquely attired. And in the streets there was the East one had expected: the children, the dirt, the disease, the undernourishment, the cries of *bakshish*, the hawkers, the touts, the glimpses of minarets. There were the reminders of imperialisms that had withdrawn in the dark, glasscased European-style shops, wilting for lack of patronage; in the sad whispering of the French hairdresser that French perfumes could no longer be obtained and that one had to make do with heavy Egyptian scents; in the disparaging references of the Lebanese business-man to 'natives', all of whom he distrusted except for his assistant who, quietly to me, spoke of the day when all the Lebanese and Europeans would be driven out of the country.

Feature by feature, the East one had read about. On the train to Cairo the man across the aisle hawked twice, with an expert tongue rolled the phlegm into a ball, plucked the ball out of his mouth with thumb and forefinger, considered it, and then rubbed it away between his palms. He was wearing a three-piece suit, and his transistor played loudly. Cairo re-vealed the meaning of the bazaar: narrow streets encrusted with filth, stinking even on this winter's day; tiny shops full of shoddy goods; crowds; the din, already barely supportable, made worse by the steady blaring of motorcar horns; medieval buildings partly collapsed, others rising on old rubble, with here and there sections of tiles, turquoise and royal blue, hinting at a past of order and beauty, crystal fountains and amorous adventures, as perhaps in the no less disordered past they always had done.

And in this bazaar, a cobbler. With white skullcap, lined face, steelrimmed spectacles and white beard, he might have posed for a photograph in the *National Geographic Magazine*: the skilled and patient Oriental craftsman. My sole was flapping. Could he repair it? Sitting almost flat on the pavement, bowed over his work, he squinted at my shoes, my trousers, my raincoat. 'Fifty piastres.' I said: 'Four'. He nodded, pulled the shoe off my foot and with a carpenter's hammer began hammering in a one-inch nail. I grabbed the shoe; he, smiling, hammer raised, held on to it. I pulled; he let go.

The Pyramids, whose function as a public latrine no guide book mentions, were made impossible by guides, 'watchmen', camel-drivers and by boys whose donkeys were all called Whisky-and-soda. *Bakshish! Bakshish!* 'Come and have a cup of coffee. I don't want you to buy anything. I just want to have a little intelligent conversation. Mr Nehru is a great man. Let us exchange ideas. I am a graduate of the university.' I took the desert bus back to Alexandria and, two days before the appointed time, retreated to the Greek freighter.

Then came the tedium of the African ports. Little clearings, one felt them, at the edge of a vast continent; and here one knew that Egypt, for all its Negroes, was not Africa, and for all its minarets and jibbahs, not the East: it was the last of Europe. At Jeddah the jibbahs were cleaner, the American automobiles new and numerous and driven with great style. We were not permitted to land and could see only the life of the port. Camels and goats were being unloaded by cranes and slings from dingy tramp steamers on to the piers; they were to be slaughtered for the ritual feast that marks the end of Ramadan. Swung aloft, the camels splayed out their suddenly useless legs; touching earth, lightly or with a bump, they crouched; then they ran to their fellows and rubbed against them. A fire broke out in a launch; our freighter sounded the alarm and within minutes the fire engines arrived. 'Autocracy has its charms,' the young Pakistani student said.

We had touched Africa, and four of the passengers had not been inoculated against yellow fever. A Pakistan-fed smallpox epidemic was raging in Britain and we feared stringency in Karachi. The Pakistani officials came aboard, drank a good deal, and our quarantine was waived. At Bombay, though, the Indian officials refused alcohol and didn't even finish the Coca-Cola they were offered. They were sorry, but the four passengers would have to go to the isolation hospital at Santa Cruz; either that or the ship would have to stay out in the stream. Two of the passengers without inoculations were the captain's parents. We stayed out in the stream.

It had been a slow journey, its impressions varied and superficial. But it had been a preparation for the East. After the bazaar of Cairo the bazaar of Karachi was no surprise; and *bakshish* was the same in both languages. The change from the Mediterranean winter to the sticky high summer of the Red Sea had been swift. But other changes had been slower. From Athens to Bombay another idea of man had defined itself by degrees, a new type of authority and subservience. The physique of Europe had melted away first into that of Africa and then, through Semitic Arabia, into Aryan Asia. Men had been diminished and deformed; they begged and whined. Hysteria had been my reaction, and a brutality dictated by a new awareness of myself as a whole human being and a determination, touched with fear, to remain what I was. It mattered little through whose eyes I was seeing the East; there had as yet been no time for this type of self-assessment.

Superficial impressions, intemperate reactions. But one memory had stayed with me, and I had tried to hold it close during that day out in the stream at Bombay, when I had seen the sun set behind the Taj Mahal Hotel and had wished that Bombay was only another port such as those we had touched on the journey, a port that the freighter passenger might explore or reject.

It was at Alexandria. Here we had been pestered most by horsecabs. The horses were ribby, the coachwork as tattered as the garments of the drivers. The drivers hailed you; they drove their cabs beside you and left you only when another likely fare appeared. It had been good to get away from them, and from the security of the ship to watch them make their assault on others. It was like watching a silent film: the victim sighted, the racing cab, the victim engaged, gesticulations, the cab moving beside the victim and matching his pace, at first brisk, then exaggeratedly slow, then steady.

Then one morning the desert vastness of the dock was quickened with activity, and it was as if the silent film had become a silent epic. Long rows of two-toned taxicabs were drawn up outside the terminal building; scattered all over the dock area, as though awaiting a director's call to action, were black little clusters of horsecabs; and steadily, through the dock gates, far to the right, more taxis and cabs came rolling in. The horses galloped, the drivers' whip hands worked. It was a brief exaltation. Soon enough for each cab came repose, at the edge of a cab-cluster. The cause of the excitement was presently seen: a large white liner, possibly carrying tourists, possibly carrying ten-pound immigrants to Australia. Slowly, silently, she idled in. And more taxis came pelting through the gates, and more cabs, racing in feverishly to an anti-climax of nosebags and grass.

The liner docked early in the morning. It was not until noon that the first passengers came out of the terminal building into the wasteland of the dock area. This was like the director's call. Grass was snatched from the asphalt and thrust into boxes below the drivers' seats; and every passenger became the target of several converging attacks. Pink, inexperienced, timid and vulnerable these passengers appeared to us. They carried baskets and cameras; they wore straw hats and bright cotton shirts for the Egyptian winter (a bitter wind was blowing from the sea). But our sympathies had shifted; we were on the side of the Alexandrians. They had waited all morning; they had arrived with high panache and zeal; we wanted them to engage, conquer and drive away with their victims through the dock gates.

But this was not to be. Just when the passengers had been penned by cabs and taxis, and gestures of remonstrance had given way to stillness, so that it seemed escape was impossible and capture certain, two shiny motorcoaches came through the dock gates. From the ship they looked like expensive toys. They cleared a way through taxis and cabs, which closed in again and then opened out to permit the coaches to make a slow, wide turn; and where before there had been tourists in gay cottons there was now only asphalt. The cabs, as though unwilling to accept the finality of this disappearance, backed and moved forward as if in pursuit. Then without haste they made their way back to their respective stations, where the horses retrieved from the asphalt what grass had escaped the hurried snatch of the drivers.

All through the afternoon the cabs and taxis remained, waiting for passengers who had not gone on the coaches. These passengers were few; they came out in ones and twos; and they appeared to prefer the taxis. But the enthusiasm of the horsecabs did not wane. Still, when a passenger appeared, the drivers jumped on to their seats, lashed their thin horses into action and rattled away to engage, transformed from idlers in old overcoats and scarves into figures of skill and purpose. Sometimes they engaged; often then there were disputes between drivers and the passengers withdrew. Sometimes a cab accompanied a passenger to the very gates. Sometimes at that point we saw the tiny walker halt; and then, with triumph and relief, we saw him climb into the cab. But this was rare.

The light faded. The cabs no longer galloped to engage. They wheeled and went at walking pace. The wind became keener; the dock grew dark; lights appeared. But the cabs remained. It was only later, when the liner blazed with lights, even its smokestack illuminated, and hope had been altogether extinguished, that they went away one by one, leaving behind shreds of grass and horse-droppings where they had stood.

Later that night I went up to the deck. Not far away, below a lamp standard stood a lone cab. It had been there since the late afternoon; it had withdrawn early from the turmoil around the terminal. It had had no fares, and there could be no fares for it now. The cab-lamp burned low; the horse was eating grass from a shallow pile on the road. The driver, wrapped against the wind, was polishing the dully gleaming hood of his cab with a large rag. The polishing over, he dusted; then he gave the horse a brief, brisk rub down. Less than a minute later he was out of his cab again, polishing, dusting, brushing. He went in; he came out. His actions were compulsive. The animal chewed; his coat shone; the cab gleamed. And there were no fares. And next morning the liner had gone, and the dock was desert again.

Now, sitting in the launch about to tie up at the Bombay pier where the names on cranes and buildings were, so oddly, English; feeling unease at the thought of the mute animal crouching on the floor at his master's back, and a similar unease at the sight of figures—not of romance, as the first figures seen on a foreign shore ought to be—on the pier, their frailty and raggedness contrasting with the stone buildings and metal cranes; now I tried to remember that in Bombay, as in Alexandria, there could be no pride in power, and that to give way to anger and contempt was to know a later self-disgust.

*

And of course Coelho, guide, fixer, knower of government forms, was right. Bombay was rigorously dry, and my two opened bottles of spirit were seized by the customs officers in white, who summoned a depressed-looking man in blue to seal them 'in my presence'. The man in blue worked at this manual and therefore degrading labour with slow relish; his manner proclaimed him an established civil servant, however degraded. I was given a receipt and told that I could get the bottles back when I got a liquor permit. Coelho wasn't so sure; these seized bottles, he said, had a habit of breaking. But his own worries were over. There had been no general search; his Greek doll had passed without query. He took it and his fee and disappeared into Bombay; I never saw him again.

To be in Bombay was to be exhausted. The moist heat sapped energy and will, and some days passed before I decided to recover my bottles. I decided in the morning; I started in the afternoon. I stood in the shade of Churchgate Station and debated whether I had it in me to cross the exposed street to the Tourist Office. Debate languished into daydream; it was minutes before I made the crossing. A flight of steps remained. I sat below a fan and rested. A lure greater than a liquor permit roused me: the office upstairs was airconditioned. There India was an ordered, even luxurious country. The design was contemporary; the walls were hung with maps and coloured photographs; and there were little wooden racks of leaflets and booklets. Too soon my turn came; my idleness was over. I filled in my form. The clerk filled in his, three to my one, made entries in various ledgers and presented me with a sheaf of foolscap papers: my liquor permit. He had been prompt and courteous. I thanked him. There was no need, he said; it was only a little paperwork.

One step a day: this was my rule. And it was not until the following afternoon that I took a taxi back to the docks. The customs officers in white and the degraded man in blue were surprised to see me.

'Did you leave something here?'

'I left two bottles of liquor.'

'You didn't. We seized two bottles from you. They were sealed in your presence.'

'That's what I meant. I've come to get them back.'

'But we don't keep seized liquor here. Everything we seize and seal is sent off at once to the New Customs House.'

My taxi was searched on the way out.

The New Customs House was a large, two-storeyed PWD building, governmentally gloomy, and it was as thronged as a courthouse. There were people in the drive, in the galleries, on the steps, in the corridors. 'Liquor, liquor,' I said, and was led from office to office, each full of shrunken, bespectacled young men in white shirts sitting at desks shaggily stacked with paper. Someone sent me upstairs. On the landing I came upon a barefooted group seated on the stone floor. At first I thought they were playing cards: it was a popular Bombay pavement pastime. But they were sorting parcels. Their spokesman told me I had been misdirected; I needed the building at the back. This building, from the quantity of ragged clothing seen in one of the lower rooms, appeared to be a tenement; and then, from the number of broken chairs and dusty pieces of useless furniture seen in another room, appeared to be a junkshop. But it was the place for unclaimed baggage and was therefore the place I wanted. Upstairs I stood in a slow queue, at the end of which I discovered only an accountant.

'You don't want me. You want that officer in the white pants. Over there. He is a nice fellow.'

I went to him.

'You have your liquor permit?'

I showed him the stamped and signed foolscap sheaf.

'You have your transport permit?'

It was the first I had heard of this permit.

'You must have a transport permit.'

I was exhausted, sweating, and when I opened my mouth to speak I found I was on the verge of tears. 'But they *told* me.'

He was sympathetic. 'We have told them many times.'

I thrust all the papers I had at him: my liquor permit, my customs receipt, my passport, my receipt for wharfage charges, my Tourist Introduction Card.

Dutifully he looked through what I offered. 'No. I would have known at once whether you had a transport permit. By the colour of the paper. A sort of buff.'

'But what is a transport permit? Why didn't they give it to me? Why do I need one?'

'I must have it before I can surrender anything.'

'Please.'

'Sorry.'

'I am going to write to the papers about this.'

'I wish you would. I keep telling them they must tell people about this transport permit. Not only for you. We had an American here yesterday who said he was going to break the bottle as soon as he got it.'

'Help me. Where can I get this transport permit?'

'The people who gave you the receipt should also give you the transport permit.'

'But I've just come from them.'

'I don't know. We keep on telling them.'

'Back to the Old Customs,' I said to the taxi-driver.

This time the police at the gates recognised us and didn't search the car. This dock had been my own gateway to India. Only a few days before everything in it had been new: the sticky black asphalt, the money-changers' booths, the stalls, the people in white, khaki or blue: everything had been studied for what it portended of India beyond the gates. Now already I had ceased to see or care. My stupor, though, was tempered by the thought of the small triumph that awaited me· I had trapped those customs officers in white and that degraded mar in blue.

They didn't look trapped.

'Transport permit?' one said. 'Are you sure?'

'Did you tell them you were leaving Bombay?' asked a second.

'*Transport* permit?' said a third and, walking away to a fourth, asked, 'Transport permit, ever hear of *transport* permit?'

He had. 'They've been writing us about it.'

A transport permit was required to transport liquor from the customs to a hotel or house.

'Please give me a transport permit.'

'We don't issue transport permits. You have to go—' He looked up at me and his manner softened. 'Here, let me write it down for you. And look, I will also give you your code-number. That will help them out at the New Customs.'

The taxi-driver had so far been calm; and it seemed now that my journeys had fallen into a pattern that was familiar to him. I began to read out the address that had been given me. He cut me short and without another word buzzed through the thickening afternoon traffic to a large brick building hung with black-and-white government boards.

'You go,' he said sympathetically. 'I wait.

Outside every office there was a little crowd.

'Transport permit, transport permit.'

Some Sikhs directed me round to the back to a low shed next to a gate marked *Prohibited Area*, out of which workers came, one after the other, raising their hands while armed soldiers frisked them.

'Transport permit, transport permit.'

I entered a long corridor and found myself among some Sikhs. They were lorry-drivers.

'Liquor permit, liquor permit.'

And at last I reached the office. It was a long low room at ground level, hidden from the scorching sun and as dark as a London basement, but warm and dusty with the smell of old paper, which was everywhere, on shelves rising to the grey ceiling, on desks, on chairs, in the hands of clerks, in the hands of khaki-clad messengers. Folders had grown dog-eared, their colours faded, their spines abraded to transparency, their edges limp with reverential handling; and to many were attached pink slips, equally faded, equally limp, marked URGENT, VERY URGENT, or IMMEDIATE. Between these mounds and columns and buttresses of paper, clerks were scattered about unimportantly, men and women, mild-featured, Indian-pallid, high-shouldered; paper was their perfect camouflage. An elderly bespectacled man sat at a desk in one corner, his face slightly puffy and dyspeptic. Tremulous control of the

paper-filled room was his: at his disappearance the clerks
might be altogether overwhelmed.

'Transport permit?'

He looked up slowly. He showed no surprise, no displeasure
at being disturbed. Papers, pink-slipped, were spread all over
his desk. A table fan, nicely poised, blew over them without
disturbance.

'Transport permit.' He spoke the words mildly, as though
they were rare words but words which, after searching for
only a second in the files of his mind, he had traced. 'Write an
application. Only one is necessary.'

'Do you have the form?'

'No forms have been issued. Write a letter. Here, have a
sheet of paper. Sit down and write. To the Collector, Excise
and Prohibition, Bombay. Do you have your passport? Put
down the number. Oh, and you have a Tourist Introduction
Card. Put down that number too. I will expedite matters.'

And while I wrote, noting down the number of my Tourist
Introduction Card, TIO (L) 156, he, expediting matters,
passed my documents over to a woman clerk, saying, 'Miss
Desai, could you start making out a transport permit?' I
thought I detected an odd pride in his voice. He was like a man
still after many years discovering the richness and variety of
his work and subduing an excitement which he nevertheless
wished to communicate to his subordinates.

I was finding it hard to spell and to frame simple sentences.
I crumpled up the sheet of paper.

The head clerk looked up at me in gentle reproof. 'Only one
application is necessary.'

At my back Miss Desai filled in forms with that blunt,
indelible, illegible pencil which government offices throughout
the former Empire use, less for the sake of what is written than
for the sake of the copies required.

I managed to complete my application.

And at this point my companion slumped forward on her
chair, hung her head between her knees and fainted.

'Water,' I said to Miss Desai.

She barely paused in her writing and pointed to an empty dusty glass on a shelf.

The head clerk, already frowningly preoccupied with other papers, regarded the figure slumped in front of him.

'Not feeling well?' His voice was as mild and even as before. 'Let her rest.' He turned the table fan away from him.

'Where is the water?'

Giggles came from women clerks, hidden behind paper.

'Water!' I cried to a male clerk.

He rose, saying nothing, walked to the end of the room and vanished.

Miss Desai finished her writing. Giving me a glance as of terror, she brought her tall bloated pad to the head clerk.

'The transport permit is ready,' he said. 'As soon as you are free you can sign for it.'

The male clerk returned, waterless, and sat down at his desk.

'Where is the water?'

His eyes distastefully acknowledged my impatience. He neither shrugged nor spoke; he went on with his papers.

It was worse than impatience. It was ill-breeding and ingratitude. For presently, sporting his uniform as proudly as any officer, a messenger appeared. He carried a tray and on the tray stood a glass of water. I should have known better. A clerk was a clerk; a messenger was a messenger.

The crisis passed.

I signed three times and received my permit.

The head clerk opened another folder.

'Nadkarni,' he called softly to a clerk. 'I don't understand this memo.'

I had been forgotten already.

It was suffocatingly hot in the taxi, the seats scorching. We drove to the flat of a friend and stayed there until it was dark.

A friend of our friend came in.

'What's wrong?'

'We went to get a transport permit and she fainted.' I did not wish to sound critical. I added, 'Perhaps it's the heat.'

'It isn't the heat at all. Always the heat or the water with you people from outside. There's nothing wrong with her. You make up your minds about India before coming to the country. You've been reading the wrong books.'

The officer who had sent me on the track of the transport permit was pleased to see me back. But the transport permit wasn't enough. I had to go to Mr Kulkarni to find out about the warehouse charges. When I had settled what the charges were I was to come back to that clerk over there, with the blue shirt; then I had to go to the cashier, to pay the warehouse charges; then I had to go back to Mr Kulkarni to get my bottles.

I couldn't find Mr Kulkarni. My papers were in my hand. Someone tried to take them. I knew he was expressing only his kindness and curiosity. I pulled the papers back. He looked at me; I looked at him. I yielded. He went through my papers and said with authority that I had come to the wrong building.

I screamed: '*Mr Kulkarni!*'

Everyone around me was startled. Someone came up to me, calmed me down and led me to the adjoining room where Mr Kulkarni had been all along. I rushed to the head of the queue and began to shout at Mr Kulkarni, waving my papers at him. He got hold of them as I waved and began to read. Some Sikhs in the queue complained. Mr Kulkarni replied that I was in a hurry, that I was a person of importance, and that in any case I was younger. Curiously, they were pacified.

Mr Kulkarni called for ledgers. They were brought to him. Turning the crisp pages, not looking up, he made a loose-wristed gesture of indefinable elegance with his yellow pencil. The Sikhs at once separated into two broken lines. Mr Kulkarni put on his spectacles, studied the calendar on the far wall, counted on his fingers, took off his spectacles and returned to his ledgers. He made another abstracted gesture with his pencil and the Sikhs fell into line again, obscuring the calendar.

Upstairs again. The clerk with the blue shirt stamped on Mr Kulkarni's sheet of paper and made entries in two ledgers. The cashier added his own stamp. I paid him and he made entries in two more ledgers.

'It's all right,' the officer said, scanning the twice-stamped and thrice-signed sheet of paper. He added his own signature. 'You're safe now. Go down to Mr Kulkarni. And be quick. They might be closing any minute.'

Part I

1. A RESTING-PLACE FOR THE IMAGINATION

These Antipodes call to one's mind old recollections of childish doubt and wonder. Only the other day I looked forward to this airy barrier as a definite point in our journey homewards; but now I find it, and all such resting-places for the imagination, are like shadows, which a man moving onwards cannot catch.

CHARLES DARWIN: *Voyage of the Beagle*

You've been reading the wrong books, the businessman said. But he did me an injustice. I had read any number of the books which he would have considered right. And India had in a special way been the background of my childhood. It was the country from which my grandfather came, a country never physically described and therefore never real, a country out in the void beyond the dot of Trinidad; and from it our journey had been final. It was a country suspended in time; it could not be related to the country, discovered later, which was the subject of the many correct books issued by Mr Gollancz and Messrs Allen and Unwin and was the source of agency despatches in the *Trinidad Guardian*. It remained a special, isolated area of ground which had produced my grandfather and others I knew who had been born in India and had come to Trinidad as indentured labourers, though that past too had fallen into the void into which India had fallen, for they carried no mark of indenture, no mark even of having been labourers.

There was an old lady, a friend of my mother's family. She was jewelled, fair and white-haired; she was very grand. She spoke only Hindi. The elegance of her manner and the grave handsomeness of her husband, with his thick white moustache, his spotless Indian dress and his silence, which compensated

29

for his wife's bustling authority, impressed them early upon
me as a couple who, though so friendly and close—they ran a
tiny shop not far from my grandmother's establishment—as
to be considered almost relations, were already foreign. They
came from India; this gave them glamour, but the glamour was
itself a barrier. They not so much ignored Trinidad as denied
it; they made no attempt even to learn English, which was what
the children spoke. The lady had two or three gold teeth and
was called by everyone Gold Teeth Nanee, Gold Teeth
Grandmother, the mixture of English and Hindi revealing to
what extent the world to which she belonged was receding.
Gold Teeth was childless. This probably accounted for her
briskness and her desire to share my grandmother's authority
over the children. It did not make her better liked. But she had
a flaw. She was as greedy as a child; she was a great uninvited
eater, whom it was easy to trap with a square of laxative
chocolate. One day she noticed a tumbler of what looked like
coconut milk. She tasted, she drank to the end, and fell ill;
and in her distress made a confession which was like a reproach.
She had drunk a tumbler of blanco fluid. It was astonishing
that she should have drunk to the end; but in matters of food
she was, unusually for an Indian, experimental and pertinacious. She was to carry the disgrace till her death. So one
India crashed; and as we grew older, living now in the town,
Gold Teeth dwindled to a rustic oddity with whom there could
be no converse. So remote her world seemed then, so dead;
yet how little time separated her from us!

Then there was Babu. Moustached, as grave and silent as
Gold Teeth's husband, he occupied a curious position in my
grandmother's household. He too was born in India; and why
he should have lived alone in one room at the back of the
kitchen I never understood. It is an indication of the narrowness of the world in which we lived as children that all I knew
about Babu was that he was a *kshatriya*, one of the warrior
caste: this solitary man who, squatting in his dark room at
the end of the day, prepared his own simple food, kneading
flour, cutting vegetables and doing other things which I had
always thought of as woman's work. Could this man from the

warrior caste have been a labourer? Inconceivable then; but later, alas, when such disillusionment meant little, to be proved true. We had moved. My grandmother required someone to dig a well. It was Babu who came, from that back room where he had continued to live. The well deepened; Babu was let down in a hammock, which presently brought up the earth he had excavated. One day no more earth came up. Babu had struck rock. He came up on the hammock for the last time and went away back into that void from which he had come. I never saw him again and had of him as a reminder only that deep hole at the edge of the cricket ground. The hole was planked over, but it remained in my imagination a standing nightmare peril to energetic fielders chasing a boundary hit.

More than in people, India lay about us in things: in a string bed or two, grimy, tattered, no longer serving any function, never repaired because there was no one with this caste skill in Trinidad, yet still permitted to take up room; in plaited straw mats; in innumerable brass vessels; in wooden printing blocks, never used because printed cotton was abundant and cheap and because the secret of the dyes had been forgotten, no dyer being at hand; in books, the sheets large, coarse and brittle, the ink thick and oily; in drums and one ruined harmonium; in brightly coloured pictures of deities on pink lotus or radiant against Himalayan snow; and in all the paraphernalia of the prayer-room: the brass bells and gongs and camphor-burners like Roman lamps, the slender-handled spoon for the doling out of the consecrated 'nectar' (peasant's nectar: on ordinary days brown sugar and water, with some shreds of the tulsi leaf, sweetened milk on high days), the images, the smooth pebbles, the stick of sandalwood.

The journey had been final. And it was only on this trip to India that I was to see how complete a transference had been made from eastern Uttar Pradesh to Trinidad, and that in days when the village was some hours' walk from the nearest branch-line railway station, the station more than a day's journey from the port, and that anything up to three months' sailing from Trinidad. In its artefacts India existed whole in Trinidad. But our community, though seemingly self-contained, was imperfect. Sweepers we had quickly learned to do without. Others supplied the skills of carpenters, masons and cobblers. But we were also without weavers and dyers, workers in brass and makers of string-beds. Many of the things in my grand-mother's house were therefore irreplaceable. They were cherished because they came from India, but they continued to be used and no regret attached to their disintegration. It was an Indian attitude, as I was to recognise. Customs are to be maintained because they are felt to be ancient. This is con-tinuity enough; it does not need to be supported by a cultiva-tion of the past, and the old, however hallowed, be it a Gupta image or a string-bed, is to be used until it can be used no more.

To me as a child the India that had produced so many of the persons and things around me was featureless, and I thought of the time when the transference was made as a period of darkness, darkness which also extended to the land, as darkness surrounds a hut at evening, though for a little way around the hut there is still light. The light was the area of my experience, in time and place. And even now, though time has widened, though space has contracted and I have travelled lucidly over that area which was to me the area of darkness, something of darkness remains, in those attitudes, those ways of thinking and seeing, which are no longer mine. My grand-father had made a difficult and courageous journey. It must have brought him into collision with startling sights, even like the sea, several hundred miles from his village; yet I cannot help feeling that as soon as he had left his village he ceased to see. When he went back to India it was to return with more things of India. When he built his house he ignored every colonial style he might have found in Trinidad and put up a heavy, flat-roofed oddity, whose image I was to see again and again in the small ramshackle towns of Uttar Pradesh. He had abandoned India; and, like Gold Teeth, he denied Trinidad. Yet he walked on solid earth. Nothing beyond his village had stirred him; nothing had forced him out of himself; he carried his village with him. A few reassuring relationships, a strip of land, and he could satisfyingly recreate an eastern Uttar Pradesh village in central Trinidad as if in the vastness of India.

We who came after could not deny Trinidad. The house we lived in was distinctive, but not more distinctive than many. It was easy to accept that we lived on an island where there were all sorts of people and all sorts of houses. Doubtless they too had their own things. We ate certain food, performed certain ceremonies and had certain taboos; we expected others to have their own. We did not wish to share theirs; we did not expect them to share ours. They were what they were; we were what we were. We were never instructed in this. To our condition as Indians in a multi-racial society we gave no thought. Criticism from others there was, as I now realise, but it never penetrated the walls of our house, and I cannot as a child remember hearing any discussion about race. Though permeated with the sense of difference, in racial matters, oddly, I remained an innocent for long. At school I was puzzled by the kinky hair of a teacher I liked; I came to the conclusion that he was still, like me, growing, and that when he had grown a little more his hair would grow straighter and longer. Race was never discussed; but at an early age I understood that Muslims were somewhat more different than others. They were not to be trusted; they would always do you down; and point was given to this by the presence close to my grandmother's house of a Muslim, in whose cap and grey beard, avowals of his especial difference, lay every sort of threat. For the difference we saw as the attribute of every group outside our own was more easily discernible in other Indians and more discernible yet in other Hindus. Racial awareness was to come; in the meantime—and until how recently—for the social antagonisms that give savour to life we relied on the old, Indian divisions, meaningless though these had become.

Everything beyond our family had this quality of difference. This was to be accepted when we went abroad and perhaps even forgotten, as for instance at school. But the moment any intercourse threatened, we scented violation and withdrew. I remember—and this was later, after this family life had broken up—being taken to visit one family. They were not related. This made the visit unusual; and because it became fixed in my mind, no doubt from something that had been said, that they were Muslims, everything about them had heightened difference. I saw it in their appearance, their house, their dress and presently, as I had been fearing, in their food. We were offered some vermicelli done in milk. I believed it to be associated with some unknown and distasteful ritual; I could not eat it. They were in fact Hindus; our families were later joined by marriage.

Inevitably this family life shrank, and the process was accelerated by our removal to the capital, where there were few Indians. The outside world intruded more. We became secretive. But once we made an open assault on the city. My grandmother wished to have a *kattha* said, and she wished to have it said under a pipal tree. There was only one pipal tree in the island; it was in the Botanical Gardens. Permission was applied for. To my amazement it was given; and one Sunday morning we all sat under the pipal tree, botanically labelled, and the pundit read. The crackling sacrificial fire was scented with pitch-pine, brown sugar and ghee; bells were rung, gongs struck, conch-shells blown. We attracted the silent interest of a small mixed crowd of morning strollers and the proselytising attentions of a Seventh Day Adventist. It was a scene of pure pastoral: aryan ritual, of another continent and age, a few hundred yards from the governor's house. But this is a later appreciation. For those of us at school at the time the public ceremony had been a strain. We were becoming selfconscious, self-assessing: our secret world was shrinking fast. Still, very occasionally, some devout Hindu of the few in Port of Spain might wish to feed some brahmins. We were at hand. We went; we were fed; we received gifts of cloth and money. We never questioned our luck. Luck indeed it seemed, for immediately afterwards, walking back home in trousers and shirt, we became ordinary boys again.

To me this luck was touched with fraudulence. I came of a family that abounded with pundits. But I had been born an unbeliever. I took no pleasure in religious ceremonies. They were too long, and the food came only at the end. I did not understand the language—it was as if our elders expected that our understanding would be instinctive—and no one explained the prayers or the ritual. One ceremony was like another. The images didn't interest me; I never sought to learn their significance. With my lack of belief and distaste for ritual there also went a metaphysical incapacity, this again a betrayal of heredity, for my father's appetite for Hindu speculation was great. So it happened that, though growing up in an orthodox family, I remained almost totally ignorant of Hinduism. What, then, survived of Hinduism in me? Perhaps I had received a certain supporting philosophy. I cannot say; my uncle often put it to me that my denial was an admissible type of Hinduism. Examining myself, I found only that sense of the difference of people, which I have tried to explain, a vaguer sense of caste, and a horror of the unclean.

It still horrifies me that people should put out food for animals on plates that they themselves use; as it horrified me at school to see boys sharing Popsicles and Palates, local iced lollies; as it horrifies me to see women sipping from ladles with which they stir their pots. This was more than difference; this was the uncleanliness we had to guard against. From all food restrictions sweets were, curiously, exempt. We bought cassava pone from street stalls; but black pudding and souse, favourite street-corner and sports-ground dishes of the Negro proletariat, were regarded by us with fascinated horror. This might suggest that our food remained what it always had been. But this was not so. It is not easy to understand just how com- munication occurred, but we were steadily adopting the food styles of others: the Portuguese stew of tomato and onions, in which almost anything might be done, the Negro way with yams, plantains, breadfruit and bananas. Everything we adopted became our own; the outside was still to be dreaded, and my prejudices were so strong that when I left Trinidad, shortly before my eighteenth birthday, I had eaten in restaurants only three times. The day of my swift transportation to New York was a day of misery. I spent a frightened, hungry day in that city; and on the ship to Southampton I ate mainly the sweets, which encouraged the steward to say when I tipped him, 'The others made pigs of themselves. But you sure do like ice cream'.

Food was one thing. Caste was another. Though I had quickly grown to see it as only part of our private play, it was capable on occasion of influencing my attitude to others. A distant relation was married; it was rumoured that her husband was of the *chamar*, or leather-worker, caste. The man was rich and travelled; he was successful in his profession and was later to hold a position of some responsibility. But he was a *chamar*. The rumour was perhaps unfounded—few marriages are not attended by disparagement of this sort—but the thought still occurs whenever we meet and that initial sniffing for difference is now involuntary. He is the only person thus coloured for me; the marriage took place when I was very young. In India people were also to be tainted by their caste, especially when this was announced beforehand, approvingly or disapprovingly. But caste in India was not what it had been to me in Trinidad. In Trinidad caste had no meaning in our day-to-day life; the caste we occasionally played at was no more than an acknowledgment of latent qualities; the assurance it offered was such as might have been offered by a palmist or a reader of handwriting. In India it implied a brutal division of labour; and at its centre, as I had never realised, lay the degradation of the latrine-cleaner. In India caste was unpleasant; I never wished to know what a man's caste was.

I had no belief; I disliked religious ritual; and I had a sense of the ridiculous. I refused to go through the *janaywa*, or thread ceremony of the newborn, with some of my cousins. The ceremony ends with the initiate, his head shaved, his thread new and obvious, taking up his staff and bundle—as he might have done in an Indian village two thousand years ago—and announcing his intention of going to Kasi-Banaras to study. His mother weeps and begs him not to go; the initiate insists that he must; a senior member of the family is summoned to plead with the initiate, who at length yields and lays down his staff and bundle. It was a pleasing piece of theatre. But I knew that we were in Trinidad, an island separated by only ten miles from the South American coast, and that the appearance in a Port of Spain street of my cousin, perhaps of no great academic attainment, in the garb of a Hindu mendicant-scholar bound for Banaras, would have attracted unwelcome attention. So I refused; though now this ancient drama, absurdly surviving in a Trinidad yard, seems to me touching and attractive.

I had contracted out. Yet there is a balancing memory. In the science class at school one day we were doing an experiment with siphons, to an end which I have now forgotten. At one stage a beaker and a length of tube were passed from boy to boy, so that we might suck and observe the effects. I let the beaker pass me. I thought I hadn't been seen, but an Indian boy in the row behind, a Port of Spain boy, a recognised class tough, whispered, 'Real brahmin.' His tone was approving. I was surprised at his knowledge, having assumed him, a Port of Spain boy, to be ignorant of these things; at the unexpected tenderness of his voice; and also at the bringing out into public of that other, secret life. But I was also pleased. And with this pleasure there came a new tenderness for that boy, and a sadness for our common loss: mine, which he did not suspect, the result of my own decision or temperament, his, which by his behaviour he openly acknowledged, the result of history and environment: a feeling which was to come to me again more strongly and much later, in entirely different circumstances, when the loss was complete, in London.

I have been rebuked by writers from the West Indies, and notably George Lamming, for not paying sufficient attention in my books to non-Indian groups. The confrontation of different communities, he said, was the fundamental West Indian experience. So indeed it is, and increasingly. But to see the attenuation of the culture of my childhood as the result of a dramatic confrontation of opposed worlds would be to distort the reality. To me the worlds were juxtaposed and mutually exclusive. One gradually contracted. It had to; it fed only on memories and its completeness was only apparent. It was yielding not to attack but to a type of seepage from the other. I can speak only out of my own experience. The family life I have been describing began to dissolve when I was six or seven; when I was fourteen it had ceased to exist. Between my brother, twelve years younger than myself, and me there is more than a generation of difference. He can have no memory of that private world which survived with such apparent solidity up to only twenty-five years ago, a world which had lengthened out, its energy of inertia steadily weakening, from the featureless area of darkness which was India.

That this world should have existed at all, even in the consciousness of a child, is to me a marvel; as it is a marvel that we should have accepted the separateness of our two worlds and seen no incongruity in their juxtaposition. In one world we existed as if in blinkers, as if seeing no more than my grandfather's village; outside, we were totally self-aware. And in India I was to see that so many of the things which the newer and now perhaps truer side of my nature kicked against —the smugness, as it seemed to me, the imperviousness to criticism, the refusal to *see*, the double-talk and double-think— had an answer in that side of myself which I had thought buried and which India revived as a faint memory. I understood better than I admitted. And to me it is an additional marvel that an upbringing of the kind I have described, cut short and rendered invalid so soon, should have left so deep an impression. Indians are an old people, and it might be that they continue to belong to the old world. That Indian reverence for the established and ancient, however awkward, however indefensible, however little understood: it is part of the serious buffoonery of Ancient Rome, an aspect of the Roman *pietas* I had rejected tradition; yet how can I explain my feeling of outrage when I heard that in Bombay they used candles and electric bulbs for the Diwali festival, and not the rustic clay lamps, of immemorial design, which in Trinidad we still used? I had been born an unbeliever. Yet the thought of the decay of the old customs and reverences saddened me when the boy whispered 'Real brahmin', and when, many years later, in London, I heard that Ramon was dead.

He was perhaps twenty-four. He died in a car crash. It was fitting. Motorcars were all that mattered to him; and it was to continue to handle them that he came to London, abandoning mother and father, wife and children. I met him almost as soon as he had arrived. It was in a dingy Chelsea boarding-house whose façade was like all the other façades in that respectable, rising street: white, the area railings black, the door an oblong of vivid colour. Only milk bottles and a quality of curtaining betrayed the house where, in a passageway, below the diffused, misty glow of a forty-watt bulb, I first saw Ramon. He was short, his hair thick and curling at the ends, his features blunt, like his strong stubby fingers. He wore a moustache and was unshaved; and in his pullover, which I could see had belonged to someone else who had made the pilgrimage to London from Trinidad and had taken back the pullover as a mark of the voyager to temperate climes, he looked shabby and unwashed.

He was of a piece with the setting, the green grown dingy of the walls, the linoleum, the circles of dirt around door handles, the faded upholstery of cheap chairs, the stained wall-paper; the indications of the passage of numberless transients to whom these rooms had never been meant for the arranging of their things; the rim of soot below the windowsill, the smoked ceiling, the empty fireplace bearing the marks of a brief, ancient fire and suggesting a camping ground; the carpets smelly and torn. He was of a piece, yet he was alien. He be-longed to unfenced backyards and lean-tos, where, pulloverless and shirtless, he might wander in the cool of the evening, about him the unfading bright green of Trinidad foliage, chickens settling down for the night, while in a neighbouring yard a coalpot sent up a thin line of blue smoke. Now, at a similar time of day, he sat choked in someone else's pullover on a low bed, how often used, how little cleaned, in the dim light of a furnished room in Chelsea, the electric fire, its dull reflector seemingly spat upon and sanded, making little impression on the dampness and cold. His fellow voyagers had gone out. He was not bright, as they were; he cared little about dress; he could not support or share their high spirits.

He was shy, and spoke only when spoken to, responding to questions like a man who had nothing to hide, a man to whom the future, never considered, held no threat and possibly no purpose. He had left Trinidad because he had lost his driving licence. His career of crime had begun when, scarcely a boy, he was arrested for driving without a licence; later he was arrested for driving while still banned. One offence led to another, until Trinidad had ceased to be a place where he could live; he needed to be in motorcars. His parents had scraped together some money to send him to England. They had done it because they loved him, their son; yet when he spoke of their sacrifice it was without emotion.

He was incapable of assessing the morality of actions; he was a person to whom things merely happened. He had left his wife behind; she had two children. 'And I believe I have something else boiling up for me.' The words were spoken without the Trinidad back-street pride. They recorded a fact; they passed judgment neither on his desertion nor his virility.

His name was Spanish because his mother was part Venezuelan; and he had spent some time in Venezuela until the police had hustled him out. But he was a Hindu and had been married according to Hindu rites. These rites must have meant as little to him as they did to me, and perhaps even less, for he had grown up as an individual, had never had the protection of a family life like mine, and had at an early age been transferred to a civilisation which remained as puzzling to him as this new transference to Chelsea.

He was an innocent, a lost soul, rescued from animality only by his ruling passion. That section of the mind, if such a section exists, which judges and feels was in him a blank, on which others could write. He wished to drive; he drove. He liked a car; he applied his skill to it and drove it away. He would be eventually caught; that he never struggled against or seemed to doubt. You told him, 'I need a hubcap for my car. Can you get me one?' He went out and took the first suitable hubcap he saw. He was caught; he blamed no one. Things happened to him. His innocence, which was not mere simpleness, was frightening. He was as innocent as a complicated machine. He could be animated by his wish to please. There was an unmarried mother in the house; to her and her child he was unfailingly tender, and protective, whenever that was required of him.

But there was his ruling passion. And with motorcars he was a genius. The word quickly got around; and it was not unusual some weeks later to see him in grease-stained clothes working on a run-down motorcar, while a cavalry-twilled man spoke to him of money. He might have made money. But all his profits went on fresh cars and on the fines he had already begun to pay to the courts for stealing this lamp and that part which he had needed to complete a job. It was not necessary for him to steal; but he stole. Still, the news of his skill went round, and he was busy.

Then I heard that he was in serious trouble. A friend in the boarding-house had asked him to burn a scooter. In Trinidad if you wished to burn a motorcar you set it alight on the bank of the muddy Caroni river and rolled it in. London, too, had a river. Ramon put the scooter into the van which he owned at the time and drove down one evening to the Embankment. Before he could set the scooter alight a policeman appeared, as policemen had always appeared in Ramon's life.

I thought that, as the scooter hadn't been burnt, the case couldn't be serious.

'But no,' one man in the boarding-house said. 'This is conspi-ra-cy.' He spoke the word with awe; he too had been booked as a conspirator.

So Ramon went up to the assizes, and I went to see how the case would go. I had some trouble finding the correct court— 'Have you come to answer a summons yourself, sir?' a police-man asked, his courtesy as bewildering as his question—and when I did find the court, I might have been back in St Vincent Street in Port of Spain. The conspirators were all there, looking like frightened students. They wore suits, as though all about to be interviewed. They, so boisterous, so anxious to antagonise their neighbours in the Chelsea street—they had taken to clipping one another's hair on the pavement of a Sunday morning (the locals washing their cars the while), as they might have done in Port of Spain—now succeeded in giving an opposed picture of themselves.

Ramon stood apart from them, he too wearing a suit, but with nothing in his face or in his greeting to show that we were meeting in circumstances slightly different from those in the boarding-house. A girl was attached to him, a simple creature,

dressed as for a dance. Not anxious they seemed, but blank;
she too was a person to whom things difficult or puzzling kept
happening. More worried than either of them was Ramon's
employer, a garage-owner. He had come to give evidence about
Ramon's 'character', and he again was in a suit, of stiff brown
tweed. His face was flushed and puffy, hinting at some type of
heart disorder; his eyes blinked continually behind his pink-
rimmed spectacles. He stood beside Ramon.

'A good boy, a good boy,' the garage-owner said, tears coming to his eyes. 'It's only his company.' It was strange that this
simple view of the relationships of the simple could hold so
much force and be so moving.

The trial was an anti-climax. It began sombrely enough,
with police evidence and cross-examinations. (Ramon was
quoted as saying at the moment of arrest: 'Yes, copper, you
got me now, sah'. This I rejected.) Ramon was being defended
by a young court-supplied lawyer. He was very brisk and
stylish, and beside himself with enthusiasm. He showed more
concern than Ramon, whom he had needlessly encouraged to
cheer up. Once he caught the judge out on some point of legal
etiquette and in an instant was on his feet, administering a
shocked, stern rebuke. The judge listened with pure pleasure
and apologised. We might have been in a nursery for lawyers:
Ramon's lawyer the star pupil, the judge the principal, and
we in the gallery proud parents. When the judge began his
summing up, speaking slowly, in a voice court-house rich,
sombreness altogether disappeared. It was clear he was not
used to the ways of Trinidad. He said he found it hard to regard
an attempt to burn a scooter on the Embankment as more
than a foolish students' prank; however, an intention to de-
fraud the insurance company was serious . . . There was an
Indian lady in the gallery, of great beauty, who smiled and had
to suppress her laughter at every witticism and every elegant
phrase. The judge was aware of her, and the summing up was
like a dialogue between the two, between the elderly man,
confident of his gifts, and the beautiful, appreciative woman.
The tenseness of the jury—a bespectacled, hatted woman sat
forward, clutching the rail as if in distress—was irrelevant;

and no one, not even the police, seemed surprised at the verdict of not guilty. Ramon's lawyer was exultant. Ramon was as serene as before; his fellow conspirators suddenly appeared utterly exhausted.

Soon enough, however, Ramon was in trouble again, and this time there was no garage-owner to speak for him. He had, I believe, stolen a car or had pillaged its engine beyond economic repair; and he was sent to prison for some time. When he came out he said he had spent a few weeks in Brixton. 'Then I went down to a place in Kent.' I heard this from his former co-accused in the boarding-house. There Ramon had become a figure of fun. And when I next heard of him he was dead, in a car crash.

He was a child, an innocent, a maker; someone for whom the world had never held either glory or pathos; someone for whom there had been no place. 'Then I went down to a place in Kent.' He was guiltless of humour or posturing. One place was like another; the world was full of such places in which, unseeing, one passed one's days. He was dead now, and I wished to offer him recognition. He was of the religion of my family; we were debased members of that religion, and this very debasement I felt as a bond. We were a tiny, special part of that featureless, unknown country, meaningful to us, if we thought about it, only in that we were its remote descendants. I wished his body to be handled with reverence, and I wished it to be handled according to the old rites. This alone would spare him final nonentity. So perhaps the Roman felt in Cappadocia or Britain; and London was now as remote from the centre of our world as, among the ruins of some Roman villa in Gloucestershire, Britain still feels far from home and can be seen as a country which in an emblematic map, curling at the corners, is partly obscured by the clouds blown by a cherub, a country of mist and rain and forest, from which the traveller is soon to hurry back to a warm, familiar land. For us no such land existed.

I missed Ramon's funeral. He was not cremated but buried, and a student from Trinidad conducted the rites which his caste entitled him to perform. He had read my books and did not want me to be there. Denied a presence I so much wished, I had to imagine the scene: a man in a white dhoti speaking gibberish over the corpse of Ramon, making up rites among the tombstones and crosses of a more recent religion, the mean buildings of a London suburb low in the distance, against an industrial sky.

But how could the mood be supported? Ramon died fittingly and was buried fittingly. In addition to everything else, he was buried free, by a funeral agency whose stalled hearse, encountered by chance on the road only a few days before his death, he had set going again.

The India, then, which was the background of my childhood was an area of the imagination. It was not the real country I presently began to read about and whose map I committed to memory. I became a nationalist; even a book like Beverley Nichols's *Verdict on India* could anger me. But this came almost at the end. The next year India became independent; and I found that my interest was failing. I now had almost no Hindi. But it was more than language which divided me from what I knew of India. Indian films were both tedious and disquieting; they delighted in decay, agony and death; a funeral dirge or a blind man's lament could become a hit. And there was religion, with which, as one of Mr Gollancz's writers had noted with approval, the people of India were intoxicated. I was without belief or interest in belief; I was incapable of worship, of God or holy men; and so one whole side of India was closed to me.

Then there came people from India, not the India of Gold Teeth and Babu, but this other India; and I saw that to this country I was not at all linked. The Gujerati and Sindhi merchants were as foreign as the Syrians. They lived enclosed lives of a narrowness which I considered asphyxiating. They were devoted to their work, the making of money; they seldom went out; their pallid women were secluded; and all day their houses screeched with morbid Indian film songs. They contributed nothing to the society, nothing even to the Indian community. They were reputed among us to be sharp businessmen. In so many ways, as I now see, they were to us what we were to the other communities. But their journey had not been final; their private world was not shrinking. They made regular trips to India, to buy and sell, to marry, to bring out recruits; the gap between us widened.

I came to London. It had become the centre of my world and I had worked hard to come to it. And I was lost. London was not the centre of my world. I had been misled; but there was nowhere else to go. It was a good place for getting lost in, a city no one ever knew, a city explored from the neutral heart outwards until, after years, it defined itself into a jumble of clearings separated by stretches of the unknown, through which the narrowest of paths had been cut. Here I became no more than an inhabitant of a big city, robbed of loyalties, time passing, taking me away from what I was, thrown more and more into myself, fighting to keep my balance and to keep alive the thought of the clear world beyond the brick and asphalt and the chaos of railway lines. All mythical lands faded, and in the big city I was confined to a smaller world than I had ever known. I became my flat, my desk, my name.

As India had drawn near, I had felt more than the usual fear of arrival. In spite of myself, in spite of lucidity and London and my years, and over and above every other fear, and the memory of the Alexandrian cab-driver, some little feeling for India as the mythical land of my childhood was awakened. I knew it to be foolish. The launch was solid enough and dingy enough; there was a tariff for fair weather and foul weather; the heat was real and disagreeable; the city we could see beyond the heat-mist was big and busy; and its inhabitants, seen in other vessels, were of small physique, betokening all the fearful things that had soon to be faced. The buildings grew larger. The figures on the docks became clearer. The buildings spoke of London and industrial England; and how, in spite of knowledge, this seemed ordinary and inappropriate! Perhaps all lands of myth were like this: dazzling with light, familiar to drabness, the margin of the sea unremarkably littered, until the moment of departure.

And for the first time in my life I was one of the crowd. There was nothing in my appearance or dress to distinguish me from the crowd eternally hurrying into Churchgate Station. In Trinidad to be an Indian was to be distinctive. To be anything there was distinctive; difference was each man's attribute. To be an Indian in England was distinctive; in Egypt it was more so. Now in Bombay I entered a shop or a restaurant and awaited a special quality of response. And there was nothing. It was like being denied part of my reality. Again and again I was caught. I was faceless. I might sink without a trace into that Indian crowd. I had been made by Trinidad and England; recognition of my difference was necessary to me. I felt the need to impose myself, and didn't know how.

'You require dark glasses? From your accent, sir, I perceive that you are perhaps a student, returned from Europe. You will understand therefore what I am about to say. Observe how these lenses soften glare and heighten colour. With the manufacture of these lenses I assure you that a new chapter has been written in the history of optics.'

So I was a student, perhaps returned from Europe. The patter was better than I had expected. But I didn't buy the lenses the man offered. I bought Crookes, hideously expensive, in a clip-on Indian frame which broke almost as soon as I left the shop. I was too tired to go back, to talk in a voice whose absurdity I felt whenever I opened my mouth. Feeling less real than before behind my dark glasses, which rattled in their broken frame, the Bombay street splintering into dazzle with every step I took, I walked, unnoticed, back to the hotel, past the fat, impertinent Anglo-Indian girl and the rat-faced Anglo-Indian manager in a silky fawn-coloured suit, and lay down on my bed below the electric ceiling fan.

2. DEGREE

They tell the story of the Sikh who, returning to India after many years, sat down among his suitcases on the Bombay docks and wept. He had forgotten what Indian poverty was like. It is an Indian story, in its arrangement of figure and properties, its melodrama, its pathos. It is Indian above all in its attitude to poverty as something which, thought about from time to time in the midst of other preoccupations, releases the sweetest of emotions. This is poverty, our especial poverty, and how sad it is! Poverty not as an urge to anger or improving action, but poverty as an inexhaustible source of tears, an exercise of the purest sensibility. 'They became so poor that year,' the beloved Hindi novelist Premchard writes, 'that even beggars left their door empty-handed.' That, indeed, is our poverty: not the fact of beggary, but that beggars should have to go from our doors empty-handed. This is our poverty, which in a hundred Indian short stories in all the Indian languages drives the pretty girl to prostitution to pay the family's medical bills.

India is the poorest country in the world. Therefore, to see its poverty is to make an observation of no value; a thousand newcomers to the country before you have seen and said as you. And not only newcomers. Our own sons and daughters, when they return from Europe and America, have spoken in your very words. Do not think that your anger and contempt are marks of your sensitivity. You might have seen more: the smiles on the faces of the begging children, that domestic group among the pavement sleepers waking in the cool Bombay morning, father, mother and baby in a trinity of love, so self-contained that they are as private as if walls had separated them from you: it is your gaze that violates them, your sense of outrage that outrages them. You might have seen the boy sweeping his area of pavement, spreading his mat, lying down; exhaustion and undernourishment are in his tiny body and shrunken face, but lying flat on his back, oblivious of you and the thousands who walk past in the lane between sleepers' mats and house walls bright with advertisements and election slogans, oblivious of the warm, over-breathed air, he plays with fatigued concentration with a tiny pistol in blue plastic. It is your surprise, your anger that denies him humanity. But wait. Stay six months. The winter will bring fresh visitors. Their talk will also be of poverty; they too will show their anger. You will agree; but deep down there will be annoyance; it will seem to you then, too, that they are seeing only the obvious; and it will not please you to find your sensibility so accurately parodied.

Ten months later I was to revisit Bombay and to wonder at my hysteria. It was cooler, and in the crowded courtyards of Colaba there were Christmas decorations, illuminated stars hanging out of windows against the black sky. It was my eye that had changed. I had seen Indian villages: the narrow, broken lanes with green slime in the gutters, the choked back-to-back mud houses, the jumble of filth and food and animals and people, the baby in the dust, swollen-bellied, black with flies, but wearing its good-luck amulet. I had seen the starved child defecating at the roadside while the mangy dog waited to eat the excrement. I had seen the physique of the people of Andhra, which had suggested the possibility of an evolution downwards, wasted body to wasted body, Nature mocking herself, incapable of remission. Compassion and pity did not answer; they were refinements of hope. Fear was what I felt. Contempt was what I had to fight against; to give way to that was to abandon the self I had known. Perhaps in the end it was fatigue that overcame me. For abruptly, in the midst of hysteria, there occurred periods of calm, in which I found that I had grown to separate myself from what I saw, to separate the pleasant from the unpleasant, the whole circular sky ablaze at sunset from the peasants diminished by its glory, the beauty of brassware and silk from the thin wrists that held them up for display, the ruins from the child defecating among them, to separate things from men. I had learned too that escape was always possible, that in every Indian town there was a corner of comparative order and cleanliness in which one could recover and cherish one's self-respect. In India the easiest and most necessary thing to ignore was the most obvious. Which no doubt was why, in spite of all that I had read about the country, nothing had prepared me for it.

But in the beginning the obvious was overwhelming, and there was the knowledge that there was no ship to run back to, as there had been at Alexandria, Port Sudan, Djibouti, Karachi. It was new to me then that the obvious could be separated from the pleasant, from the areas of self-respect and self-love. Marine Drive, Malabar Hill, the lights of the city at night from Kamala Nehru Park, the Parsi Towers of Silence: these are what the tourist brochures put forward as Bombay, and these were the things we were taken to see on three successive days by three kind persons. They built up a dread of what was not shown, that other city where lived the hundreds of thousands who poured in a white stream in and out of Churchgate Station as though hurrying to and from an endless football match. This was the city that presently revealed itself, in the broad, choked and endless main roads of suburbs, a chaos of shops, tall tenements, decaying balconies, electric wires and advertisements, the film posters that seemed to derive from a cooler and more luscious world, cooler and more luscious than the film posters of England and America, promising a greater gaiety, an ampler breast and hip, a more fruitful womb. And the courtyards behind the main streets: the heat heightened, at night the sense of outdoors destroyed, the air holding on its stillness the odours of mingled filth, the windows not showing as oblongs of light but revealing lines, clothes, furniture, boxes and suggesting an occupation of more than floor space. On the roads northwards, the cool redbrick factories set in gardens: Middlesex it might have been, but not attached to these factories any semi-detached or terrace houses, but that shanty town, that rubbish dump. And, inevitably, the prostitutes, the 'gay girls' of the Indian news- papers. But where, in these warrens where three brothels might be in one building and not all the sandal-oil perfumes of Lucknow could hide the stench of gutters and latrines, was the gaiety? Lust, like compassion, was a refinement of hope. Be- fore this one felt only the fragility of one's own sexual im- pulses. One hesitated to probe, to imagine; one concentrated on one's own revulsion. Men with clubs stood guard at the entrances. Protecting whom from what? In the dim, stinking corridors sat expressionless women, very old, very dirty, shrivelled almost to futility; and already one had the feeling that people were negligible: these were the sweepers, the servants of the gay girls of the Bombay poor, doubtless lucky because employed: a frightening glimpse of India's ever reced- ing degrees of degradation.

Degrees of degradation, because gradually one discovers that in spite of its appearance of chaos, in spite of all the bustling white-clad crowds which by their number would appear to defy or to make worthless any attempt at categorisa- tion, this degradation is charted, as the Indian landscape itself which, from the train no more than a jumble of tiny irregularly shaped fields, private follies of which no official organisation would take cognisance, has yet been measured and surveyed and sketched and remains recorded in all its absurdity in the various collectorates, where the title deeds, wrapped in red cloth or yellow cloth, rise in bundles from floor to ceiling. This is the result of an English endeavour answering the Indian need: definition, distinction. To define is to begin to separate oneself, to assure oneself of one's position, to be withdrawn from the chaos that India always threatens, the abyss at whose edge the sweeper of the gay girl sits. A special type of hat or turban, a way of cutting the beard or a way of not cutting the beard, the Western-style suit or the unreliable politicians' khadi, the caste mark of the Kashmiri Hindu or Madras brahmin: this gives proof of one's community, one's worth as a man, one's function, as the title deed in the collector- ate gives proof of one's ownership of part of the earth.

The prompting is universal, but the Indian practice is purely of India. 'And do thy duty, even if it be humble, rather than another's, even if it be great. To die in one's duty is life: to live in another's is death.' This is the Gita, preaching degree fifteen hundred years before Shakespeare's Ulysses, preaching it today. And the man who makes the dingy bed in the hotel room will be affronted if he is asked to sweep the gritty floor. The clerk will not bring you a glass of water even if you faint. The architecture student will consider it a degradation to make drawings, to be a mere draughtsman. And Ramnath, the steno-grapher, so designated on the triangular block of wood that stands on his desk, will refuse to type out what he has taken down in shorthand.

Ramnath was a clerk in a government department. He earned 110 rupees a month and was happy until Malhotra, a 600-rupee-a-month officer, came to his department. Malhotra was an Indian from East Africa; he had been educated at an English university, and had just returned from a European posting. Ramnath and his 110-rupee colleagues secretly scoffed at Europe-returned Indians, but they were all a little frightened of Malhotra, whose reputation was terrifying. He was supposed to know every paragraph of the Civil Service code; he knew his privileges as well as his responsibilities.

Soon enough Ramnath was summoned to Malhotra's office, and there a letter was dictated to him at speed. Ramnath was happily able to catch it all and he returned to the desk marked 'Steno' with a feeling of satisfaction. No further summons came that day; but one came early next morning and when Ramnath went in he found Malhotra quite pale with anger. His neatly trimmed moustache bristled; his eyes were hard. He was freshly bathed and shaved, and Ramnath could feel the difference between his own loose white trousers and open-necked, long-tailed blue shirt and Malhotra's European-tailored grey suit set off by the university tie. Ramnath re-mained composed. The anger of a superior, for whatever reason, was as natural as Ramnath's own abuse of the sweeper who twice daily cleaned out his tenement privy in Mahim.

In such relationships anger and abuse were almost without meaning; they merely marked proper distinctions.

'That letter you took yesterday,' Malhotra said. 'Why wasn't it returned for signature yesterday afternoon?'

'It wasn't? I am sorry, sir. I will see about it now.' Ramnath took his leave and presently returned. 'I have spoken about it to the typist, sir. But Hiralal has had quite a lot of work these last few days.'

'Hiralal? Typist? Don't you type?'

'Oh no, sir. I am a steno.'

'And what do you think a steno is? In future you type out the letters I give you, do you hear?'

Ramnath's face went blank.

'Do you hear?'

'That is not my job, sir.'

'We'll see about that. Take another letter now. And I want this one back before lunch.'

Malhotra dictated. Ramnath made his squiggles with a dancing pen, bowed when the dictating was over, and left the room. In the afternoon Malhotra buzzed for him.

'Where is that letter you took this morning?'

'It is with Hiralal, sir.'

'And yesterday's letter is still with Hiralal. Didn't I tell you that you must type out the letters I give you?'

Silence.

'Where is my letter?'

'It is not my job, sir.'

Malhotra banged the table. 'But we went through all that this morning.'

This was what Ramnath also felt. 'I am a steno, sir. I am not a typist.'

'I am going to report you, Ramnath, for insubordination.'

'That is your right, sir.'

'Don't *talk* to me like that! You won't type my letters. Let me have it from you like that. Say, "I won't type your letters".'

'I am a steno, sir.'

Malhotra dismissed Ramnath and went to see the head of his department. He was made to wait a little in the ante-room before he was called in. The head was tired, tolerant. He understood the impatience of a man like Malhotra, fresh from Europe. But no one before had required a steno to type. Of course, a steno's duties might be said to include typing. But that would be extending the definition of the word. Besides, this was India, and in India it was necessary to take people's feelings into consideration.

'If that is your attitude, sir, then I am sorry to say that you leave me with no alternative but to take the matter to the Union Public Service Commission. I shall report Ramnath for insubordination to you. And through you I shall ask for a full-scale inquiry into the duties of stenos.'

The head sighed. Malhotra wasn't going to get far in the service. That was clear; but he had his rights, and a demand for an inquiry would at some time, though not immediately, create a good deal of trouble: papers, questions, reports.

'Try a little persuasion, Malhotra.'

'I take it, sir, that this is your last word on the subject?'

'Last word?' The head was vague. 'My last word . . . '

The telephone rang; the head seized it, smiling at Malhotra. Malhotra rose and withdrew.

There was no letter awaiting signature on Malhotra's desk. He buzzed for Ramnath and very promptly Ramnath appeared. His triumph could scarcely be concealed by his excessive gravity, his bowed shoulders, his pad pressed to his blue-shirted breast, his gaze fixed on his shoes. He knew that Malhotra had been to see the head, and that not even a rebuke had resulted.

'A letter, Ramnath.'

Pad fell open; pen squiggled above and below ruled lines. But as he squiggled, Ramnath's assurance gave way to terror. What he was taking down was Malhotra's request for his sacking, for insubordination, for inefficiency as a stenographer, and for insolence. This committing of a thing to paper was threatening enough. What was worse was that the letter would have to be typed out by Hiralal. For Ramnath now there seemed only a choice of humiliations. Controlling his terror, he took the letter down, waited with bowed head to be dismissed, and when dismissal came, fled to the office of the head of the department. He waited a long time in the ante-room; he went in; and in no time he came out again.

At five that afternoon Ramnath tapped at Malhotra's door and stood in the doorway. In a trembling hand he held some typewritten sheets; and as soon as Malhotra looked up, Ramnath's eyes filled with tears.

'Ah,' Malhotra said. 'Hiralal has been catching up with his work, I see.'

Saying nothing, Ramnath shot to the side of Malhotra's desk, placed the typewritten sheets on the green blotting pad and, in a continuation of this downward action, dropped to the floor and touched Malhotra's polished shoes with his clasped palms.

'Get up! Get up! Did Hiralal type this?'

'I did! I did!' Ramnath was sobbing on the worn floor mat.

'Treat you people like people, and the net result is that you get insubordinate. Treat you like animals, and then you behave like this.'

Sobbing, embracing the shoes, polishing them with his palms, Ramnath agreed.

'You will type my letters from now on?'

Ramnath struck his forehead on Malhotra's shoes.

'All right. We'll tear this letter up. This is how we get through our work in this department.'

Sobbing, banging his forehead on Malhotra's shoes, Ramnath waited until the interleaved scraps of top copy and carbon fell into the wastepaper basket. Then he rose, his eyes dry, and ran out of the room. The day's work was over; now, with the great jostling crowds, home to Mahim. He had yet to accustom himself to the humiliations of the new world. He had been violated in the tenderest area of his self-esteem, and fear of the abyss alone had given him the strength to endure such a violation. It was a little tragedy. He had learned to obey; he would survive.

Countless such tragedies are marked on the hearts of those whom one sees in those brisk white-clad crowds, hurrying to and from their homes like city-workers in every city of the world, people for whom all the advertisements are meant, all the electric trains run, to whom the film posters are directed, all the extravagantly coloured women with big breasts and big hips, descendants of those figures of old Indian sculpture which, until separated from the people who created them, are like a tragic folk longing.

For Malhotra, too, with his Italian-styled suit and English university tie, the society and its violations were new. East Africa, the English university and the years in Europe had made him just enough of a colonial to be out of place in India. He had no family to speak of. He was only a 600-rupee-a-month man, and his place was therefore with 600-rupee-a-month men. But at that level there were no outsiders, no one who, like Malhotra, had rejected the badges of food and caste and dress. He wished to marry; it was also what his parents wished for him. But his colonial eye made him aspire too high. 'Don't call us. We will call you.' 'We thank you for your interest, and we will let you know as soon as the numerous applications have been gone through.' 'We don't appreciate 600 rupees a month.' This was what the son of one family said. And below that there was, in Malhotra's view, little more than village society. No marriage, then, for him; and the years were going by, and his parents were breaking their hearts. He could only share his bitterness with his friends.

Malik was one of these. He too was a 'new man'. He and Malhotra were bound only by their common bitterness, for Malik was an engineer and earned 1,200 rupees a month. He lived in a well-appointed flat in one of the finer areas of Bombay. By the standards of London he was well off. By the standards of Bombay he was over-privileged. But he was miserable. European engineers less qualified than himself earned three times as much for their services as experts and advisers; the mere fact that they were Europeans commended them to Indian firms. This was his story. A new man, he remained a stranger in Bombay, more of an outsider than any visiting European technician, to whom many doors were open. Malik's qualifications for the young business executive or 'box-wallah' society seemed high, but at our first meeting he told me of the probing by which he was continually rejected. He was an engineer; that was good. That he was Scandinavia-returned was impressive. That he worked for an established firm with European connections made him more than promising. Then: 'Do you own a car?' Malik didn't. The probing was abandoned; no one was even interested in his parentage.

He spoke sadly in his passé modernistic flat, which he was beginning to let go: the irregular bookshelves, the irregular ceramics, the irregular coffee table. For all this there was no audience, and it was like the scrupulous preparation for going out of a girl whom no one will notice. It is with contemporary furniture as with contemporary clothes: sad unless there is someone who notices and cares. On the irregular coffee table there was a large photograph in a gilt frame of a pretty white girl with dark hair and high cheekbones. I asked no questions, but Malhotra told me later that the girl had died years before in her Northern land. While we talked and drank the tape-recorder played songs Malik had recorded in his student days in Europe, songs which even I could recognise as old. And in that Bombay flat, surrounded by the dramatic squares of light and darkness of other metropolitan blocks, below us the glittering arc of Marine Drive, in that room with the central photograph of the dead girl and the sour background of dead songs, we looked through the well-thumbed photograph albums: Malik in overcoat, Malik and his friends, Malik and the girl, against snow or pine-covered mountains, against open-air cafés: Malik and Malhotra sharing the past (Ibsen in the original on the irregular bookshelves), 600-rupee-a-month and 1,200-rupee-a-month men temporarily forgetting their humiliations in memories of a past acceptance, when to be a man and a student was enough, and to be Indian gave glamour.

Jivan was thirteen or fourteen when he left his village to look for work in Bombay. He had no friends in the city and nowhere to go. He slept on the pavements. At last he found a job in a printery in the Fort area. He earned fifty rupees a month. He did not look for lodgings; he continued to sleep on that stretch of pavement which custom had now made his. Jivan could read and write; he was intelligent and anxious to please; and after some months he was chasing advertisements for a magazine his firm printed. His wages steadily rose and it seemed he was set for success and high responsibility in the firm. Then one day, without warning, he went to his employer and gave notice.

'It is my luck,' his employer said. 'I can never keep good people. I train them. Then they leave me. What's this new job you've found?'

'I have none, sir. I was hoping you would find one for me.'

'Oho! It's another rise you're after.'

'No, sir. It isn't money I want. It's this cycling about. It was all right when I was younger. But now I would like an office job. I want a desk of my own. I will even take less money if I can get an office job. I hope you will help me find one.'

Jivan's mind was made up. His employer was a kind-hearted man and he recommended Jivan for a clerkship in another firm. Here, as a clerk, Jivan rose fast. He was as loyal and hardworking as he had been in the printery; and he had the magic touch. Soon he was almost running the firm. After some time he had saved eight thousand rupees, slightly more than six hundred pounds. He bought a taxi and hired it out at twenty rupees a day: Malhotra's salary. He still worked for his firm. He still slept on the pavements. He was twenty-five years old.

Vasant grew up in a Bombay slum. He was very young when he left school to look for work. He took to hanging around the stock exchange. His face became familiar and the stockbrokers sent him on little errands. They began to use him as a telegraph-runner. One day a stockbroker gave Vasant a message but no money. 'It's all right,' the stockbroker said. 'They'll bill me at the end of the month.' So Vasant discovered that if you sent telegrams in some number the telegraph office gave you credit for a month. He offered a service to stock-brokers: he would collect all their telegrams from their offices, file them, and he would ask for money only at the end of the month. He charged a small fee; he made a little money; he even managed to rent a little cubby-hole of a 'telegraph office'. He read all the stockbrokers' telegrams: his knowledge of the market grew. He began to deal himself. He became rich. Now he was old and established. He had a respectably furnished office in a suitable block. He had a receptionist, secretaries, clerks. But this was mainly for show. He continued to do all his important work in his cramped little 'telegraph office'; he could think nowhere else. When he was poor he had never eaten during the day. The habit remained with him. If he ate during the day he became sluggish.

The worker in leather is among the lowest of the low, the most tainted of the tainted, and it was unusual, especially in the far South, where caste distinctions are rigid, to find two brahmin brothers making leather goods. Their establishment was small and self-contained: house, workshops and vegetable gardens on a plot of four acres. One brother, lean, nervous, hunted orders in the town and with his quick eyes observed foreign designs in briefcases, diary bindings, camera cases; the other brother, plump, placid, superintended the work. The greatest praise, which made them both smirk and squirm with pleasure, was: 'But you didn't make this here. It looks foreign. American, *I* would say'. They both had progressive views about what the lean brother, in khaki shorts and vest on this Sunday morning, referred to as 'labour relations'. 'You've got to keep them happy. I can't do the work. I can't get my children to do it. You've got to keep them happy.' An 'ar-chin', picked off the streets, got one rupee a day; when he was fourteen or fifteen he could get four rupees a day; the 'maistry' got one hundred and twenty rupees a month, with a yearly bonus of about two hundred and forty rupees. 'Yes,' the other brother said. 'You have to keep them happy.' They were proud that everything in their workshops was made by hand, but their ambition was to create an 'industrial estate' which would bear their name. They had come from a poor family. They had begun by making envelopes. They still made envelopes. In one corner of the workshop a boy was standing on a neat stack of envelope sheets; a 'maistry', wielding a broad-bladed chopper, chopped the paper close to the boy's toes; elsewhere boys were folding up the paper that had been cut to the pattern required. The brothers were worth seventy thousand pounds.

Adventure is possible. But a knowledge of degree is in the bones and no Indian is far from his origins. It is like a physical yearning: the tycoon in his cubby-hole, the entrepreneur clerk sleeping on the pavement, the brahmin leather-goods manu-facturers anxious to protect their children against caste contamination. However incongruous the imported mechanics of the new world—stockbrokers, telegrams, labour relations, advertisements—might seem, they have been incorporated into the rule of degree. Few Indians are outsiders. Malik and Malhotra are exceptional. They are not interested in the type of adventure the society can provide; their aspirations are alien and disruptive. Rejecting the badges of dress and food and function, rejecting degree, they find themselves rejected. They look for Balzacian adventure in a society which has no room for Rastignacs.

'When unrighteous disorder prevails, the women sin and are impure; and when women are not pure, Krishna, there is disorder of castes, social confusion.' This is the Gita again. And in India there is no social confusion, no disorder of castes, no adventure, in spite of the bingo on Sunday mornings in the old British clubs, in spite of the yellow-covered overseas editions of the *Daily Mirror* which the ladies in their graceful saris seize with eager manicured hands, and the copy of *Woman's Own* which the dainty shopper, basket-carrying servant respectfully in her train, presses to one breast like a badge of caste; in spite of the dance floors of Bombay, Delhi and Calcutta: those sad bands, those sad Anglo-Indian girls at the microphone, and the air full of dated slang. 'Oh, just bung your coat down there.' 'I say, by Jove!' And the names fly: Bunty, Andy, Freddy, Jimmy, Bunny. They are real, the men who answer to these names, and they answer them well:

their jackets and ties and collars and accents do make them
Bunty and Andy and Freddy. But they are not wholly what they
seem. Andy is also Anand, Danny Dhandeva; their marriages
have been strictly arranged, their children's marriages will be
arranged; the astrologer will be earnestly consulted and horo-
scopes will be cast. For every man and woman on the dance
floor is marked by destiny, on every one Fate has its eye. The
Parsis, perhaps Freddy's lesser friends or relations, in their
enclosure between decks on the holiday steamer from Goa,
might loudly sing, their pleasure heightened by the confusion
of the native crowd, *Barbara Allen* and *The Ash Grove* and *I
Don't Have a Wooden Heart*. But that little corner of merry
England which they have created in Bombay is also Druidical.
It worships fire; its ways are narrow and protective, and at the
end lie the Towers of Silence and the grim rites behind those
walls whose main portals are marked with a symbol from the
ancient world.

The outer and inner worlds do not have the physical separateness which they had for us in Trinidad. They coexist; the society
only pretends to be colonial; and for this reason its absurdities
are at once apparent. Its mimicry is both less and more than a
colonial mimicry. It is the special mimicry of an old country
which has been without a native aristocracy for a thousand
years and has learned to make room for outsiders, but only at
the top. The mimicry changes, the inner world remains constant: this is the secret of survival. And so it happens that, to
one whole area of India, a late seventeenth-century traveller like
Ovington remains in many ways a reliable guide. Yesterday the
mimicry was Mogul; tomorrow it might be Russian or American; today it is English.

Mimicry might be too harsh a word for what appears so
comprehensive and profound: buildings, railways, a system of
administration, the intellectual discipline of the civil servant
and the economist. Schizophrenia might better explain the
scientist who, before taking up his appointment, consults the
astrologer for an auspicious day. But mimicry must be used
because so much has been acquired that the schizophrenia is
often concealed; because so much of what is seen remains

simple mimicry, incongruous and absurd; and because no
people, by their varied physical endowments, are as capable
of mimicry as the Indians. The Indian army officer is at a first
meeting a complete English army officer. He even manages to
look English; his gait and bearing are English; his mannerisms,
his tastes in drink are English; his slang is English. In the
Indian setting this Indian English mimicry is like fantasy. It is
an undiminishing absurdity; and it is only slowly that one
formulates what was sensed from the first day: this is a mimicry
not of England, a real country, but of the fairytale land of
Anglo-India, of clubs and sahibs and syces and bearers. It is
as if an entire society has fallen for a casual confidence trickster.
Casual because the trickster has gone away, losing interest in
his joke, but leaving the Anglo-Indians flocking to the churches
of Calcutta on a Sunday morning to assert the alien faith, more
or less abandoned in its country of origin; leaving Freddy
crying, 'Just bung your coat down there, Andy;' leaving the
officer exclaiming, 'I say, by Jove! I feel rather bushed.'
Leaving 'civil lines', 'cantonments', leaving people 'going off
to the hills': magic words now fully possessed, now spoken as
of right, in what is now at last Indian Anglo-India, where
smartness can be found in the cosy proletarian trivialities of
Woman's Own and the *Daily Mirror* and where Mrs Hauksbee,
a Millamant of the suburbs, is still the arbiter of elegance.

But room has been left at the top, and out of this mimicry a
new aristocracy is being essayed, not of politicians or civil
servants, but of the business executives of foreign, mostly
British, firms. To them, the box-wallahs as they are called, have
gone the privileges India reserves for the foreign and conquer-
ing; and it is to this new commercial caste that both Malik,
the engineer 'drawing' twelve hundred rupees a month, and
Malhotra, the government servant drawing six hundred, aspire
with despair and, despairing, seek to ridicule. We are now as
far above them as they are above Ramnath, with his flapping
Indian-style white cotton trousers, boarding the crowded
suburban electric train to get to his tenement room in Mahim;
as far above them as Ramnath is above the sweeper of the 'gay
girl' in Forras Road. We have left even the lower-class Parsis

far below; we can hardly hear them singing *Flow Gently, Sweet Afton* on the holiday steamer from Goa.

Bunty the box-wallah. He is envied and ridiculed throughout India. Much is made of the name, and even Bunty, from the security of his aristocracy, sometimes pretends to find its origin in the box of the street pedlar, though it is more likely that the name derives from the Anglo-Indian office box, the burden in the old days of a special servant, of which Kipling speaks so feelingly in *Something of Myself*. Bunty is envied for his luxurious company flat, his inflated salary and his consequent ability, in an India which is now independent, guiltlessly to withdraw from India. For this withdrawal he is also ridiculed. He is an easy target. He is new to the caste, but the caste is old and, though essentially engaged in trade, it has been ennobled by the glamour of the conqueror, the rewards of trade, and now by Bunty himself, whom these two things in conjunction have attracted.

Bunty comes of a 'good' family, Army, ICS; he might even have princely connections. He is two or three generations removed from purely Indian India; he, possibly like his father, has been to an Indian or English public school and one of the two English universities, whose accent, through all the encircling hazards of Indian intonation, he strenuously maintains. He is a blend of East and West; he is 'broad-minded'. He permits his name to be corrupted into the closest English equivalent, like place names in the mouth of the conqueror. So Firdaus becomes Freddy, Jamshed Jimmy, and Chandrashekhar, which is clearly impossible, becomes the almost universal Bunty or Bunny. Bunty knows it will count in his favour, as a mark of his broadmindedness, though at this level it requires a minimum of heroism, if he makes a mixed marriage; if, say, as a Punjabi Hindu he marries a Bengali Muslim or a Bombay Parsi. Freed of one set of caste rules, he obeys another, and these are as nice: to introduce Jimmy, whose airconditioned office is shared and has hard furnishings, into the home of Andy, who has an office to himself with soft furnishings, is to commit a blunder.

Bunty's grandfather might have conducted his business over

a hookah or while reclining on bolsters in a dreadfully furnished
room. Bunty discusses business over drinks at the club or on
the golf course. There is no need for the golf course: the box-
wallah circle is tiny. But it is a condition of Bunty's employ-
ment that he play golf, in order to make suitable 'contacts',
and on the golf courses of clubs all over the country he can be
seen with an equally unhappy Andy, who, as he goes out into
the drizzle of Bangalore, might remark that it is rather like the
rain of England. There are other traditions, which vary from
city to city. In Calcutta there is the Friday afternoon revelry at
Firpo's restaurant on Chowringhee. In the days of the British
this celebrated the departure of the mail boat for England and
marked the end of the four-and-a-half-day week. Letters to
England now go by air; but Bunty is caste-minded; he maintains the tradition, unembarrassed by its origin.

It is easy for Indians to make fun of Bunty for being called
'daddy' by his English-speaking children; for his imitated
manners: he rises when ladies come into a room; for his foreign
interest in interior decoration; for the spotless bathroom and
adequate towels he provides for his guests (such attentions in
India being beneath the notice of all but the latrine-cleaner: the
Indian lavatory and the Indian kitchen are the visitor's nightmare). But Bunty is no fool. He has withdrawn from India,
but he does not wish to be a European. He sees the glamour of
Europe; but, being in almost daily contact with Europeans, he
is compelled by his pride to be Indian. He strives too hard
perhaps to blend East with West; his patronage of Indian arts
and crafts is a little like that of the visitor. In his drawing-room,
hung with contemporary Indian fabrics, the odd sketch from
Kangra, Basohli or Rajasthan or a piece of the bright bazaar
art of Jamini Roy stands beside the Picasso lithograph or the
Sisley reproduction. His food is a mixture of Indian and
European; his drink is wholly European.

But this mixture of East and West in Bunty's home tells
more of the truth about Bunty than either his friends or
enemies believe. For Bunty is only pretending to be a colonial.
He sees himself as every man's equal and most men's superior;
and in him, as in every Indian, the inner world continues whole

and untouched. Bunty might relish the light, attractive complexions of his wife and children. He might be at especial pains to draw your attention to the complexions of his children, and he might do so by some flippant denigratory assessment. But their paleness is not a European paleness, which to Bunty is reminiscent of the Indian albino; and indeed about the European, however to be imitated, fawned upon and resented, there still remains some stigma of the *mleccha*, the unclean. Bunty's caste is European; but Bunty carries within himself a strong sense of aryan race and ancientness as exclusive possessions. It is for this reason that the Anglo-Indian half-breed, however pale, however anglicised, can form no respectable part of Bunty's society unless graced by some notable family connection; for this group there can be no room in India except as outsiders and not at the top. (Nor would they wish there to be room. Their dream is of England; and to England they come—the paler go to Australia, white—and they congregate in sad little colonies in places like Forest Hill, busy churchgoers in short dresses which, in India anti-Indian, in London are un-English and colonial; and they read *Woman's Own* and the *Daily Mirror* on the day of publication: a dream of romance fulfilled.) Towards Europe Bunty is like the puritan seducer: he despises even while he violates.

On Sunday morning Bunty entertains his friends to drinks in his flat. This might be on Malabar Hill if it is in Bombay; if in Calcutta, it will be well hidden from the *bustees* which provide factory labour.

'I had a round of golf yesterday with the Deputy Director . . . ' This is from Andy.

'Well, the Director told me . . . '

Bunty and Andy are not discussing business. They are talking of the Chinese invasion. Even now, however, they appear to be taking delight in their new closeness to power. It is not for this reason alone that their gossip is disturbing. It is a unique type of gossip. How can it be described? It is unslanted; it states facts and draws no conclusions. It makes one long to shake them by the shoulder and say, 'Express your prejudices. Say at least, "If I had the power I would do this". Say that you are on the side of this and against that. Don't just go on calmly reporting unrelated little disasters. Get angry. Get excited. Get worried. Try to link all that you have been saying. Make some sort of pattern out of it, however prejudiced. Then at least I will understand. Right now you are behaving as though you are talking of well-known history.'

It is with this gossip that one begins to doubt what Bunty and Andy show of themselves and one begins to feel that they are not what they seem, that there are areas to which they can retreat and where they are hard to get at. The flat now seems to hang in a void. India is a stone's throw away, but in the flat it is denied: the beggars, the gutters, the starved bodies, the weeping swollen-bellied child black with flies in the filth and cowdung and human excrement of a bazaar lane, the dogs, ribby, mangy, cowed and cowardly, reserving their anger, like the human beings around them, for others of their kind. The decoration of the flat is contemporary; many of its ingredients are Indian; but it is based on nothing. On the shelves there are novels that might be found on shelves in a dozen other countries: vulgarity nowadays is international and swift. But novels imply an interest in people. This flat holds a rejection of concern. And did not that educated brahmin read the romances of Denise Robins, which lay on his shelves next to the bulky volumes of ancient astrological prophecies published by the Madras Government? Did not that young man, a student at Punjab University, read the paperbound volumes of the Schoolgirl's Own Library for relaxation? Will not Bunty's wife fall on the *Daily Mirror* and *Woman's Own* in the club? Will she not consult her astrologer?

Somewhere there has been a failure of communication, unrecognised because communication seems to have been established. In the cafés there are earnest groups of the young who talk about 'theatre' and the need for bringing theatre to the 'people'. They are like their counterparts in England, whom, like the army officers, they even manage physically to resemble; and like their counterparts in England, by theatre they mean *Look Back in Anger*, professionally abbreviated to *Look Back*. A willingness to accept, an underlying, unwitting rejection of the values implied: in Bunty's rooms, the irritating gossip going on, the Chinese about to break through into Assam, the mimicry is no longer as funny as the sight on that first day in Bombay, after the exhaustion and hysteria, of the banner hung across the hot, squalid street advertising the Oxford and Cambridge Players' production of *The Importance of Being Earnest*.

Withdrawal, denial, confusion of values: these are vague words. We need more direct evidence; and a little, I feel, is provided by a recent Indian novel, *The Princes*, by Manohar Malgonkar, published in London by Hamish Hamilton in 1963. *The Princes* is the medieval tragedy of a medieval Indian petty prince who loses power with Independence and feels the humiliation of his fall so deeply that he goes out unarmed after a wounded tiger and is killed. It is an honest book, and the writing is not without skill. Malgonkar has a feeling for outdoor life and his descriptions of hunting and shooting can convey the enchantment of these pastimes even to those who do not practise them.

The Prince is descended from casteless Deccani bandits who, when they acquired political power, surrendered a lakh of rupees to the pundits in exchange for caste privileges. The treasures they amassed remain in the state treasury, objects of almost religious awe, guarded by a special group of retainers. For the ruling house these treasures are a private delectation, a reminder of the past; it is unthinkable that they should be used to improve the impoverished state. The Prince is opposed to progress. He states the view quite bluntly; and when the British decide to build a dam in territory adjacent to the state, he persuades his aboriginal subjects who live in the area to be affected to vote against the scheme. The Prince gives five annual scholarships, each worth £70, to deserving boys. On himself he is more lavish. He has two palaces, thirty motorcars and annual pocket money of £70,000. To spend £1,500 to bring down a courtesan from Simla is as nothing. He has much time to devote to his hobbies. He is an excellent shot and a fearless tracker of wounded tigers. 'I am rich and well-born,' he says, quoting the Gita. 'Who else is equal to me?' He matches words with action. When the nationalists of the state occupy the administration building in 1947 he goes in alone, ignoring the crowd, and hauls down the Indian flag. He is unable to accommodate himself to the handsome terms of the Home Ministry in Delhi, and when he sees that it is too late to save his state and his powers he is heartbroken. He does not rage or weep. Quoting that line of the Gita, he goes out unarmed after a wounded tiger and is killed. He was rich and high; he has fallen.

It is a medieval concept of tragedy.

> *Reduce we all our lessons unto this:*
> *To rise, sweet Spenser, therefore live we all.*
> *Spenser, all live to die, and rise to fall.*

But what is puzzling is that it should be so presented to us by the Prince's son, who is the narrator. He was born in 1920, educated at an English-style English-staffed public school for the sons of princes, and served as an officer in the army during the war. 'Indeed it seems to me,' he says, 'that with the passing of the years I have come to identify myself more and more with [my father's] values.' After the public school which sought to root out snobbery between princes of big states and princes of little states; after the army; after the love affair with an Anglo-Indian girl, encountered in Simla.

The British certainly knew all about resisting change. It was spring in the Himalayas, and Simla was exactly as it had been fifty years ago or a hundred, and Mrs Hauksbee might have been living just around the corner.

'I like your perfume, whatever it is.'

'Chanel number five. I had just a scrap left, but I had to wear it—for going out with a prince.'

'Why, thanks! I'll buy some more.'

After the clubs of Delhi:

'Rumpus?' I exclaimed. 'Why not? Of course we can have a rumpus. One is not a father every day, dammit! What sort of a rumpus had you in mind?' I was certainly learning to handle conversation, now that I had been in New Delhi for nearly two years; meaningless, insincere, but light. You had to keep it frothy, that was all that mattered.

This is how far we will appear to move from the Prince and his derelict principality and the local primary school where, at the beginning of the story, the narrator, Abhayraj, and his half-brother Charudutt are pupils. They are kept separate from the untouchables, who sit on the floor at the back. One morning during the break a game of mango-seed football starts in the verandah. The untouchables watch from a distance. One joins in, trips Charudutt. The caste boys, Abhayraj included, abuse the untouchables: 'Cow-eaters, stinkers, cow-skinners.' And they throw the offending untouchable boy and his satchel into the pond. 'Bastard!' the boy shouts from the pond at Charudutt. 'You are no prince. You are a whore's son.'

It is this word, bastard, which interests Abhayraj. He asks his English tutor, Mr Moreton, what the word means. Mr Moreton hesitates. 'I could understand his embarrassment. He was a sensitive man, and he knew about Charudutt and about the numerous *upraja* sons in our family—children born to rulers out of wedlock.' This is the sensitivity of Mr Moreton. Neither tutor nor pupil speaks of the scene in the school grounds.

The untouchable boy, Kanakchand, has no books the next day. He is put out of the class and in the afternoon Abhayraj sees him 'miserable and downcast, still squatting on the wall'. He is still there the following morning. Abhayraj speaks to him and finds out that he cannot stay at home because he will be flogged if his father gets to know that his books have been destroyed; he cannot go into the class because he has no books and no money to buy new ones. Abhayraj gives Kanakchand all the books in his own satchel. Among them, however, is the *Highroads Treasury*, which is not a school book but a gift from Mr Moreton. Mr Moreton, by some chance, asks after the book that day; the truth is told him; he understands. The next morning Kanakchand comes to Abhayraj and returns the *Highroads Treasury*. 'It was a present. Here, I have brought it back.'

It is a brutal but touching episode, rendered with fidelity, from the taunting to the forgetting to the impulse of pity and generosity. Now comes the sentence which distorts it all, which cuts the ground from under our feet. 'He was as sound as a silver rupee when he began,' Abhayraj comments. 'What made him turn so sour and twisted in later life?' Kanakchand sound as a silver rupee! Kanakchand, untouchable, cow-eater, stinker, squatting on the floor at the back of the class, sitting on the fountain wall for two days because he has lost his books! Did his soundness lie in his acceptance of degree? Did it lie in his refusal to steal from someone who had made him a valuable gift?

The friendship develops. One day Kanakchand makes a gift to Abhayraj of enormous bean-seeds, good for nothing except looking at and holding in the hands, and Abhayraj is 'vaguely distressed at my first contact with the playthings on the floor of the forest'. And more is to come. 'I did not realise it then, but Kanakchand was my first direct contact with the quivering poverty of India.' It is a singular word, this *quivering*. At first it seems unnecessary; then it seems theatrical yet oddly matter-of-fact; then it seems a concession to a convention of feeling.

Kanakchand's poverty is certainly theatrical. His lunch is one black roti, chillis and an onion.

It seemed that even the onion was something of a treat, and that bajra or millet bread and chilli powder mixed with groundnut oil formed his main meal of the day. I watched with fascination as he ate, hungrily and with relish . . . He wolfed the very last crumb, biting alternately on the charred bajra roti and the onion. And when he finished the very last mouthful, he licked his fingers clean.

It is like a description of the feeding habits of a rare animal. Poverty as occasional spectacle: this is our poverty. Abhayraj offers Kanakchand a chocolate. Kanakchand throws it, wrapper and all, into his mouth. Abhayraj exclaims. Kanakchand spits it out and—sound as a silver rupee, remember—makes this curious statement: 'Oh, I didn't know. I thought Bal-raje was playing some kind of joke on me—making me eat green paper.'

Kanakchand is intelligent but his English is poor. To win one of the Prince's five scholarships to a high school he has to write an English essay. Abhayraj writes the essay for him; Kanachand wins the scholarship; and the day arrives for the Prince to make the presentation. Kanakchand's parents are present, 'deliriously happy'. 'Truth, honesty, faith in God and above all, loyalty,' the Prince begins his speech, 'add up to far more than the gaining of worldly rewards.' With this he raises his riding crop and strikes Kanakchand to the floor, strikes him twice again and 'wiped his hands delicately on a handkerchief'. Abhayraj is horrified. He persuades his mother to provide for Kanakchand's education. But Abhayraj notes that Kanakchand never shows any 'gratitude'; and Abhayraj is tormented, not by Kanakchand's humiliation, but by 'the guilt of turning a high-spirited, ambitious boy into a malevolent revolutionary': again that distorting gloss, that cutting of the ground from under our feet.

The years pass. Kanakchand becomes important in the nationalist movement. He wishes to be avenged, and with Independence vengeance is his. He is now presented to us as physically repulsive and contemptible, overbearing at one moment, instinctively cringing at the next. The Prince's little principality disappears. Kanakchand, adding insult to injury, leads a demonstration through the streets, chanting, 'The raj is dead!'

> That, I thought, was the one thing I would never forgive Kanakchand. He was hitting at a man who had already fallen but was putting up a brave front. He was humiliating some-one who still held that he had no equal among men. That, truly, was the vengeance of sheep, as my father had said.

The stiff upper lip reinforcing a medieval conception of degree, public school fairplay stimulating an opposed passion: the confusion is now apparent. It is with more than public school righteousness, though it might seem that in its name alone action is being taken, that Abhayraj makes a vow. He will

avenge his father. He will do so by inflicting an old
humiliation—in retrospect how deserved, answering how apt
an assessment of degree—on Kanakchand. He will flog him
in public; he will flog him with a riding crop. 'He was one of
those who would always squeal, one of those unfortunates
who had not learned to take their punishment without showing
it.' This is the action with which the book ends. This is what is
presented for our approval; this is what, after the tragedy of
the Prince's fall, restores calm of mind to the narrator and is
meant to restore it to us.

The poverty of India is *quivering*. The guilt Abhayraj
carries for his father's flogging of Kanakchand, not public
school material in the final analysis, is only the guilt of turning
a high-spirited boy into a revolutionary. And all the cruelty of
India is magicked away in text-book Western phrases which
are as empty as that *quivering*: the narrator sees his father
denying 'basic rights' to 'the people', he talks of the 'collective
wish of the people'. Nowhere do I see the India I know: those
poor fields, those three-legged dogs, those sweating red-coated
railway porters carrying heavy tin trunks on their heads. 'The
mountains were rainwashed, the sky was a bright blue and the
air was stiff with the scent of pine and flowers and charged with
an almost electric silence broken by the sharp warnings of the
rickshaw pullers.' It is so the rickshaw puller appears, beast of
burden more degrading than degraded: unseen, the source
only of a holiday sound, part of the atmosphere of a Simla
romance. This is the Indian withdrawal and denial; this is
part of the confusion of Indian Anglo-India.

So too it comes to the traveller. The poor become faceless.
Then all the rest, the dance floors, the Western mimicry, might
be subjects for gentle satire. But first the background, the
obvious, must be ignored.

3. THE COLONIAL

Well, India is a country of nonsense.

M. K. GANDHI

The man moves briskly among the passengers on the crowded
suburban train, distributing leaflets. The leaflets are smudged
and dog-eared; in three languages they tell of the misfortunes
of a refugee family. Some passengers read the leaflets; many
more don't. The train comes into a station. The leaflet-
distributor goes out through one door and a woman and a boy
enter through another. The leaflet didn't promise this. It
promised an impoverished Bengali woman and her six starving
children, not this small boy, blind, thin, half-naked, scaly with
dirt, whining at a low, steady pitch, tears streaming out of raw
red eyes, his arms held aloft in supplication. The boy is
manœuvred and propelled through the coach by the woman,
who weeps and whines and briskly, without acknowledgement,
collects the small coins which the passengers, barely looking
up, hand to her. She does not pause to plead with those who
don't give. By the time the train stops she and the boy are at
the door, ready to change coaches. They go out. Another man
comes in. He too is in a rush. He pushes through the coach,
retrieving what leaflets he can before the next station.

It has been swift; everyone, passengers included, is well-
drilled; there has been little stir. Stencilled notices in three
languages on the grimy woodwork warn against alms-giving,
as they warn against accepting cigarettes from strangers since
'these may be doped'. But it is good to give to the beggar. He
follows a holy calling; he can exercise the pity and virtue of
even the poor. Possibly the boy had been blinded to work this
suburban route; and the organisation was certainly at fault in

issuing the wrong leaflets. But this is not important. What matters is the giving to the beggar, the automatic act of charity which is an automatic reverence to God, like the offering of a candle or a spin of the prayer-wheel. The beggar, like the priest, has his function; like the priest, he might need an organisation.

But here is an observer who dissents:

> If I had the power, I would stop every *sadavrata* where free meals are given. It has degraded the nation and it has en-couraged laziness, idleness, hypocrisy and even crime. Such misplaced charity adds nothing to the wealth of the country, whether material or spiritual . . . . I know that it is . . . much more difficult to organise an institution where honest work has to be done before meals are served . . . . But I am con-vinced that it will be cheaper in the long run, if we do not want to increase in geometrical progression the race of loafers which is fast overrunning this land.

It is the attitude of the foreigner who does not understand the function of the beggar in India and is judging India by the standards of Europe. He is too radical to succeed and of course in this matter of beggary he has failed.

Shankaracharya Hill, overlooking the Dal Lake, is one of the beauty spots of Srinagar. It has to be climbed with care, for large areas of its lower slopes are used as latrines by Indian tourists. If you surprise a group of three women, companion-ably defecating, they will giggle: the shame is yours, for exposing yourself to such a scene.

In Madras the bus station near the High Court is one of the more popular latrines. The traveller arrives; to pass the time he raises his dhoti, defecates in the gutter. The bus arrives; he boards it; the woman sweeper cleans up after him. Still in Madras, observe this bespectacled patriarch walking past the University on the Marina. Without warning he raises his dhoti, revealing a backside bare save for what appears to be a rope-like G string; he squats, pisses on the pavement, leisurely rises;

the dhoti still raised, he rearranges his G-string, lets the dhoti
fall, and continues on his promenade. It is a popular evening
walk, this Marina; but no one looks, no face is averted in
embarrassment.

In Goa you might think of taking an early morning walk
along the balustraded avenue that runs beside the Mandovi
River. Six feet below, on the water's edge, and as far as you
can see, there is a line, like a wavering tidewrack, of squatters.
For the people of Goa, as for those of imperial Rome, defecating is a social activity; they squat close to one another; they
chatter. When they are done they advance, trousers still down,
backsides bare, into the water, to wash themselves. They climb
back on to the avenue, jump on their cycles or get into their
cars, and go away. The strand is littered with excrement; amid
this excrement fish is being haggled over as it is landed from
the boats; and every hundred yards or so there is a blue-and-
white enamelled notice in Portuguese threatening punishment
for soiling the river. But no one notices.

Indians defecate everywhere. They defecate, mostly, beside
the railway tracks. But they also defecate on the beaches; they
defecate on the hills; they defecate on the river banks; they
defecate on the streets; they never look for cover. Muslims,
with their tradition of purdah, can at times be secretive. But
this is a religious act of self-denial, for it is said that the peasant,
Muslim or Hindu, suffers from claustrophobia if he has to
use an enclosed latrine. A handsome young Muslim boy, a
student at a laughable institute of education in an Uttar
Pradesh weaving town, elegantly dressed in the style of Mr
Nehru, even down to the buttonhole, had another explanation.
Indians were a poetic people, he said. He himself always sought
the open because he was a poet, a lover of Nature, which was
the matter of his Urdu verses; and nothing was as poetic as
squatting on a river bank at dawn.

These squatting figures—to the visitor, after a time, as
eternal and emblematic as Rodin's Thinker—are never spoken
of; they are never written about; they are not mentioned in
novels or stories; they do not appear in feature films or
documentaries. This might be regarded as part of a permissible

prettifying intention. But the truth is that *Indians do not see these squatters* and might even, with complete sincerity, deny that they exist: a collective blindness arising out of the Indian fear of pollution and the resulting conviction that Indians are the cleanest people in the world. They are required by their religion to take a bath every day. This is central; and they have devised minute rules to protect themselves from every conceivable contamination. There is only one pure way to defecate; in love-making only the left hand is to be used; food is to be taken only with the right. It has all been regulated and purified. To observe the squatters is therefore distorting; it is to fail to see through to the truth. And the ladies at the Lucknow club, after denying that Indians defecate in public, will remind you, their faces creased with distaste, of the habits of Europe—the right hand used for love-making, toilet paper and food, the weekly bath in a tub of water contaminated by the body of the bather, the washing in a wash-basin that has been spat and gargled into—proving by such emotive illustrations not the dirtiness of Europe but the security of India. It is an Indian method of argument, an Indian way of seeing: it is so that squatters and wayside filth begin to disappear.

But here is that observer again:

Instead of having graceful hamlets dotting the land, we have dung-heaps. The approach to many villages is not a refreshing experience. Often one would like to shut one's eyes and stuff one's nose; such is the surrounding dirt and offending smell.

The one thing which we can and must learn from the West is the science of municipal sanitation.

By our bad habits we spoil our sacred river banks and furnish excellent breeding grounds for flies .... A small spade is the means of salvation from a great nuisance. Leaving night-soil, cleaning the nose, or spitting on the road is a sin against God as well as humanity, and betrays a sad want of consideration for others. The man who does not cover his waste deserves a heavy penalty even if he lives in a forest.

The observer is seeing what no Indian sees. But he has now
declared his foreign inspiration. The celebrated Indian daily
bath he frequently dismisses as 'a kind of bath'. He is unwilling
to see beyond the ritual act to the intention, and in the intention
to find reality. Sanitation is one of his obsessions. And just as
in London he had read books on vegetarianism and clothes-
washing and in South Africa books on bookkeeping, so he
has read books on this subject.

> In his book on rural hygiene Dr Poore says that excreta
> should be buried in earth no deeper than nine to twelve
> inches. The author contends that superficial earth is charged
> with minute life, which, together with light and air which
> easily penetrate it, turn the excreta into good soft sweet-
> smelling soil within a week. Any villager can test this for
> himself.

It is the characteristic note of this observer. His interest in
sanitation, which is properly the concern of the latrine-cleaner,
is not widely shared. The briefest glimpse of the lavatories at
New Delhi's international airport is sufficient. Indians defecate
everywhere, on floors, in urinals for men (as a result of yogic
contortions that can only be conjectured). Fearing contamination, they squat rather than sit, and every lavatory cubicle
carries marks of their misses. No one notices.

In Europe and elsewhere the favoured bunk in a railway
sleeper is the top bunk. It is more private and less liable to
disturbance from dangling feet or opening doors. In India,
however, where the top bunk has the added advantage of being
freer of dust, the lower bunk is preferred, not because it is
easier to spread one's bedding on it—there are porters and
servants to do that—but because climbing to the top bunk
involves physical effort, and physical effort is to be avoided as a
degradation.

On this express to Delhi my sleeper had been booked by a
high railway official and I was naturally given the lower bunk.
My travelling companion was about forty. He wore a suit; he

might have been a senior clerk or a university teacher. He was not happy about the top bunk. He complained about it first to the porter and then, after the train had started, to himself. I offered to change with him. His sourness vanished. But he simply stood where he was and did nothing. His bedding had been spread for him on the top bunk by the porter, and he was waiting until we got to the next station, two hours distant, so that he might get a porter to take it down for him. I wished to settle down. I began to do the porter's job. He smiled but offered no help. I lost my temper. His face acquired that Indian expressionlessness which indicates that communication has ceased and that the Indian has withdrawn from a situation he cannot understand. Labour is a degradation; only a foreigner would see otherwise:

> Divorce of the intellect from body-labour has made of us the shortest-lived, most resourceless and most exploited nation on earth.

The observer, the failed reformer, is of course Mohandas Gandhi. Mahatma, great-souled, father of the nation, deified, his name given to streets and parks and squares, honoured everywhere by statues and *mandaps* and in Delhi by Rajghat, which the visitor must approach barefooted over scorching sand, his portrait garlanded in every *pan*-shop, hung in hundreds of offices, bare-chested, bespectacled, radiating light and goodness, his likeness so familiar that, simplified to caricature and picked out in electric lights, it is now an accepted part of the decorations of a wedding house, he is nevertheless the least Indian of Indian leaders. He looked at India as no Indian was able to; his vision was direct, and this directness was, and is, revolutionary. He sees exactly what the visitor sees; he does not ignore the obvious. He sees the beggars and the shameless pundits and the filth of Banaras; he sees the atrocious sanitary habits of doctors, lawyers and journalists. He sees the Indian callousness, the Indian refusal to see. No Indian attitude escapes him, no Indian problem; he looks down to the roots of the static, decayed society. And the picture of India which comes out of his writings and exhortations over more than thirty years still holds: this is the measure of his failure.

He saw India so clearly because he was in part a colonial. He settled finally in India when he was forty-six, after spending twenty years in South Africa. There he had seen an Indian community removed from the setting of India; contrast made for clarity, criticism and discrimination for self-analysis. He emerged a colonial blend of East and West, Hindu and Christian. Nehru is more Indian; he has a romantic feeling for the country and its past; he takes it all to his heart, and the India he writes about cannot easily be recognised. Gandhi never loses the critical, comparing South African eye; he never rhapsodises, except in the vague Indian way, about the glories of ancient India. But it is Gandhi, and not Nehru, who will give as much emphasis to the resolutions passed at a Congress gathering as to the fact that the Tamilian delegates ate by themselves because they would have been polluted by the sight of non-Tamilians, and that certain delegates, forgetting that there were no excrement-removers at hand, used the verandah as a latrine.

It is a correct emphasis, for more than a problem of sanitation is involved. It is possible, starting from that casual defecation in a verandah at an important assembly, to analyse the whole diseased society. Sanitation was linked to caste, caste to callousness, inefficiency and a hopelessly divided country, division to weakness, weakness to foreign rule. This is what Gandhi saw, and no one purely of India could have seen it. It needed the straight simple vision of the West; and it is revealing to find, just after his return from South Africa, how Gandhi speaks Christian, Western, simplicities with a new, discovering fervour: 'Before the Throne of the Almighty we shall be judged, not by what we have eaten nor by whom we have been touched but by whom we have served and how. Inasmuch as we serve a single human being in distress, we shall find favour in the sight of God.' The New Testament tone is not inappropriate. It is in India, and with Gandhi, that one can begin to see how revolutionary the now familiar Christian ethic must once have been. Hindus might try to find in this ideal of service the 'selfless action' of the Gita. But this is only Indian distortion, the eternal Indian attempt to incorporate and nullify. The Gita's selfless action is a call to self-fulfilment and at the same time a restatement of degree; it is the opposite of the service which Gandhi, the Indian revolutionary, is putting forward as a practicable day-to-day ideal.

The spirit of service, excrement, bread-labour, the dignity of scavenging, and excrement again: Gandhi's obsessions— even when we remove nonviolence, when we set aside all that he sought to make of himself, and concentrate on his analysis of India—seem ill-assorted and sometimes unpleasant. But they hang together; they form a logical whole; they answer the directness of his colonial vision.

Study these four men washing down the steps of this unpalatable Bombay hotel. The first pours water from a bucket, the second scratches the tiles with a twig broom, the third uses a rag to slop the dirty water down the steps into another bucket, which is held by the fourth. After they have passed, the steps are as dirty as before; but now above the blackened skirting-tiles the walls are freshly and dirtily splashed. The bathrooms and lavatories are foul; the slimy woodwork has rotted away as a result of this daily drenching; the concrete walls are green and black with slime. You cannot complain that the hotel is dirty. No Indian will agree with you. Four sweepers are in daily attendance, and it is enough in India that the sweepers attend. They are not required to *clean*. That is a subsidiary part of their function, which is to *be* sweepers, degraded beings, to go through the motions of degradation. They must stoop when they sweep; cleaning the floor of the smart Delhi café, they will squat and move like crabs between the feet of the customers, careful to touch no one, never looking up, never rising. In Jammu City you will see them collecting filth from the streets with their bare hands. This is the degradation the society requires of them, and to this they willingly submit. They are dirt; they wish to appear as dirt.

Class is a system of rewards. Caste imprisons a man in his function. From this it follows, since there are no rewards. that duties and responsibilities become irrelevant to position. A man is his proclaimed function. There is little subtlety to India. The poor are thin; the rich are fat. The petty Marwari merchant in Calcutta eats quantities of sweets to develop the layers of fat that will proclaim his prosperity. 'You look fat and fresh today' is a compliment in the Punjab. And in every Uttar Pradesh town you might see the rich and very fat man in cool, clean white sitting in a cycle-rickshaw being pedalled by a poor and very thin man, prematurely aged, in rags. Beggars whine. Holy men give up all. Politicians are grave and unsmiling. And the cadet of the Indian Administrative Service, when asked why he has joined the service, replies after some thought, 'It gives me prestige'. His colleagues, who are present, do not disagree. It is an honest reply; it explains why, when the Chinese invade, the administration in Assam will collapse.

Service is not an Indian concept, and the providing of services has long ceased to be a concept of caste. The function of the businessman is to make money. He might wish to sell shoes to Russia. He therefore sends good samples; the order obtained, he sends a shipload of shoes with cardboard soles. Overcoming foreign distrust of Indian business practices, he gets an order from Malaya for drugs. And sends coloured water. It is not his duty as a merchant to supply genuine drugs or good shoes or any shoes or drugs at all; his duty is, by whatever means, to make money. The shoes are sent back; there are complaints about the coloured water. This is the merchant's luck; these are the trials he has to endure. He hops from enterprise to enterprise, from shoes to drugs to tea. A tea plantation is a delicate organisation; he soon works it to ruin. Shortsightedness and dishonesty do not enter into it. The merchant is simply fulfilling his function. Later, fulfilling another aspect of his function, he might give up his money altogether and end his days as a mendicant sadhu.

The tailor in Madras will give you trousers with a false hem. At the first shrinking the trousers are useless. But his label is in the waistband and he begged you to give his name to others. He can make money only if he gets customers; and he will get customers, not by making good trousers, but by getting his name known. And here is a shirtmaker distributing leaflets to announce the opening of his establishment. The Japanese have driven him out of West Africa. 'Their finish was better.' He speaks without rancour; that defeat was just part of his luck. His response to it is not to improve his finish but, abandoning 'the black Negro savages of Africa', to start afresh in this Indian town. The shirt he makes you is atrocious. The cuffs are an inch too narrow, the tail is several inches too short; and after the first wash the whole thing shrinks. He has made a little extra money by saving on material; for this reason he remains warm towards you and whenever he sees you he presses you to have another shirt made. (If you had gone to him with an introduction and had therefore been represented to him as someone capable of doing him harm, it would have been in his interest to be extravagantly generous; the shirt might even have been a little too large.) Every morning he pauses at the door of his shop, bows and touches the dust of the threshold to his forehead. This is how he guards his luck; his enterprise is a contract between God and himself alone.

'After acceptance she should please him; when he is infatuated with her she should suck him dry of his wealth and at last abandon him. This is the duty of a public woman.' The *Kama Sutra*, it might be said, reveals a society in undress; and no Indian manual is so old that it has ceased to be relevant. It is perhaps inevitable that a religion which teaches that life is illusion should encourage a balancing pragmatism in earthly, illusory relationships. The duty of the public woman—and mark that word duty—resembles the duty of the businessman: if you want to find sharp practice and monopolies preached as high virtues you can do no better than read some of the tales of the Indian classical period. The cow is holy. It is to be reverenced by being allowed to live, even if it has to be turned out into grassless city streets; even if it has been knocked down by a lorry on the Delhi-Chandigarh road and lies dying slowly in its blood for a whole afternoon, it remains holy: the villagers will stand by to see that no one attempts to take its life. The black buffalo, on the other hand, creature of darkness, is always fat and sleek and well looked after. It is not holy; it is only more expensive. The *Kama Sutra* lists fifteen situations in which adultery is permissible; the fifth situation is 'when such clandestine relations are safe and a sure method of earning money'; and at the end of the list comes the warning that 'it must be distinctly understood that it [adultery] is permitted for these purposes alone and not for the satisfaction of mere lust'. This moral ambiguity is in keeping with what the *Kama Sutra*, like other Indian manuals, lays down as the duties of the cultured man: 'to engage in activities that do not endanger one's prospects in the other world, that do not entail loss of wealth and that are withal pleasant'.

In the introduction to *Tales of Ancient India*, a selection of translations from the Sanskrit, published by the University of Chicago Press in 1959, J. A. B. Van Buitenen writes:

If I have toned down the 'spiritual', it is because sometimes one wishes to protest against the image of Indian spirituality —here as well as in India. The classical civilisation was not overly spiritual. Even its skull-bearing hermits and vagrant saints had the zest to find humour in a funeral pyre. The homely Buddha of history becomes a towering pantheon of tier upon tier of beings teeming with a restless splendour that owes little to resignation. For a brief span even free will could be an issue. There was a spirit abroad that fleetingly allowed itself to be captured in a living form before it lost itself in formless spirituality. It is hard to believe that so much life would die even in a thousand years.

Caste, sanctioned by the Gita with almost propagandist fervour, might be seen as part of the older Indian pragmatism, the 'life' of classical India. It has decayed and ossified with the society, and its corollary, function, has become all: the sweeper's inefficiency and the merchant's shortsighted ruthlessness are inevitable. It is not easy to get candidates for a recently instituted award for brave children. Children do not wish their parents to know that they have risked their lives to save others. It isn't that Indians are especially cowardly or have no admiration for courage. It is that bravery, the willingness to risk one's life, is the function of the soldier and no one else. Indians have been known to go on picnicking on a river bank while a stranger drowned. Every man is an island; each man to his function, his private contract with God. This is the realisation of the Gita's selfless action. This is caste. In the beginning a no doubt useful division of labour in a rural society, it has now divorced function from social obligation, position from duties. It is inefficient and destructive; it has created a psychology which will frustrate all improving plans. It has led to the Indian passion for speech-making, for gestures and for symbolic action.

Symbolic action: tree-planting week (seventy percent of the trees planted die from lack of attention after the speeches), smallpox eradication week (one central minister is reported to have refused to be vaccinated for religious reasons, and vaccination certificates can be bought for a few shillings from various medical men), anti-fly week (declared in one state before the flies came), children's day (a correct speech by Mr Nehru about children on the front page of the newspaper and on the back page a report that free milk intended for poor children had found its way to the Calcutta open market), malaria eradication week (HELP ERADICATE MALARIA daubed, in English, on the walls of illiterate Hindi-speaking villages).

When action is so symbolic, labels are important, for things and places as well as for people. An enclosed open space, its purpose made clear by its fixtures, nevertheless carries a large board: CHILDREN'S PLAYGROUND. Another open space with a stage at one end has the sign: OPEN AIR THEATRE. The jeep that leads a state governor's cavalcade is marked in white: PILOT JEEP. New Delhi is a jumble of labels; the effect is of a civil service bazaar. Even ancient and holy buildings are disfigured. The eighth-century temple at the top of Shankara-charya Hill in Srinagar is hung at the gateway with a multi-coloured sign which would serve a haberdasher's shop. Set into the ancient stonework of one of the temples at Mahabali-puram near Madras is a plaque commemorating the minister who inaugurated the work of restoration. The Gandhi Mandap in Madras is a small colonnaded structure; carved on it are the names of the members of the committee that put the mandap up; the list is taller than a man.

The machinery of the modern state exists. The buildings exist; they are labelled; they sometimes anticipate need, and such anticipation can often be its own sufficient fulfilment. Consider the credits at the bottom of a Tourist Department leaflet: *Designed and produced by the Directorate of Advertising and Visual Publicity, Ministry of Information and Broadcasting, for the Department of Tourism, Ministry of Transport and Communications.* The structure is too perfect, too well labelled. It is not surprising that sometimes it proclaims no more than good intentions. The copies of *Family Planning News* that I saw contained little news of families that had been planned and many photographs of charming ladies in those wonderful saris, planning family planning. Traffic lights are part of the trappings of the modern city. Lucknow therefore has them; but they are only decorations, and dangerous, because ministers are required by their dignity never to halt at lights; and there are forty-six ministers in this state. The sweetshops of Gorakhpur are required to have glasscases; the cases accordingly stand, quite empty, next to the heaps of exposed sweets. There is that fine new theatre at Chandigarh; but who will write the plays?

When a crisis occurs, as during the Chinese invasion, the symbolic nature of the structure is made plain. Speeches are made and reported at length. Many gestures—the woman Minister of Health giving blood, somebody else giving jewellery—are given publicity. Various services are suspended. Then no one seems to know what to do next. Perhaps a Defence of the Realm Act? Dora, everyone calls it, adding a comforting familiarity to a correct label; and for a few days it is spoken like a magic word. The British proclaimed Dora in 1939. Now the Indian Government does the same. The British dug trenches. So they dig trenches in Delhi, but only symbolically, here and there, and dangerously, in public parks, below trees. The trenches answer the insatiable Indian need for open-air latrines. And, needless to say, supplies for the army, symbolically armed, find their way to the Calcutta open market.

*

An eastern conception of dignity and function, reposing on symbolic action: this is the dangerous, decayed pragmatism of caste. Symbolic dress, symbolic food, symbolic worship: India deals in symbols, inaction. Inaction arising out of proclaimed function, function out of caste. Untouchability is not the most important effect of the system; a western conception of dignity alone has made it so. But at the heart of the system lies the degradation of the latrine-cleaner, and that casual defecation in a verandah which Gandhi observed in 1901.

'The moment untouchability goes the caste system will be purified.' It sounds like a piece of Gandhian and Indian double-think. It might even be interpreted as a recognition of the inevitability of caste. But it is a revolutionary assessment. Land reform does not convince the brahmin that he can put his hand to the plough without disgrace. Making awards to children for bravery does not lessen the feeling that it is unpardonable to risk one's life to save another. Reserving government jobs for untouchables helps nobody. It places responsibility in the hands of the unqualified; and the position of untouchable civil servants, whose reputations always go before them, is intolerable. It is the system that has to be re-generated, the psychology of caste that has to be destroyed. So Gandhi comes again and again to the filth and excrement of India, the dignity of latrine-cleaning; the spirit of service; bread-labour. From the West his message looks limited and cranky; but it is only that to a concerned colonial vision of India he is applying Western simplicities.

India undid him. He became a mahatma. He was to be reverenced for what he was; his message was irrelevant. He roused India to all her 'formless spirituality'; he awakened all the Indian passion for self-abasement in the presence of the virtuous, self-abasement of which the *Kama Sutra* would have approved, since it ensured a man's prospects in the other world, did not encourage him to any prolonged and difficult labour, and was withal pleasant. Symbolic action was the curse of India. Yet Gandhi was Indian enough to deal in symbols. So, latrine-cleaning became an occasional ritual, virtuous because sanctioned by the great-souled; the degradation of the latrine-cleaner continued. The spinning-wheel did not dignify labour; it was only absorbed into the great Indian symbolism, its significance rapidly fading. He remains a tragic paradox. Indian nationalism grew out of Hindu revivalism; this revivalism, which he so largely encouraged, made his final failure certain. He succeeded politically because he was reverenced; he failed because he was reverenced. His failure is there, in his writings: he is still the best guide to India. It is as if, in England, Florence Nightingale had become a saint, honoured by statues everywhere, her name on every lip; and the hospitals had remained as she had described them.

His failure is deeper. For nothing so shakes up the Indian in order that he might be made more securely static, nothing so stultifies him and robs him of his habitual grace, as the possession of a holy man.

'Is this the train for Delhi?' I cried to a peasant group, bounding, with seconds to spare, into a compartment at Mora-dabad station.

'Where on earth do you think you are? Speak Hindi if you want an answer. Hindi alone here.'

This was from the head of the group. He was not a nationalist, propagating the national language. At any other time he would have been civil and even deferential. But now he was the possessor of a saffron-clad holy man, fat and sleek and oily—there is little subtlety to India—before whom the women and children of the group were abasing themselves.

It is so with Indians and Gandhi. He is the latest proof of their spirituality; he strengthens the private contract with God of all who revere him. Nothing remains of Gandhi in India but this: his name and the worship of his image; the seminars about nonviolence, as though this was all he taught; prohibition, rich in symbolism and righteousness, proclaimed as a worthy goal even at the height of the China crisis; and the politician's garb.

Observe this village politician, austerely and correctly clad, speaking of the mahatma and the motherland at a country meeting.

'To get elected,' the Indian Administrative Service

officer tells me, 'that man had seventeen people murdered.'

There is no inconsistency; the mahatma has been absorbed into the formless spirituality and decayed pragmatism of India. The revolutionary became a god and his message was thereby lost. He failed to communicate to India his way of direct looking. And strange: in twelve months I could find no one among his ordinary worshippers who could tell me exactly what he looked like. It was not a question to put to Indians, who have no descriptive gift, but the replies were astonishing. For some he was tiny; for one man in Madras he was six feet tall. For some he was dark; for some he was exceedingly fair. Yet all remembered him; many even had personal photographs. These did not help: the image was too familiar. So it is when legends are complete. Nothing can add to them or take away from them. The image is fixed, simplified, unalterable; witness is of no account. Nearly every word Gandhi spoke and wrote is recorded; the Gandhi bibliography is immense. But in India he has already receded; he might have lived in the days when scribes wrote on leaves and strips of brass and people travelled on foot.

4. ROMANCERS

The titles of Indian films never ceased to attract me. They were straightforward, but they held infinite suggestion. *Private Secretary:* in India, where adventure of the sort implied was limited, where kisses were barred from the screen, the mind could play with such a title: the 'progressive' girl, the attractive office job (typewriter, white telephone), the mixing of the sexes; irregular love; family life threatened; tragedy. I never saw the film. I saw only the poster: a body, if I remember rightly, lay on an office floor. *Junglee* (untamed) was another title: a woman against a background of Himalayan snow. For *Maya* (cosmic illusion, vanity) a woman was shown weeping big, bitter tears. *Jhoola* (the swing) promised gaiety, many songs and dances. Then, as sinister in suggestion as *Private Secretary, Paying Guest.*

We were paying guests. It was in Delhi, the city of symbols, first of the British Raj and now of the independent Indian republic: a jungle of black-and-white noticeboards mushrooming out of feverish administrative activity, the Indian Council for this and Academy for that, the Ministry for this and the Department for that, the buildings going up all the time, monstrous bird's nests of bamboo scaffolding: a city ever growing, as it has been for the last forty years, a city of civil servants and contractors. We were paying guests; and our host was Mrs Mahindra, the wife of a contractor.

She sent her car to meet us at the railway station. It was an attention we were grateful for. To step out of the third-class airconditioned coach on to the smooth hot platform was to feel one's shirt instantly heated, to lose interest, to wonder

88

with a dying flicker of intellectual curiosity why anyone in India bothered, why anyone had bothered with India. On that platform, oven-dry, competitive activity was yet maintained. The porters, blazing in red tunics and red turbans, hustled about, screeching for custom. The successful staggered beneath metal trunks sprayed with fine dust after the journey from Bombay: one trunk, two trunks, three trunks. The fans spun frenziedly above us. The beggars whined. The man from the Bhagirath Hotel waved his grubby folder. Remembering that for antarctic explorers surrender was easy and that the enduring, the going on, was the act of bravery, I reached out for the folder and, standing in the midst of noise and activity in which I had lost interest and which now seemed to swing outwards from me in waves, I read with slow concentration, in which everything was distorted and dissolving:

Arrive a Delhi au terme d'un equisant voyage, c'est avec le plus grand plaisir que j'ai pris le meilleur des repos au Bahgitath Hotel, dant les installations permettent de se remettre de ses fetigues dans un cadre agreable. J'ai particulierment apprecie la gentillesse et l'hospitolite de le direction et do personnel. Je ne peploie q'ue chose, c'est de n'avoir pu arroser les excellents repos des baissens alcoolirees aux quelles nous mettent le cour en joie.

28-7-61   Fierre Bes Georges, Gareme (Seine) France

Baissens alcoolirees: yearning had glided into delirium. *Et Monsieur, qu'est-ce-qu-il peploie? Je ne peploie qu'ue chose. Arrosez les excellents repos.* On the shining concrete the figures were stretched out, Indian sleepers on an Indian railway station. The unemployed porters squatted. The beggar woman, whining, even she squatted. *Arrosez les excellent repos.* But there were no fountains. The streets were wide and grand, the roundabouts endless: a city built for giants, built for its vistas, for its symmetry: a city which remained its plan, unquickened and unhumanised, built for people who would be protected from its openness, from the whiteness of its light, to whom the trees were like the trees on an architect's drawing, decorations, not intended to give shade: a city built like a monument. And everything labelled, as on an architect's drawing; every moving thing dwarfed, the man on his bicycle, with his black, black shadow; an endless, ever spreading city which encouraged no repose, which sent people scuttling through its avenues and malls, as these scooter-rickshaws scuttled noisily in and out of the traffic, shrunk to less than human size in the presence of the monumental city.

The house was in one of the New Delhi 'colonies' or residential settlements, abrupt huddles of fantasy and riotous modern lines after the exposed austerity of the centre. It was as though an Indian village had been transformed into concrete and glass, and magnified. The houses were not yet coherently numbered; and the narrow nameless lanes were full of bewildered Sikhs seeking houses by plot numbers, whose sequence was chronological, indicating date of purchase. Dust; concrete white and grey; no trees; each Sikh attached to a brisk, black shadow.

We sat in front of an empty, unsmoked fireplace below an electric fan and rested with glasses of Coca-Cola.

'Duffer, that Bihari boy,' Mrs Mahindra said, apologising for her chauffeur and making conversation.

She was plump, still young, with large staring eyes. She had little English, and when words failed her she gave a giggle and looked away. She said *Mm*, her eyes became vacant, and her right hand went to her chin.

The house was new and on this ground floor smelled of concrete and paint. The rooms were not yet fully decorated; the furnishings were sparse. But there were fans everywhere; and the bathroom fittings, from Germany, were rare and expensive.

'I am craze for foreign,' Mrs Mahindra said. 'Just craze for foreign.'

She marvelled at our suitcases and at what they contained. She fingered with reverence and delight.

'Craze, just craze for foreign.'

Widening her eyes, it might have been in fear, it might have been in admiration, she told us of her husband, the contractor. He had a hard life. He was always travelling about in forests and jungles and living in tents. She had to stay behind and do the housekeeping.

'Three thousand rupees a month allowance. These days cost-of-living that-is-no-joke.'

She was not really boasting. She came from a simple family and she accepted her new wealth as she would have accepted poverty. She was anxious to learn, anxious to do the correct thing, anxious for our foreign approval. Did we like the colours of her curtains? The colours of her walls? Look, that lamp bracket there was foreign, from Japan. There wasn't a thing which was not foreign except, as she confessed when we went up to her dining-room for lunch, for this brass dish-warmer.

She sat with us, not eating, staring at our plates, hand supporting her chin, widening her eyes dreamily and smiling whenever our glances met. She was new to the business, she said with a giggle. She had not had any paying guests before, and so we must forgive her if she treated us like her children.

Her sons arrived. They were in their teens, tall, and as cool towards us as their mother was demonstrative. They joined us at the table. Mrs Mahindra spooned out from the dishes into their plates, spooned out into our plates.

Suddenly she giggled and nodded towards her elder son.

'I want him to marry foreign.'

The boy didn't react.

We talked about the weather and the heat.

'The heat doesn't affect us,' the boy said. 'Our bedrooms are airconditioned.'

Mrs Mahindra caught our eyes and gave a mischievous smile.

She insisted on taking us out with her that afternoon to do a little shopping. She wanted to buy curtains for one of the downstairs rooms. But, we said, the curtains she had shown us in that room were brand new and very elegant. No, no, she said; we were only being polite. She wanted to buy new curtains that afternoon and she wanted our foreign advice.

So we drove back into the centre. She pointed out the monuments: Humayun's Tomb, India Gate, Rashtrapati Bhavan.

'New Delhi, New Delhi,' she sighed. '*Capital* of India.'

We went from shop to shop, and I began to fade. Fading, I relapsed into mechanical speech. 'Look,' I said to the boy, pointing to a heap of slippers that were extravagantly of the orient, their tapering embroidered points curling back on themselves. 'Look, those are rather amusing.'

'They are too common for us.'

His mother was known to the shop assistants. She engaged them all in friendly conversation. They offered her chairs. She sat; she fingered; she talked. Bolt after bolt was unwrapped for her. Blandly she watched and blandly she walked away. Her movements were easy; no one appeared to be offended. She knew what she wanted, and at last she found it.

She asked us to study the fireplace that evening. It was of irregular shape and had been designed by her husband, who had also designed the irregular recesses, for electric lights, in the stone fence.

'Modern. Modern. *All* modern.'

In the morning the painters came to repaint the newly painted, unused room to match the curtains that had been bought the previous afternoon.

She came into our room as we lay stripped below the ceiling fan after breakfast. She sat on the edge of the bed and talked. She examined this stocking, that shoe, that brassiere; she asked prices. She lured us out to watch the painters at work; she held the material against the paint and asked whether they went well together.

She had nothing to do except to spend three thousand rupees a month. She had one especial friend. 'Mrs M. *Mehta. Secretary.* Women's *League*. Mrs M. Mehta. Airconditioners and other electrical gadgets.' The name and the words were familiar from advertisements. Regularly Mrs Mahindra visited Mrs M. Mehta; regularly she consulted her astrologer; regularly she shopped and went to the temple. Her life was full and sweet.

A tall man of about fifty came to the house in the afternoon. He said he was answering an advertisement in the newspaper; he wished to lease the ground floor which we were occupying. He wore a double-breasted grey suit and spoke English with a strained army accent.

'Mm.' Mrs Mahindra looked away.

The man in the grey suit continued to speak in English. He represented a large firm, he said. A firm with foreign connections.

'Mm.' Her eyes became vacant; her palm went to her chin.

'No one will sleep here.' He was faltering a little; perhaps it had occurred to him that his firm was not as desirable as the 'diplomatic' foreigners so many advertisements solicited. 'We will give you a year's rent in advance and sign a lease for three years.'

'Mm.' She said, replying in Hindustani to his English that she would have to talk to her husband. And then there were so many other people who were interested.

'We intend to use the premises just as offices.' His dignity was beginning to yield to a certain exasperation. 'And all we would like is for a caretaker to sleep here at night. The house will remain as your home. We will give you twelve thousand rupees right away.'

She stared in her abstracted way, as though sniffing the new paint and thinking about the curtains.

'Duffer,' she said when he had gone. 'Talking English. *Barra sahib*. Duffer.'

The next morning she was glum.

'*Letter*. My husband's *father* is coming. Today. Tomorrow.' The prospect clearly depressed her. 'Talk, talk, thatisnojoke.'

When we came back to the house that afternoon we found her sitting, sad and dutiful, with a white-haired man in Indian dress. She already seemed to have shrunk a little; she looked chastened, even embarrassed. It was our foreignness she stressed when she introduced us. Then she looked away, became abstracted and took no further part in the conversation.

The white-haired man looked us over suspiciously. But he was, as Mrs Mahindra had hinted, a talker; and he regarded himself and especially his age, which was just over sixty, with wonder. It was not his adventures he spoke of so much as the habits he had formed in those sixty years. He rose at four every morning, he said; he went for a four or five-mile walk; then he read some chapters of the Gita. He had followed this routine for forty years, and it was a routine he would recommend to any young man.

Mrs Mahindra sighed. I felt she had taken a lot already and I thought I would release her. I tried to get the old man to talk of his past to me. He had no adventures to relate; he just had a list of places he had lived in or worked in. I asked precise questions; I made him describe landscapes. But Mrs Mahindra, not understanding my purpose, not accepting—or perhaps by duty not able to accept—the release I offered, sat and suffered. In the end it was the old man whom I drove away. He went and sat by himself in the small front garden.

'Naughty, naughty,' Mrs Mahindra said, giving me a smile of pure exhaustion.

'Summer is here,' the old man said after dinner. 'I have been sleeping out in the open for a fortnight. I always find that I begin to sleep out in the open a few weeks before other people.'

'Will you be sleeping out in the open tonight?' I asked.

'Of course.'

He slept just outside the door. We could see him, and no doubt he could see us. At four—so it was reasonable to assume —we heard him rise and get ready for his walk: lavatory chain, gargling, clattering, doors. We heard him return. And when we got up we found him reading the Gita.

'I always read a few pages of the Gita after I come back from my walk,' he said.

After that he idled about the house. He had nothing to do. It was difficult to ignore him; he required to be spoken to. He talked, but I began to feel that he also monitored.

We returned in the afternoon to a painful scene: the inter-viewing of another applicant for the ground floor. The applicant was uneasy; the old man, who was putting the questions, was polite but reproving; and the object of his reproof, I felt, was Mrs Mahindra, whose face was almost hidden in the top end of her sari.

We lost some of Mrs Mahindra's attentions. In no time at all she had dwindled into the Indian daughter-in-law. We heard little now of her craze for foreign. We had become liabilities. And when, attending to her father-in-law's conversation, she caught our eyes, her smile was tired. It held no conspiracy, only dutiful withdrawal. We had found her, on that first day, in a brief moment of sparkle.

We had to go to the country that weekend, and it was with a feeling almost of betrayal that we told her we were going to leave her alone with her father-in-law for a few days. She brightened at the news; she became active. We must just go, she said, and not worry about a thing. We didn't have to pack everything away; she would look after our room. She helped us to get ready. She gave us a meal and stood in the irregularly pointed stone gateway and waved while the Bihari chauffeur, duffer as we remembered, drove us off. Plump, saddened, wide-eyed Mrs Mahindra!

A weekend in the country! The words suggest cool clumps of trees, green fields, streams. Our thoughts were all of water as we left Delhi. But there was no water and little shade. The road was a narrow metal strip between two lanes of pure dust. Dust powdered the roadside trees and the fields. Once we drove for miles over a flat brown wasteland. At the end of the journey lay a town, and a communal killing. The Muslim murderer had fled; the dead Hindu had to be mourned and cremated in swift secrecy before daybreak; and afterwards troublemakers of both sides had to be watched. This occupied our host for almost all the weekend. We remained in the inspection house, grateful for the high ceiling, below the spinning fan. On one wall there was a framed typewritten digest of rules and regulations. Set into another wall was a fireplace. The winters it promised seemed so unlikely now; and it was as though one was forever doomed to be in places at the wrong time, as though one was forever feeling one's way through places where every label was false: the confectionery machine on the railway platform that hadn't worked for years, the advertisement for something that was no longer made, the timetable which was out of date. Above the mantelpiece there was a photograph of a tree standing on eroded earth beside a meagre stream; and in that photograph, in its message of exhaustion and persistence, there was something which already we could recognise as of India.

We returned to Delhi by train below a darkening sky. We waited for the storm to break. But what looked like raincloud was only dust. The tea boy cheated us (and on this run several months later that same boy was to cheat us again); a passenger complained of corruption; one story excited another. And the wind blew and the dust penetrated everywhere, dust which, the engineers tell us, can get in where water can't. We longed for the town, for hot baths and airconditioning and shuttered rooms.

The lower floor of the Mahindras' house was in darkness. The door was locked. We had no key. We rang, and rang. After some minutes a whispering, tiptoeing servant let us in as though we were his private friends. Everything in our room was as we had left it. The bed was unmade; the suitcases hadn't been moved; letters and leaflets and full ashtrays were on the bedside table; dust had settled on the static disarray. We were aware of muted activity upstairs, in the room with the Indian brass dish-warmer.

The sahib, the servant said, had returned from the jungle. And the sahib had quarrelled with the memsahib. 'He say, "You take *paying* guests? You take *money?*" '

We understood. We were Mrs Mahindra's first and last paying guests. We had been part of her idleness, perhaps like those men who had called to lease the ground floor. Perhaps Mrs M. Mehta, secretary of the Women's League, leased her ground floor; perhaps Mrs M. Mehta had a dazzling succession of foreign paying guests.

Dear Mrs Mahindra! She enjoyed her money and no doubt in her excitement had wished to make a little more. But her attentions had been touched with the genuine Indian warmth. We never saw her again; we never saw her sons again; we never saw her husband. Her father-in-law we only heard as, lurking in our room, we waited for him to settle down for the night. We heard him rise in the morning; we heard him leave for his walk. We gave him a few minutes. Then we crept out with our suitcases and roused one of the sleeping taxi-drivers in the

taxi-rank not far off. Through a friend we later sent the money
we owed.

The days in Delhi had been a blur of heat. The moments that
stayed were those of retreat: darkened bedrooms, lunches,
shuttered clubs, a dawn drive to the ruins of Tughlakabad, a
vision of the Flame of the Forest. Sightseeing was not easy.
Bare feet were required in too many places. The entrances to
temples were wet and muddy and the courtyards of mosques
were more scorching than tropical beaches in mid-afternoon.
At every mosque and temple there were idlers waiting to
pounce on those who did not take off their shoes. Their delight
and their idleness infuriated me. So did one notice: 'If you
think it is beneath your dignity to take off your shoes, slippers
are provided.' At Rajghat, faced with an unnecessarily long
walk over hot sand to the site of Gandhi's cremation, I refused
to follow the Tourist Department's guide and sat, a fully shod
heretic, in the shade. Blue-shirted schoolboys waited for the
Americans among the tourists. The boys were well fed and
well shod and carried their schoolbooks like emblems of their
worthiness. They ran to the old ladies. The ladies, informed of
India's poverty, stopped, opened their purses and smilingly
distributed coins and notes, while from the road the pro-
fessional beggars, denied entrance, watched enviously. The
heat was unhinging me. I advanced towards the schoolboys,
simple murder in my heart. They ran away, nimble in the heat.
The Americans looked assessingly at me: the proud young
Indian nationalist. Well, it would do. I walked back to the
coach, converting exhaustion into anger and shame.

So it had been in Delhi. I was shouting now almost as soon
as I entered government offices. At times the sight of rows of
young men sitting at long tables, buried among sheaves of
paper, young men checking slips of one sor t or another, young
men counting banknotes and tying them into bundles of a
hundred, all India's human futility, was more than I could
bear. 'Don't complain to me. Make your complaint through
proper channel.' 'Through proper channel! Proper channel!'
But it was hopeless; irony, mockery, was impossible in India.

And: 'Don't complain to me. Complain to my officer.' 'Which is your bloody officer?' All this with a liberating sense that my violent mood was inviting violence. Yet so often it was met only with a cold, puncturing courtesy; and I was reduced to stillness, shame and exhaustion.

In Lutyens's city I required privacy and protection. Only then was I released from the delirium of seeing certain aspects of myself magnified out of recognition I could sense the elegance of the city, in those colonnades hidden by signboards and straw blinds, in those vistas: the new tower at one end of the tree-lined avenue, the old dome at the other. I could sense the 'studious' atmosphere of which people had spoken in Bombay. I could sense its excitement as a new capital city, in the gatherings at the Gymkhana Club on a Sunday morning, the proconsular talk about the abominations of the Congo from former United Nations officials, in the announcements in the newspapers of 'cultural' entertainments provided by the embassies of competing governments: a city to which importance had newly come, and all the new toys of the 'diplomatic'. But to me it was a city in which I could only escape from one darkened room to another, separate from the reality of out of doors, of dust and light and lowcaste women in gorgeous saris—gorgeousness in saris being emblematic of lowness—working on building sites. A city doubly unreal, rising suddenly out of the plain: acres of seventeenth and eighteenth-century ruins, then the ultra-contemporary exhibition buildings; a city whose emblematic grandeur spoke of a rich and settled hinterland and not of the poor, parched land through which we had been travelling for twenty-four hours.

Yet that evening, lying in my bunk in the aluminium coach of the Srinagar Express and waiting for the train to leave, I found that I had begun to take a perverse delight in the violence of it all: delight at the thought of the twenty-four-hour journey that had brought me to Delhi, the thirty-six-hour journey still farther north that awaited me, through all the flatness of the Punjab to the mightiest mountain range in the world; delight at the physical area of luxury I had managed to reserve for myself, the separation from the unpleasant which I

was yet, through the easily operated rubber-beaded windows,
able to see: the red-turbanned porters, the trolleys of books
and magazines, the hawkers, the frenzied fans hanging low so
that from my bunk the platform appeared to be ceilinged by
spinning blades: once hated symbols of discomfort, now
answering all my urgency and exaltation which, fraudulent
though I knew it to be, I was already fearing to lose, for with a
twenty degree drop in temperature all would subside to
ordinariness.

The Punjab, intermittently glanced at during the night, was
silent and featureless except for the moving oblongs of light
from our train. A still hut, blacker against the flat black fields
awaiting the day-long sun: what more had I expected? In the
morning we were at Pathankot, the railhead—and how strange
again and again to hear this solitary English word, to me so
technical, industrial and dramatic, in a whole sentence of
Hindustani—the railhead for Kashmir. It was cool at the station
in the early morning; there was a hint of bush and, deceptive
though it was, of mountains close at hand. And our passengers
appeared in woollen shirts, sporty hats, jackets, cardigans,
pullovers and even gloves, the woollen garments of the Indian
summer holidays, not yet strictly needed, but an anticipation of
the holiday that had almost begun.

At first it was only the army of whose presence we were
aware on this flat scrub near the Pakistan border: signposted
camps, all whitewash and straight lines, the rows of lorries
and jeeps, the occasional manœuvres of light tanks. These men
in olive-green battledress and bush-hats might have belonged
to another country. They walked differently; they were handsome. We stopped at Jammu for lunch. Thereafter we climbed,
entering Kashmir by the road built by the Indian army in 1947
at the time of the Pakistan invasion. It grew cooler; there were
hills and gorges and a broken view, hill beyond hill, receding
planes of diminishing colour. We drove beside the Chenab
river which, as we climbed, fell beneath us into a gorge, littered
with logs.

'And where do you come from?'

It was the Indian question. I had been answering it

five times a day. And now again I went through the explanations.

He was sitting across the aisle from me. He was respectably
dressed in a suit. He was bald, with a sharp Gujerati nose, and
he looked bitter.

'And what do you think of our great country?'

It was another Indian question; and the sarcasm had to be
dismissed.

'Be frank. Tell me exactly what you think.'

'It's all right. It's very interesting.'

'Interesting. You are lucky. You should live here. We are
trapped here, you know. That's what we are. Trapped.'

Beside him sat his plump, fulfilled wife. She was less
interested in our conversation than in me. She studied me
whenever I looked away.

'Corruption and nepotism everywhere,' he said. 'Everybody
wanting to get out to United Nations jobs. Doctors going
abroad. Scientists going to America. The future is totally black.
How much, for instance, do you earn in your country?'

'About five thousand rupees a month.'

It was unfair to strike so hard. But he took it well.

'And what do you do for this?' he asked.

'I teach.'

'What do you teach?'

'History.'

He was unimpressed.

I added, 'And a little chemistry.'

'Strange combination. I'm a chemistry teacher myself.'

It happens to every romancer.

I said, 'I teach in a comprehensive school. You have to do a
little of everything.'

'I see.' Annoyance was peeping out of his puzzlement; his
nose seemed to twitch. 'Strange combination. Chemistry.'

I was worried. Several hours of our journey together still
remained. I pretended to be annoyed by a crying child. This
couldn't go on. But relief soon came. We stopped among pines
in a lay-by above a green wooded valley. We got out to stretch
our legs. It was cool. The plains had become like an illness

whose exact sensations it is impossible, after recovery, to
recall. The woollens were now of service. The holiday had
begun to fulfil itself. And when we got back into the bus I
found that the chemistry teacher had changed seats with his
wife, so that he would not have to continue talking to
me.

It was night, clear and cold, when we stopped at Banihal.
The rest house was in darkness; the electric lights had gone.
The attendants fussed around with candles; they prepared
meals. In the moonlight the terraced rice fields were like leaded
panes of old glass. In the morning their character had changed.
They were green and muddy. After the Banihal tunnel we began
to go down and down, past fairytale villages set in willow
groves, watered by rivulets with grassy banks, into the Vale
of Kashmir.

Kashmir was coolness and colour: the yellow mustard fields,
the mountains, snow-capped, the milky blue sky in which we
rediscovered the drama of clouds. It was men wrapped in
brown blankets against the morning mist, and barefooted
shepherd boys with caps and covered ears on steep wet rocky
slopes. At Qazigund, where we stopped, it was also dust in
sunlight, the disorder of a bazaar, a waiting crowd, and a smell
in the cold air of charcoal, tobacco, cooking oil, months-old
dirt and human excrement. Grass grew on the mud-packed
roofs of cottages—and at last it was clear why, in that story I
had read as a child in the *West Indian Reader*, the foolish widow
had made her cow climb up to the roof. Buses packed with men
with red-dyed beards were going in the direction from which
we had come. Another bus came in, halted. The crowd broke,
ran forward and pressed in frenzy around a window through
which a man with tired eyes held out his thin hand in benedic-
tion. He, like the others, was going to Mecca; and among these
imprisoning mountains how far away Jeddah seemed, that
Arabian pilgrim port dangerous with reefs over which the blue
water grows turquoise. In smoky kitchen shacks Sikhs with
ferocious beards and light eyes, warriors and rulers of an age
not long past, sat and cooked. Each foodstall carried an

attractive signboard. The heavy white cups were chipped; the tables, out in the open, were covered with oil-cloth in checked patterns; below them the ground had been softened to mud.

The mountains receded. The valley widened into soft, well-watered fields. The road was lined with poplars and willows drooped on the banks of clear rivulets. Abruptly, at Awantipur, out of a fairytale village of sagging wood-framed cottages there rose ruins of grey stone, whose heavy trabeate construction—solid square pillars on a portico, steep stone pediments on a colonnade around a central shrine, massive and clumsy in ruin—caused the mind to go back centuries to ancient worship. They were Hindu ruins, of the eighth century, as we discovered later. But none of the passengers exclaimed, none pointed. They lived among ruins; the Indian earth was rich with ancient sculpture. At Pandrethan, on the outskirts of Srinagar, the army camp was set about a smaller temple in a similar style. The soldiers were exercising. Army lorries and huts lay in neat rows; on the roadside there were army boards and divisional emblems.

We stopped at the octroi post, quaint medievalism, in a jam of Tata-Mercedes-Benz lorries, their tailboards decorated with flowered designs and *Horn Please* in fanciful lettering on a ground of ochre or pink. On the raised floors of shops blanket-wrapped men smoked hookahs. Skirting the town, we came to an avenue lined with giant chenar trees, whose sweet shade the Kashmiris believe to be medicinal, and turned into the yard of the Tourist Reception Centre, a new building in pale red brick. Across the road a large hoarding carried a picture of Mr Nehru, with his urging that the foreign visitor should be treated as a friend. Directly below the hoardings the Kashmiris were shouting already, with pure hostility it seemed, barely restrained by the swagger sticks of elegant turbanned policemen.

Among the shouters were the owners of houseboats or the servants of owners. It seemed scarcely conceivable that they owned anything or had anything worthwhile to offer. But the houseboats existed. They lay on the lake in a white row against floating green islands, answering the snow on the surrounding mountains. At intervals concrete steps led down from the lake boulevard to the crystal water. On the steps men sat and squatted and smoked hookahs; their *shikara* boats were a cluster of red and orange awnings and cushions; and in *shikaras* we were ferried over to the houseboats, where, mooring, and going up dainty steps, we found interiors beyond anything we had imagined: carpets and brassware and framed pictures, china and panelling and polished furniture of another age. And at once Awantipur and the rest disappeared. For here was English India. Here, offered for our inspection, were the chits, the faded recommendations of scores of years. Here were invitations to the weddings of English army officers, now perhaps grandfathers. And the houseboat man, so negligible at the Tourist Centre, so negligible as he pedalled behind our tonga, pleading with tears that we should visit his boat, himself altered: kicking off his shoes, dropping to his knees on the carpet, his manners became as delicate as the china—so rare now in India—in which he offered us tea. Here were more photographs, of his father and his father's guests; here were more recommendations; here were tales of enormous English meals.

Outside, the snow-capped mountains ringed the lake, at whose centre stood Akbar's fort of Hari Parbat; poplars marked the lake-town of Rainawari; and far away, beyond an open stretch of water, on the fresh green lower slopes of the mountains—as though the earth had been washed down through the ages to fill the crevices of rock—were the Mogul Gardens, with their terraces, their straight lines, their central pavilions, their water courses dropping from level to level down rippled concrete falls. The Mogul one could accept, and the Hindu. It was this English presence which, though the best known, from books and songs and those pale hands beside the Shalimar—not a stream as in my imagining, but the grandest of the gardens—it was this English presence which seemed hardest to accept, in this mountain-locked valley, this city of hookahs and samavars (so pronounced) where, in a dusty square on Residency Road, was the caravanserai for Tibetans with their long-legged boots, hats, plaited hair, their clothes as grimy-grey as their weatherbeaten faces, men indistinguishable from women.

But we did not take a houseboat. Their relics were still too movingly personal. Their romance was not mine, and it was impossible to separate them from their romance. I would have felt an intruder, as I felt in those district clubs where the billiard rooms were still hung with framed cartoons of the 1930s, where the libraries had gone derelict, the taste of a generation frozen, and where on the smoking room walls were stained engravings, difficult to see through the reflections on the dusty glass, of tumultous horsemen labelled 'Afridis' or 'Baluchis'. Indians could walk among these relics with ease; the romance had always been partly theirs and now they had inherited it fully. I was not English or Indian; I was denied the victories of both.

Part II

5. A DOLL'S HOUSE ON
THE DAL LAKE

HOTEL LIWARD
Prop: FLUSH SYSTEM *M. S. Butt*

The sign came later, almost at the end of our stay. 'I am honest man,' the owner of the C-class houseboat had said, as we stood before the white bucket in one of the mildewed and tainted rooms of his rotting hulk. 'And flush system, this is not *honest*.' But Mr Butt, showing us his still small sheaf of recommendations in the sitting room of the Liward Hotel, and pointing to the group of photographs on the pea-green walls, had said with a different emphasis, '*Before* flush.' We looked at the laughing faces. At least a similar betrayal could not be ours. The sign, dispelling conjecture, was placed high on the pitched roof and lit by three bulbs, and could be seen even from Shankaracharya Hill.

It seemed an unlikely amenity. The hotel stood in the lake, at one end of a plot of ground about eighty feet long by thirty wide. It was a rough two-storeyed structure with ochre concrete walls, green and chocolate woodwork, and a roof of unpainted corrugated iron. It had seven rooms altogether, one of which was the dining room. It was in reality two buildings. One stood squarely in the angle of the plot, two walls flush with the water; it had two rooms up and two rooms down. A narrow wooden gallery went right around the top floor; around two sides of the lower floor, and hanging directly above the water, there was another gallery. The other building had one room down and two up, the second of which was a many-sided semi-circular wooden projection supported on wooden poles. A wooden staircase led to the corridor that linked the two buildings; and the whole structure was capped by a pitched corrugated iron roof of complex angular design.

It had a rough-and-ready air, which was supported by our first glimpse of Mr Butt, cautiously approaching the landing stage to welcome us. He wore the Kashmiri fur cap, an abbreviation of the Russian. His long-tailed Indian-style shirt hung out of his loose trousers and dangled below his brown jacket. This suggested unreliability; the thick frames of his spectacles suggested abstraction; and he held a hammer in one hand. Beside him was a very small man, barefooted, with a dingy grey pullover tight above flapping white cotton trousers gathered in at the waist by a string. A touch of quaintness, something of the Shakespearean mechanic, was given him by his sagging woollen nightcap. So misleading can first impressions be: this was Aziz.

And flush was not yet finally installed. Pipes and bowls had been laid, but cisterns were yet to be unwrapped.

'One day,' Aziz said in English. 'Two days.'

'I like flush,' Mr Butt said.

We read the recommendations. Two Americans had been exceedingly warm; an Indian lady had praised the hotel for providing the 'secrecy' needed by honeymoon couples.

'*Before* flush,' Mr Butt said.

With this his English was virtually exhausted, and thereafter we dealt with him through Aziz.

We bargained. Fear made me passionate; it also, I realised later, made me unnaturally convincing. My annoyance was real; when I turned to walk away I was really walking away; when I was prevailed upon to return—easy, since the boatman refused to ferry me back to the road—my fatigue was genuine. So we agreed. I was to take the room next to the semi-circular sitting-room, of which I was also to have exclusive use. And I needed a reading lamp.

'Ten-twelve rupees, what is that?' Aziz said.

And, I would need a writing-table.

He showed me a low stool.

With my hands I sketched out my larger requirements.

He showed me an old weathered table lying out on the lawn. 'We paint,' he said.

I rocked the table with a finger.

Aziz sketched out two timber braces and Mr Butt, understanding and smiling, lifted his hammer.

'We fix,' Aziz said.

It was then that I felt they were playing and that I had become part of their play. We were in the middle of the lake. Beyond the alert kingfishers, the fantastic hoopoes pecking in the garden, beyond the reeds and willows and poplars, our view unbroken by houseboats, there were the snow-capped mountains. Before me a nightcapped man, hopping about restlessly, and at the end of the garden a new wooden shed, his home, unpainted and warm against the gloom of low-hanging willows. He was a man skilled in his own way with hammer and other implements, anxious to please, magically improvising, providing everything. The nightcap did not belong to a Shakespearian mechanic; it had a fairy-tale, Rumpelstiltskin, Snow White-and-the-seven-dwarfs air.

'You pay advance and you sign agreement for three months.'

Even this did not break the spell. Mr Butt wrote no English. Aziz was illiterate. I had to make out my own receipt. I had to write and sign our agreement in the back of a large, serious-looking but erratically filled ledger which lay on a dusty shelf in the dining room.

'You write three months?' Aziz asked.

I hadn't. I was playing safe. But how had he guessed?

'You write three months.'

The day before we were to move in we paid a surprise visit. Nothing appeared to have changed. Mr Butt waited at the landing stage, dressed as before and as seemingly abstracted. The table that was to have been painted and braced remained unpainted and unbraced on the lawn. There was no sign of a reading lamp. 'Second coat,' Aziz had said, placing his hand on the partition that divided bathroom from bedroom. But no second coat had been given, and the bright blue paint lay as thin and as scabrous on the new, knot-darkened wood. Dutifully, not saying a word, Mr Butt examined with us, stopping when we stopped, looking where we looked, as though he wasn't sure what, in spite of his knowledge, he might find. The bathroom was as we had left it: the lavatory bowl in position, still in its gummed paper taping, the pipes laid, the cistern absent.

'Finish,' I said. 'Finish. Give back deposit. We go. No stay here.'

He made no reply and we went down the steps. Then across the garden, from the warm wooden shack, embowered in willows, Aziz came tripping, nightcapped and pullovered. Blue paint spotted his pullover—a new skill revealed—and there was a large spot on the tip of his nose. He was carrying, as if about to offer it to us, a lavatory cistern.

'Two minutes,' he said. 'Three minutes. I fix.'

One of Snow White's own men in a woollen nightcap: it was impossible to abandon him.

Three days later we moved in. And it had all been done. It was as if all the folk at the bottom of the garden had lent a hand with broom and brush and saw and hammer. The table had been massively braced and tremendously nailed together; it was covered with an already peeling skin of bright blue paint. A large bulb, fringed at the top with a small semi-spherical metal shade, was attached to a stunted flexible arm which rested on a chromium-plated disc and was linked by incalculable tangled yards of flex—I had specified length and manœuvrability—to the electric point: this was the lamp. In the bathroom the lavatory cistern had been put in place. Aziz, like a magician, pulled the chain; and the flush flushed.

'Mr Butt he say,' Aziz said, when the waters subsided, 'this is not his hotel. This is *your* hotel.'

There were others beside Aziz and Mr Butt. There was the sweeper boy in flopping garments of requisite filth. There was Ali Mohammed. He was a small man of about forty with a cadaverous face made still more so by ill-fitting dentures. His duty was to entice tourists to the hotel, and his official dress consisted of a striped blue Indian-style suit of loose trousers and lapel-less jacket, shoes, a Kashmiri fur cap and a silver watch and chain. So twice a day he came out of the hut at the bottom of the garden and, standing with his bicycle in the *shikara*, was paddled past the tailor's one-roomed wooden shack, high and crooked above the water, past the poplars and the willows, past the houseboats, past Nehru Park, to the *ghat* and the lake boulevard, to cycle to the Tourist Reception Centre and to stand in the shade of chenars outside the entrance, with the tonga-wallahs, houseboat-owners or their agents, below the hoarding with Mr Nehru's portrait. And there was the *khansamah*, the cook. He was older than Aziz or Ali Mohammed, and more nobly built. He was a small man, but he was given height by the rightness of his proportions, his carriage, his long-tailed shirt and the loose trousers that tapered down to his well made feet. He was a brooder. His regular features were tormented by nervousness and irritability. He often came out of the kitchen and stood for minutes on the verandah of the hut, gazing at the lake, his bare feet beating the floorboards.

Our first meal was all ritual. The concrete floor of the dining room had been spread with old matting; and on the table two small plastic buckets sprouted long-stemmed red, blue, green and yellow plastic daisies. 'Mr Butt he buy,' Aziz said. 'Six rupees.' He went out for the soup; and presently we saw him and Ali Mohammad, each holding a plate of soup, coming out of the hut and walking carefully, concentrating on the soup, down the garden path.

'Hot box coming *next* week,' Aziz said.

'Hot box?'

'*Next* week.' His voice was low; he was like a sweet-tempered nurse humouring a spoilt and irascible infant. He took a napkin off his shoulder and flicked away tiny flies. 'This is *nothing*. Get little hot, little flies dead. Big flies come chase little flies. Then mosquito come bite big flies and *they* go away.'

And we believed him. He withdrew and stood outside below the projecting sitting room; and almost immediately we heard him shouting to the kitchen or to some passing lake-dweller in a voice that was entirely altered. Through the windows at our back we had a view of reeds, mountains, snow and sky;

before us from time to time we had a glimpse of Aziz's night-capped head as he peered through the as yet glassless window frame. We were in the middle of the unknown, but on our little island we were in good hands; we were being looked after; no harm could come to us; and with every dish that came out of the hut at the end of the garden our sense of security grew.

Aziz, his delight matching ours, shouted for the *khansamah*. It seemed an impertinent thing to do. A grumble, a silence, a delay showed that it was so taken. When at last the *khansamah* appeared he was without his apron; he was nervous and bashful. What would we like for dinner? What would we like for dinner? 'You want scones for tea? And pudding, what you want for pudding? Tipsy pudding? Trifle? Apple tart?'

Snow White had gone, but her imparted skills remained.

It was only early spring, and on some mornings there was fresh snow on the mountains. The lake was cold and clear; you could see the fish feeding like land animals on the weeds and on the lake bed, and when the sun came out every fish cast a shadow. It could be hot then, with the sun out, and woollen clothes were uncomfortable. But heat presently led to rain, and then the temperature dropped sharply. The clouds fell low over the mountains, sometimes in a level bank, some-times shredding far into the valleys. The temple at the top of Shankaracharya Hill, one thousand feet above us, was hidden; we would think of the lonely brahmin up there, with his woollen cap and his small charcoal brazier below his pinky-brown blanket. When the wind blew across the lake the young reeds swayed; on the rippled water reflections were abolished; the magenta discs of the lotus curled upwards; and all the craft on the lake made for shelter. Some pulled in at the hotel landing stage; occasionally their occupants went to the hut to get charcoal for their hookahs or for the mud-lined wicker braziers which they kept below their blankets. And immedi-ately after rain the lake was as glassy as could be.

The hotel stood on one of the main *shikara* lanes, the silent highways of the lake. The tourist season had not properly begun and about us there still flowed only the life of the lake. In the morning the flotilla of grass-laden *shikaras* passed, paddled by women sitting crosslegged at the stern, almost level with the water. The market-place shifted, according to custom, from day to day. Now it was directly in front of the hotel, beyond the lotus patch; now it was farther down the lane, beside the old boat that was the pettiest of petty lake shops. Often it seemed that buyer and seller would come to blows; but the threatening gestures, the raised voices, the paddling away, abuse hurled over the shoulder, the turning back, abuse continuing, all this was only the lake method of bargaining. All day the traffic continued. The cheese man, priest-like in white, sat before white conical mounds of cheese and rang his bell, he and his cheese sheltered by an awning, his paddler exposed at the stern. The milk-lady was fearfully jewelled; silver earrings hung from her distended lobes like keys from a key-ring. The confectioner's goods were contained in a single red box. The 'Bread Bun & Butter' man called every day at the hotel; on his *shikara* board N was written back to front. 'Beau-ti-ful! Mar-vellous! Lover-ly!' This was the cry of Bulbul, the flower-seller. His roses sweetened our room for a week; his sweet-peas collapsed the day they were bought. He suggested salt; his sweet-peas collapsed again; we quarrelled. But his *shikara* continued to be a moving bank of bewitching colour in the early mornings, until the season was advanced and he left us to work the more profitable A-class houseboats on Nagin Lake. The police *shikara* passed often, the sergeant paddled by constables. In the post office *shikara*, painted red, the clerk sat crosslegged at a low desk, selling stamps, cancelling letters and ringing his bell. Every tradesman had his paddler; and the paddler might be a child of seven or eight. It did not look especially cruel. Here children were, as they have until recently been elsewhere, miniature adults in dress, skills and appearance. Late at night we would hear them singing to keep their spirits up as they paddled home.

So quickly we discovered that in spite of its unkempt lushness, its tottering buildings and the makeshift instincts of its inhabitants, the lake was charted and regulated; that there were divisions of labour as of land; and that divisions of water space were to be recognised even if marked by no more than a bent and sagging length of wire. There were men of power, with areas of influence; there were regional elected courts. And such regulations were necessary because the lake was full of people and the lake was rich. It provided for all. It provided weeds and mud for vegetable plots. A boy twirled his bent pole in the water, lifted, and he had a bundle of rich, dripping lake weed. It provided fodder for animals. It provided reeds for thatching. It provided fish, so numerous in the clear water that they could be seen just below the steps of the busy *ghat*. On some days the lake was dotted with fishermen who seemed to be walking on water: they stood erect and still on the edge of their barely moving *shikaras*, their tridents raised, their eyes as sharp as those of the kingfishers on the willows.

The hot box, promised by Aziz, came. It was a large wooden crate, grey with age and exposure. It occupied one corner of the dining-room, standing on its end at a slight angle on the uneven concrete floor. It was lined on the inside with the flattened metal of various tins, one side was hinged to make a door, and it was fitted with shelves. At mealtimes a charcoal brazier stood at the bottom. So the soup no longer came in steaming plates from the kitchen; and every morning we found Ali Mohammed squatting before the brazier, his back to us, utterly absorbed, turning over slices of bread with his fingers. A dedicated toastmaker he appeared, but he was in reality listening to the fifteen-minute programme of Kashmiri devotional songs that followed the news in English on Radio Kashmir. In the curve of his back there could be sensed a small but distinct anxiety: the toast might be required too soon, we might turn to another station, or he might be called away to other duties. Already at this time he was in his official suit; and I doubt whether, if otherwise dressed, he would have turned abruptly from his toast one morning and asked, 'You want see Kashmiri dancing girl?' His top dentures projected in a sad attempt at a smile. 'I bring here.'

Something had startled where I thought I was safest. The tourist's terror of extortion gripped me. 'No, Ali. You take me see first. I like, I bring here.'

He turned to face the hot box and the toast again. It had been a momentary impulse; he never mentioned dancing girls again.

And after the hot box, improvements came fast. Two strips of torn matting were laid down the narrow, pansy-lined path that connected the kitchen with the dining-room. The strips lay at a slight angle to one another; when it rained they looked black against the lawn. And presently—the lake giving up more of its treasures—uneven lengths of old board appeared on this matting. The polisher, a silent boy, came. He polished the 'sofa-set' in the sitting room, and the old writing-table (stuffed with Russian propaganda: Ali brought back armfuls from the Russians he met at the Tourist Reception Centre). He polished the chairs and the beds and the dining table; he polished day after day, saying nothing, ate platefuls of rice in the kitchen, and at last went away, leaving the furniture almost exactly as it had been. The turf-layer came; he tore and rammed and tamped on one bare bank.

It was all activity now. But there were periods of repose, especially in the afternoons. Then Aziz squatted on the kitchen verandah before the hookah and pulled; he had changed his woollen nightcap for a fur cap and had become a workaday Kashmiri, with a gift for instantaneous repose. Visitors called, boatmen, vendors; and from the hut came sounds of romping and chatter. After one outburst of gaiety we had a glimpse of Aziz running out to the verandah without his cap, and he had changed again: he was quite bald. On sunny afternoons Mr Butt and the *khansamah* wrapped themselves in blankets from head to toe and slept on the lawn.

The painters came, to give that second coat. One was purely medieval; he had the labourer's broad friendly face and he wore a dirty cotton skullcap. The other was bare-headed and wore contemporary green overalls. But their skills matched. They painted without any preparation. They couldn't manage straight lines; they ignored the division between concrete and timber, between ceiling and walls, between glass pane and window frame. They dripped paint everywhere. Their abandon infected me. I took a brush and on an unpainted wall drew birds and animals and faces. They giggled, and drew some things of their own. The man in the overalls asked the man in the skullcap in Kashmiri: 'Shall I ask him for *bakshish?*' Skullcap looked at me. 'No, no,' he said. But when Skullcap went out of the room Overalls said in English, 'I make room nice for you. You give bakshish?'

The painters left and the glazier came to complete the dining room windows. He measured the panes by eye and hand, cut, cut again, fitted, tapped in little nails and went away. Then a new coir matting was laid down on the steps and corridors and top gallery. It was too wide for the gallery—a sewage pipe stood in the way—and it remained curled along one edge; on the steps an absence of rails made it dangerous; and after every gusty shower the matting in the corridor was soaked. Two days later a patterned green plastic tablecloth covered the dining table. And that was not the end. Overalls turned up again. He went from green door to green door, painting numbers in chocolate, wiping out inelegancies with a rag, leaving each shaggy number in a brownish blur; then he went to the kitchen and ate a plateful of rice.

Nothing more, it seemed, could be done. And when Aziz brought me coffee one morning he said, 'Sahib, I request one thing. You write Touriasm office, invite Mr Madan to tea.'

Mr Madan was the Kashmir Director of Tourism. I had met him once, and briefly. Then, in response to my plea for help in finding accommodation, he had said, 'Give me twenty-four hours'; and that was the last I had heard. I explained this to Aziz.

'You write Touriasm, invite Mr Madan to tea. Not your tea. My tea. Mr Butt tea.'

Meal by meal, waiting on us, he pressed his case. The Liward was new; it was neither houseboat nor hotel; it needed some sort of recognition from the Tourist Office. I was willing enough to write a letter of recommendation. It was the invitation to tea that worried me; and it was this that Aziz and Mr Butt, smiling shyly behind his spectacles, insisted on. So one

morning, with Mr Butt and the English-reading secretary of
the All Shikara Workers Union looking over my shoulder, I
wrote to Mr Madan and invited him to tea.

Mr Butt himself took the letter into town. At lunch Aziz
reported that Mr Madan had read the letter but had sent no
reply. Solicitous now of my own honour, Aziz added: 'But
perhaps he write and wait get typewrite and send by his own
chaprassi.'

Aziz knew the forms. But no *chaprassi* ever came with Mr
Madan's reply. I had a typewriter; a uniformed army officer
brought me invitations from the Maharaja; yet I was without
the influence to do a simple thing like getting Mr Madan to
come to tea. Perhaps it was not only language that kept Mr
Butt silent. And a further humiliation awaited me. The
secretary of the All Shikara Workers Union wished to get up a
petition to the Director of Transport for a more frequent bus
service. I drafted the petition; I typed it; I signed it. It wasn't
even acknowledged. Aziz knew the forms. So when, not long
after, I complained about the weakness of the bulbs and asked
for one to be replaced, and he said, 'Two-three rupees. You
buy, I buy—what difference?' I didn't really feel I could object.
I bought.

The season had begun. The hotel was not recognised, but
accommodation was limited in Srinagar, our prices were
reasonable, and soon we began to get guests. I had been full of
plans for publicising the hotel. I had put some of these plans
to Aziz and, through him, to Mr Butt. They smiled, grateful
for my interest; but all they wanted me to do was to talk to
those tourists in jacket and tie whom Ali brought back from
the Reception Centre. When I failed I felt humiliated. When I
succeeded I was miserable. I was jealous; I wanted the hotel
to myself. Aziz understood, and he was like a parent comforting
a child. 'You will eat first. You will eat by yourself. We give
you special. This is not Mr Butt hotel. This is your hotel.'
When he announced new guests he would say, 'Is good, sahib.
Good for hotel. Good for Mr Butt.' Sometimes he would raise
one hand and say, 'God send customer.'

I remained unhappy. Being an unorthodox hotel, we attracted the orthodox. There had been the brahmin family, the first of many, who had insisted on cooking for themselves. They shelled peas, sifted rice and cut carrots in the doorway of their room; they cooked in the broom cupboard below the steps and washed their pots and pans at the garden tap; they turned part of the new turf to mud. Others threw their rubbish on the lawn; others spread their washing on the lawn. And I believed that the idyll was at an end when Aziz announced one day, with a well managed mixture of enthusiasm and condolence, that twenty orthodox Indians were coming to the hotel for four days. Some would sleep in the dining room; we would eat in the sitting room. I was beyond condolence. Aziz recognised this and offered none. We waited. Aziz became morose, almost offended, in our presence. But the twenty did not turn up; and then for a day or two Aziz looked genuinely offended.

There were other difficulties. I had had it established that the radio in the dining room was to be turned on just before eight. As soon as we heard the pips we went down to breakfast and the news in English. One morning no pips came, only Hindi film songs and Hindi commercials for Aspro and Horlicks: the radio was tuned to Radio Ceylon. I shouted through the window for Aziz. He came up and said he had explained to the boy from Bombay about the eight o'clock news from Delhi, but the boy had paid no attention.

I had loathed the boy from Bombay on sight. He wore tight trousers and a black imitation-leather jacket; his hair was thick and carefully combed; he carried his shoulders with something of the lefthander's elegant crookedness; he had the boxer's light walk and his movements were swift and abrupt. I thought of him as the Bombay Brando; I set him against a background of swarming Bombay slum. We had not spoken. But now, leather jacket or no leather jacket, this was war.

I ran downstairs. The radio was on full blast, and Brando was sitting in a derelict wicker chair on the lawn. I lowered the volume, almost to silence at first, in my haste; and turned to Radio Kashmir. Ali was making toast; the curve of his back signalled that he wasn't going to interfere. Nothing happened during the news. As soon as it was over, however, Brando pushed violently through the curtained doorway, went to the radio, wiped out Radio Kashmir for Radio Ceylon, and pushed out again violently through the curtain.

And so now it went on, morning and evening. Aziz I knew to be neutral. Ali I thought to be on my side. He crouched silently before the hot box, deprived now of his Kashmiri devotional songs. The conflict had reached stalemate. I longed for some development and one morning I suggested to Ali that Kashmiri songs were better than the commercials from Radio Ceylon. He looked up from his toast with alarm. Then I discovered that in the few short weeks of the tourist season, of tourist transistors tuned to Radio Ceylon, his taste had changed. He liked the commercial jingles, he liked the film songs. They were modern, an accessible part of that world beyond the mountains from which the advanced, money-laden Indian tourists came. Kashmiri music belonged to the lake and the valley; it was rude. So fragile are our fairylands.

Then I went down with a stomach upset and had to stay in bed. The next morning there was a knock on the door. It was Brando.

'I didn't see you yesterday,' he said. 'They told me you were not well. How are you today?'

I said I was better and thanked him for coming. There was a pause. I tried to think of something more to say. He wasn't trying at all. He stood unembarrassed beside the bed.

'Where do you come from?' I asked.

'I come from Bombay.'

'Bombay. What part of Bombay?'

'Dadar. You know Dadar?'

It was what I had imagined. 'What do you do? Are you a medical student?'

He barely raised his left foot off the floor, and his shoulders went crooked. 'I am *guest* in the hotel.'

'Yes, I know that,' I said.

'*You* are guest in the hotel.'

'I am a guest in the hotel.'

'So *why* you say I am *medical* student? *Why?* You are guest in the hotel. I am guest in the hotel. You get sick. I come to see you. Why you say I am *medical* student?'

'I am sorry. I know that you have come to see me only because we are both guests in the hotel. But I didn't mean to offend you. I just wanted to find out what you did.'

'I work for an insurance company.'

'Thank you very much for coming to see me.'

'You are welcome, mister.'

And, leading with the left shoulder, he pushed through the curtains and left.

Thereafter courtesy was imposed on both of us. I offered him Radio Ceylon; he offered me Radio Kashmir.

'Huzoor!' the *khansamah* called one afternoon, knocking and coming into the room at the same time. 'Today my day off, and I going home *now*, huzoor.' He spoke rapidly, like a man with little time. Normally Aziz came with him to our room; but this afternoon he had managed to elude Aziz, whom I saw, through the window, reclining on a string bed in the kitchen verandah.

'My son is sick, huzoor.' He gave a crooked bashful smile and shifted about on his elegant feet.

It was not necessary. My hand was already in my pocket, detaching notes from a stapled wad of a hundred. It was all that the local State Bank of India had that week. It encouraged this type of protracted furtive activity: I knew how easy and dangerous it was to excite the Kashmiri.

'My son is sick *bad*, huzoor!'

His impatience matched mine.

'*Huzoor!*' It was an exclamation of pure displeasure. Three notes had stuck together and appeared as one. Then he smiled. 'Oh, three rupees. All right.'

'Huzoor!' the *khansamah* said one week later. 'My wife is sick, huzoor.'

At the door, fingering the notes I had given him, he stopped and said with sudden consoling conviction, 'My wife true sick bad, huzoor. Very bad. She have typhoid.'

This worried me. Possibly he wasn't being merely courteous. At dinner I asked Aziz.

'She not have typhoid.' Aziz's tight-lipped smile, suppressing laughter at my gullibility, was infuriating.

I had, however, betrayed the *khansamah*. He came no more with tales of sick relations. I did not like to think of his humiliation in the kitchen; and I liked to think least of all of Aziz's triumph over him. On that small island I had become involved with them all, and with none more so than Aziz. It was an involvement which had taken me by surprise. Up to this time a servant, to me, had been someone who did a job, took his money and went off to his own concerns. But Aziz's work was his life. A childless wife existed somewhere in the lake, but he seldom spoke of her and never appeared to visit her. Service was his world. It was his craft, his trade; it transcended the formalities of uniform and deferential manners; and it was the source of his power. I had read of the extraordinary control of eighteenth-century servants in Europe; I had been puzzled by the insolence of Russian servants in novels like *Dead Souls* and *Oblomov;* in India I had seen mistress and manservant engage in arguments as passionate, as seemingly irreparable and as quickly forgotten as the arguments between husband and wife. Now I began to understand. To possess a personal servant, whose skill is to please, who has no function beyond that of service, is painlessly to surrender part of oneself. It creates dependence where none existed; it requires requital; and it can reduce one to infantilism. I became as alert to Aziz's moods as he had been to mine. He had the power to infuriate me; his glumness could spoil a morning for me. I was quick to see disloyalty and diminishing attentions. Then I sulked; then, depending on his mood, he bade me goodnight through a messenger or he didn't bid me goodnight at all; and in the morning we started afresh. We quarrelled silently about guests of whom I disapproved. We quarrelled openly when I felt that his references to increasing food prices were leading up to a demand for more money. I wished, above all, to be sure of his loyalty. And this was impossible, for I was not his employer.

So, in my relations with him, I alternated between bullying and bribing; and he handled both.

His service, I say, transcended uniform. He wore none; and he appeared to have only one suit of clothes. They grew grimy on him, and his scent became riper and riper.

'Can you swim, Aziz?'

'O yes, sahib. I swim.'

'Where do you swim?'

'Right here on lake.'

'It must be very cold.'

'O no, sahib. Every morning Ali Mohammed and I take off clothes and swim.'

This was something; it removed one doubt. 'Aziz, get the tailor to make you a suit. I will pay.'

He became stern and preoccupied, a man worn down by duties: this was a sign of pleasure.

'How much do you think it will cost, Aziz?'

'Twelve rupees, sahib.'

And in this mood, catching sight of Ali Mohammed about to go off to the Tourist Reception Centre in his shabby striped blue suit, his waistcoat and watch-chain, I surrendered to the pathos of his appearance.

'Ali, get the tailor to make you a new waistcoat. I will pay.'

'Very good, sir.'

It was hard to tell with Ali. He always looked slightly stunned whenever he was addressed directly.

'How much will it cost?'

'Twelve rupees, sir.'

It appeared to be a popular price. I went up to my room. I had hardly settled down at the blue table when the door was roughly pushed open and I turned to see the *khansamah*, blue apron on, advancing upon me. He seemed to be in an uncontrollable rage. He put a hand on the jacket that was hanging on the back of my chair and said, 'I want a coat'. Then, as if alarmed by his own violence, he stepped back two paces. 'You give Ali Mohammed jacket and you give that man Aziz suit.'

Had they been taunting him in the kitchen? I thought of Aziz's tight-lipped smile, his stern look of a moment before:

suppressions of triumph that had inevitably to be released. Ali had been about to go off to the Tourist Reception Centre; he must have gone back to the kitchen to break the news.

'I am a poor man.' The *khansamah* made a sweeping gesture with both hands down his elegant clothes.

'How much will it cost?'

'Fifteen rupees. No, twenty.'

It was too much. 'When I leave I will give you coat. When I leave.'

He dropped to the floor and tried to seize my feet in mark of gratitude, but the legs and rungs of the chair were in the way.

He was a tormented man; and I knew, from what I heard and saw, that there were rows in the kitchen. He was careful of his honour. He was a cook. He was not a general servant; he had not learned the art of pleasing and probably despised those, like Aziz, who prospered by pleasing. I could see that he would provoke situations with which he could not cope; and after every defeat he would suffer.

It must have been a week later. For dinner he sent across meat stew and vegetable stew. The stews were identical, apart from the shreds and cubes of meat in one. I was not a meat-eater, and I was irrationally upset. I could not touch the vegetable stew. Aziz was wounded; this gave me pleasure. He went out with the stew to the kitchen, from where the *khansamah's* voice was presently heard, angrily raised. Aziz returned alone, walking carefully, as though his feet were sore. After some time there was a call from behind the curtained doorway. It was the *khansamah*. In one hand he held a frying pan, in another a fish-slice. His face was flushed from the fire and ugly with anger and insult.

'Why you don't eat my vegetable stew?'

As soon as he began to speak he lost control of himself. He stood over me and was almost screaming. 'Why you don't eat my vegetable stew?' I feared he was about to hit me with the frying pan, which he had raised, and in which I saw an omelette. Immediately after his violence, however, came his alarm, his recognition of his own weakness.

I suffered with him. But the thought of egg and oil nauseated me further; and I was surprised by the rise within myself of that deep anger which unhinges judgement and almost physically limits vision.

'Aziz,' I said, 'will you ask this person to go?'

It was brutal; it was ludicrous; it was pointless and infantile. But the moment of anger is a moment of exalted, shrinking lucidity, from which recovery is slow and shattering.

Some time later the *khansamah* left the Liward. It occurred without warning. He came up with Aziz to my room one morning and said, 'I am going, huzoor.'

Aziz, anticipating my questions, said, 'This is happy for him, sahib. Not worry. He get job family Baramula side.'

'I am going, huzoor. Give me certificate *now*.' He stood behind Aziz, and as he spoke he squinted one eye and wagged a long finger at Aziz's back.

I typed out a certificate for him right away. It was long and emotional, of no use to a future employer; it was a testimony of sympathy: I felt he was as inadequate as myself. While I wrote Aziz stood by, dusting from time to time, smiling, seeing that nothing went wrong.

'I am going *now*, huzoor.'

I sent Aziz outside, and gave the *khansamah* more money than was necessary. He took it without softening. All he did was to say slowly and with passion, 'That man Aziz!'

'This is happy for him,' Aziz said again afterwards. 'Two three days we get new *khansamah*.'

So the vision of the hotel as doll's house altered.

'Sahib, I request one thing. You write Touriasm Office, invite Mr Madan to tea.'

'But, Aziz, he didn't come the last time.'

'Sahib, you write Touriasm.'

'No, Aziz. No more invitations to tea.'

'Sahib, I request one thing. You go see Mr Madan.'

Another plot had been hatched in the kitchen. Every week Ali Mohammed had to apply for a permit to enter the police-guarded compound of the Tourist Reception Centre. This wasted some of his tourist-catching time. What he needed was a permit for the entire season, and the kitchen felt that I could get one for him.

'Do they really give these season permits, Aziz?'

'Yes, sahib. Lotta *houseboat* have season permit.'

My lake hotel, unorthodox, unrecognised, was being discriminated against. Without further inquiry, I made an appointment with Mr Madan, and when the day came Mr Butt and I rode into town on a tonga.

And they knew about me at the Tourist Office! My previous letter had made the Liward Hotel famous. There were smiles and handshakes from several officials who were delighted, if a little puzzled, by my interest. The Indian bureaucracy has its silences and delays, but it never loses or forgets any document; and it was with pure geniality that I was hustled, as the writer of an unsolicited letter of praise, into the picture-hung office of Mr Madan, the director.

His waiting visitors, his grave expectant courtesy almost made me change my mind. Now the greetings were over; something had to be said. So: Would Mr Madan please see that Ali Mohammed was given a permit for the season, if Ali Mohammed was entitled to such a permit?

'But permits are no longer required. Your friend, I imagine, has a British passport.'

I could not blame him for misunderstanding. Ali was not a tourist, I said. He wanted to meet tourists. He was a Kashmiri, a hotel servant; he wanted to get inside the Tourist Reception Centre. I knew that tourists had to be protected. Still. My trivialities burdened me. I became more and more earnest, anxious to get out of the encounter with dignity.

Mr Madan behaved well. If Ali applied, he said, he would consider the application.

I bade him good morning and walked briskly out with the news to Mr Butt.

'You see head clerk now,' Mr Butt said, and I allowed myself to be led into a room of desks and clerks.

The head clerk was not at his desk. We found him later in the corridor, a smiling well-built young man in a pale grey suit. He knew my letter; he understood my request. Let the hotel apply tomorrow; he would see what he could do.

'Tomorrow,' I said to Mr Butt. 'You come tomorrow.'

Hurriedly, I left him and made my way through the grounds of the Government Emporium, once the British Residency, to the Bund along the muddy Jhelum river. The elaborate Kashmiri woodwork of the Residency had decayed here and there; next to it a dingy little shack—very English, very Indian—proclaimed itself as the Emporium Café. But the chenar-shaded grounds remained grandiloquent, carefully irregular patches of daisies dramatising the vast lawn. The Residency stood at one end of the Bund, on which, I had often been told, no Indian was allowed in the old days. Now the turnstiles were broken. Signs forbade cycling and walking on the grass bank; but there was constant cycling, and a deep path had been worn into the bank. Cows nibbled at the front gardens of buildings which, though in reality no more than an adoption of the Kashmiri style, at first sight appeared a type of mock mock-Tudor. Some old-fashioned shops survived, roomy, dark, with many glass cases; they still seemed to hold the anticipations of a thousand Anglo-Indian 'leaves'. Faded advertisements for things like water biscuits, no longer obtainable, could still be seen; boards and walls still carried the names of British patrons, viceroys and commanders-in-chief. In a taxidermist's shop there was a framed photograph of an English cavalry officer with his polished boot on a dead tiger.

One type of glory had gone. The other brightness, of the bazaar, had not yet come. But it was on the way. 'You needn't tell me, sir. I can see from your dress and your speech that your taste is English. Step inside and let me show you my English-taste rugs. Observe. This is English taste. I *know*. Now on the other hand observe this. It is heavy, Indian and of course inferior . . . .'

Kashmirs Most Extraordinary Entertaining Rendezvous
YAP—LET'S GO TO PREMIERS RESTAURANT
Hey-Fellers-Tony is At the Mike
With All the Five Bops

Fellers enjoy the 36 Varieties of Icecreams
DRINK DRINKS
IN OUR STARLIT GOLDEN BAR

That was what the leaflets said. Now the rendezvous itself, new, contemporary—'most gayest', according to another leaflet, 'most delicious in tours'—was before me. It was too early for Tony and the Five Bops. I had a quiet, expensive litre of Indian beer and tried to put the morning's encounters out of my mind.

Later I walked down the dusty Residency Road and talked with the old bearded bookseller. He was a BA, LLB from Bombay, and a refugee from Sind. He said he was eighty. I challenged this. 'Well, I say eighty so as not to say seventy-eight.' He told me of the Pakistani invasion of 1947 and of the looting of Baramula. In this very city of Srinagar, this city of tonga-wallahs, Ali Mohammed and Yap—Let's go to Premiers five hundred rupees were being paid for eight-rupee bus seats to Jammu. 'Now there is nothing to do but laugh, and I often just sit here and read.' He read Stephen Leacock, and was addicted to the stories of Major Munro. Why did he say Major Munro? Well, he had read that Saki was Munro and a Major, and he felt it was a discourtesy to deny a favourite author his rank.

I was riding back to the hotel *ghat* on a tonga when I saw Mr Butt. I took him on. He was utterly wretched. I had left him too hurriedly. He had not understood my words and had spent all morning at the Tourist Reception Centre waiting for me.

Next morning I typed out the application for the season permit and Mr Butt took it into town. It was hot and it became hotter. Towards midday the sky darkened, the clouds lowered, the mountains became dark blue and were reflected in the water until the winds started to rage across the lake, kicking up the lotus leaves, tormenting the willows, pushing the reeds this way and that. Soon it began to rain and, after that very hot morning, it became quite cold. It was still raining when Mr Butt returned. His fur cap was soaked into mean, glistening

kinkiness; his jacket was dark with wet; his shoulders were
hunched below the turned-up collar; his shirt-tail was dripping.
I watched him walk slowly down the wet boards in the garden
to the kitchen. He kicked his shoes off and disappeared inside.
I returned to my work, and waited for the sound of happy bare
feet on the steps. But there was nothing.

And, as before, it was I who had to ask. 'Did Mr Butt get
the permit, Aziz?'

'Yes, he get permit. One week.'

One morning some days later I was having coffee in the sitting
room when the painter in the overalls pushed his head through
the doorway and said, 'You typewrite give me painting
certificate, sahib?' I did not reply.

6. THE MEDIEVAL CITY

The level of the lake dropped to the last step of the landing stage; the water became muddier and swarmed with black colonies of summer fish. The snow on the mountains to the north melted and the exposed rock looked bleached and eroded. On the cool parkland of the foothills the firs became darker blobs of green. The poplars on the lake lost their fresh greenness and the willows scattered spinning leaves in high wind. The reeds became so tall they curved, and when the wind blew they swayed and tossed like waves. The lotus leaves rose crinkled and disordered out of the water, thrust up on thick stalks. Then, like blind tulips, the lotus buds appeared, and a week later opened in explosions of dying pink. In the garden the californian poppies and the clarkia grew straggly and were pulled out; the French marigolds, which had taken the place of the pansies, thickened and put out buds. The petunias in the shade of the dining room wall were failing; they, like the geraniums, had been discoloured and weighted down with distemper from the painters' brushes. The godetias were at their peak: a mass of whipped colour, white and pink and pale violet. The sunflowers, seedlings when we arrived, were so tall, their leaves so broad, I could no longer look down into their hearts to examine the progress of the star-shaped buds. The dahlias put out one small red bloom, a touch of vivid colour against the green of reeds and willows and poplars.

We still had the kingfisher. But other birds appeared less frequently in the garden. We missed the hoopoe, with his long busy bill, his curved black and white wing stripes, his crest fanning out as he landed. With the heat the little flies died, as

Aziz had said; and their place was taken by the house-fly. The flies I had known so far were shy of man; these settled on my face and hands even while I worked, and for several mornings in succession I was awakened before six by the buzzing of a single, Flit-surviving fly. Aziz promised mosquitoes; they would rout the flies. To him a fly was an act of God; one afternoon I saw him happily asleep in the kitchen, his cap on, his face black with still, contented flies.

I had asked for Flit, and more Flit. Now I asked for ice.

'Anybody don't like ice,' Aziz said. 'Ice is heating.'

And this reply led to one of our silences.

On very hot days the mountains to the north were hidden by haze from morning till evening. When the sun began to go down an amber light filled the valley and the mist rose slowly between the poplars on the lake. Each tree was distinct; and from Shankaracharya Hill Srinagar, smoking, appeared to be a vast industrial town, the poplars as erect as chimneys. Against this the fort of Akbar, standing on its reddish hill in the centre of the lake, was silhouetted: the sun to the left, a white disc slowly turning pale yellow, the mountains fading from grey to nothing as they receded.

Beyond the Bund it was a medieval town, and it might have been of medieval Europe. It was a town, damp or dusty, of smells: of bodies and picturesque costumes discoloured and acrid with grime, of black, open drains, of exposed fried food and exposed filth; a town of prolific pariah dogs of disregarded beauty below shop platforms, of starved puppies shivering in the damp caked blackness below butchers' stalls hung with bleeding flesh; a town of narrow lanes and dark shops and choked courtyards, of full, ankle-length skirts and the innumerable brittle, scarred legs of boys. Yet much skill had gone into the making of these huddled wooden buildings; much fine fantastic carving and woodwork remained, not at first noticeable, for everything had been weathered to grey-black; and there were odd effects of beauty, as when every brass and burnished copper vessel in a shop of brass and copper vessels glinted in the gloom. For against this drabness, an overwhelming impression of muddiness, of black and grey and brown, colour stood out and was enticing: the colours of sweets, yellow and glistening green, however fly-infested. Here one was able to learn again the attraction of primary, heraldic colours, the colours of toys, and of things that shone, and to rediscover that child's taste so long suppressed, which is also peasant's taste, erupting here, as in the rest of India, in tinsel and coloured lights and everything we had all once considered pretty. Out of these cramped yards, glimpsed through filth-runnelled alleyways, came bright colours in glorious patterns on rugs and carpets and soft shawls, patterns and colours derived from Persia, in Kashmir grown automatic, even in all their rightness and variety, and applied with in-discriminate lavishness on a two-thousand-rupee carpet or an old blanket which, when worked, would sell for twelve rupees. In this medieval dirt and greyness beauty was colour, equally admired in a fine rug, a pot of plastic daisies or, as once in Europe, in a fantastic costume.

As complementary as colour was gaiety. The town slept during the winter. The tourists went away, hotels and house-boats closed, and in their dark, small-windowed rooms the Kashmiris wrapped themselves in blankets and idled over charcoal braziers until the spring. The spring brought sun and dust and fairs, colour and noise and exposed food. Nearly every fortnight there seemed to be a fair in some part of the Valley. Each was like the other. In each might be found the picture-seller, his stock spread out on the ground: thin wall-scrolls with violently coloured drawings of Indian and Arabian mosques, objects of desired pilgrimage, flattened out of per-spective; photographs of film stars; coloured pictures of political leaders; innumerable paperbacked booklets. There were stalls of cheap toys and cheap clothes; there were tea-tents and sweet-trays. A Hindu holy man of terrifying aspect sat in the dust behind his small dry vials that contained charms of 'eye of newt and tongue of dog'. And always there was amplified music. On the lake, too, the playground now not only of the tourists but also of the people of the town, there was music: from the *doongas*, smaller unpainted houseboats, hired complete with kitchen-women and pole-man. He walked slowly back and forth past the cabins, now carrying his pole, now leaning on it, separate from the revelry within but seemingly content; a woman, possibly his wife, bundled in dirty skirts and heavy with silver jewellery, sat solitary at the high stern, steering with a long paddle. It was movement for the sake of movement. The *doongas* went nowhere in particular and were never beyond shouting distance of gardens or houses; they called here, moored there for the night. A *doonga* party could last for days; people might get off at some point to attend to their affairs on land and might rejoin the boat later at another point. A dull, strenuous entertainment it seemed to me; but my winters were full. The fair in the grove at Ganderbal, a few miles to the northwest, climaxed the season. All the *doongas* and *shikaras* made their way there and moored for the night: movement for the sake of movement, crowd for the sake of crowd, noise for the sake of noise.

And in this medieval town, as in all medieval towns, the people were surrounded by wonders. About them in Srinagar were the gardens of the Mogul emperors. The pavilions were neglected but they were still whole. On Sundays the fountains of Shalimar still played, with here and there a bent or broken nozzle. But the builders had receded beyond history into legend: fabulous personages of whom little was known except that they were *very* handsome or *very* brave or *very* wise, with wives who were *very* beautiful. 'That?' said the Kashmir; engineer, waving towards Akbar's late-sixteenth-century fort in the Dal Lake. 'That is five thousand years old.' In the Hazratbal mosque on the lake there was a hair from the beard of the Prophet Mohammed. It had been brought through untold dangers to Kashmir, the medical student told me, by 'a man'. Who was this man? What did he do? Where did he come from? My student couldn't say; he knew only that once, when this man was in an especially dangerous situation, he had gashed himself in the arm and in the gash had concealed the holy hair. It was an authentic relic, there could be no doubt of that. It was so potent that birds never flew over the chapel in which it was kept and cows, sacred to Hindus, never sat with their backs to the chapel.

God watched over them all, and they responded with enthusiasm. Mohurram was the month in which for ten days they mourned Hussain, the Prophet's descendant, murdered at Kerbala. The wails and songs of the Shias came to us over the water at night. Aziz, of the Sunni sect, said with a smile, 'Shia not Muslim.' Yet on the seventh morning, when on the radio the well-known story of Kerbala was being told, tears came to Aziz's eyes, his face grew small, and he hurried out of the dining room, saying, 'I can't stop. I don't like listen.'

There was to be a Shia procession at Hasanbad; there would be people whipping themselves with chains. Aziz, recovered from the morning's emotion, insisted that we should go, and made the arrangements. We went by *shikara*, quickly penetrating into the green-scummed, willow-hung water highways of the lake town, past the dirty yards terminating in broken concrete steps, gutters running down their sides, on which men and women and children were washing clothes, our own washerman, I was sorry to see, among them. The highways were altogether foul, smelling of the sewer; but at every yard children, miniature adults, rushed out to greet us: 'Salaam!'

At Hasanbad we moored among dozens of *shikaras*, many brilliantly canopied, walked past the foundations of a ruin of which we had never heard, and found ourselves in the middle of a dusty summer fair. The streets had been swept; water carts laid the dust. There were awnings and stalls. The well-to-do among the women in the crowd were veiled in black or brown from head to well-shod feet; they were in groups of two or three, and through the grilled netting over their eyes we felt ourselves scrutinised. It was the poor who were unveiled; here, as everywhere else, to be conservative and correct was the privilege of the rich or the rising. We passed a father and his daughter; he was letting her play with his whip, as yet unused.

Beyond this open, almost country, road lay the narrow main street. Here the crowd was thick. Many men wore black shirts;

one boy was carrying a black flag. Soon we saw some flagellants. Their clothes were stiff with blood. The procession had not yet begun and they walked idly up and down the centre of the road, between the admiring crowds, jostling those who tomorrow might once again be their betters. In the corbelled upper storeys of the narrow houses every crooked window, of Kashmiri tininess, framed a medieval picture: the intent faces of women and girls, the girls fresh-complexioned, the women, from their long seclusion, pallid, all cut out against the sharp blackness of window space. Below, in the choked road, were lorryloads of police. Some boys were tormenting the puppies below the butcher's stall; we heard the puppies kicked, a surprisingly loud sound to come from such small bodies; we heard the yelps and whines. Hawkers called; stranded cars hooted. Over it all lay the microphone-magnified voice of the mullah—the microphone an Indian inevitability—reciting the story of Kerbala. His voice held anguish and hysteria; at times it seemed he would break down; but he went feverishly on and on. He was reciting from under an awning hung across the street and was hidden by the crowd, some of whom carried coloured pennants.

More flagellants appeared. The back of one was obscenely cut up; blood, still fresh, soaked his trousers. He walked briskly up and down, deliberately bumping into people and frowning as though offended. His whip hung from his waist. It was made up of perhaps six metal chains, eighteen inches long, each ending in a small bloody blade; hanging from his waist, it looked like a fly-whisk. As disquieting as the blood were the faces of some of the enthusiasts. One had no nose, just two punctures in a triangle of pink mottled flesh; one had grotesquely raw bulging eyes; there was one with no neck, the flesh distended straight from cheek to chest. In their walk was pride; they behaved like busy men with no time for trivialities. I suspected some of the bloody garments. Some looked too dry; they might have been last year's, they might have been borrowed, or the blood might have been animal's blood. But there was no denying the integrity of the man whose nearly bald head was roughly bandaged, the blood still streaming down. The glory lay in blood; he who displayed the most was the most certain of attention.

We left the hot crowded street and made our way into the open. We sat in a scuffed, dusty graveyard, beside some boys playing an incomprehensible medieval game with pebbles. Until that morning religious enthusiasm had been a mystery to me. But in that street, where only the police lorries and the occasional motorcar and the microphone and perhaps the ice-cream sold by hawkers in shallow round tins were not of the middle ages, the festival of blood had seemed entirely natural. It was these American girls now approaching who were inexplicable and outlandish; not content with the attention they would normally attract, they wore body-accentuating garments which would have been outrageous in London. The flagellant who, ignoring them, began to get out of his blood-stained clothes on the canal steps, in full view of everyone, and was presently naked, was of a piece with the setting and the holiday mood of the day. This was his day; today he had licence. He had earned it by his bloody back. He had turned dull virtue into spectacle.

Religious enthusiasm derived, in performance and admiration, from simplicity, from a knowledge of religion only as ritual and form. 'Shia not Muslim,' Aziz had said. The Shia, he added, demonstrating, bowed in this way when he said his prayers; the Muslim, now, bowed in this. Christians were closer to Muslims than to Hindus because Christians and Muslims buried their dead. 'But, Aziz, many Christians are cremated.' 'They not Christian.' The medical student, explaining the difference between Islam and Sikhism, which he particularly detested, said that Muslims slaughtered their animals by bleeding them slowly to death, uttering prayers the while. Sikhs struck off an animal's head at one blow, without prayers. He sketched out the gesture, involuntarily shook his head with repulsion, and put his hand over his face. On the day of Id Mr Butt gave us a cake iced *Id Mubarak*, Id Greetings. The day took us by surprise; *shikara*-loads of Kashmiris, men, women and children, were ferried about the lake all morning, subdued and stiff and startling in clean clothes of white and blue. It was a day of visits and gifts and feasting; but, too, for the Kashmiri, the year's solitary day of cleanliness, a penitential debauch of soap and water and itching new cloth. Yet neither the medical student nor the engineer nor the merchant, all of whom came to visit us and offered gifts, could explain the significance of the day. It was only what we had seen; it was a day when Muslims had to eat meat.

Religion was spectacle, and festivals, women veiled ('so that men wouldn't get excited and think bad things,' the merchant said), women bred and breeding like battery hens; it was the ceremonial washing of the genitals in public before prayers; it was ten thousand simultaneous prostrations. It was this complete day-filling, season-filling mixture of the gay, the penitential, the hysterical and, importantly, the absurd. It answered every simple mood. It was life and the Law, and its forms could admit of no change or query, since change and query would throw the whole system, would throw life itself, in danger. 'I am a bad Muslim,' the medical student had said at our first meeting. 'How can I believe that the world was made in six days? I believe in evolution. My mother would grow mad if I said these things to her.' But he rejected none of the forms, no particle of the Law; and was more of a religious fanatic than Aziz who, secure in his system, inspected other systems with tolerant interest. The sputniks had momentarily shaken some in their faith, for the upper atmosphere had been decreed closed to all but Mohammed and his white horse. But doctrine could be made to accommodate this—what the Russians had done was to send up their sputniks on the white horse—and the faith could survive because doctrine was not as important as the forms it had bred. The abandoning of the veil was more to be feared and resisted than the theory of evolution.

These forms had not developed over the centuries. They had been imposed whole and suddenly by a foreign conqueror, displacing another set of forms, once no doubt thought equally unalterable, of which no trace remained. The medieval mind could assess a building as five thousand years old, and do so casually; with like facility it buried events three and four hundred years old. And it was because it was without a sense of history that it was capable of so complete a conversion. Many Kashmiri clan names—like that of Mr Butt himself—were often still purely Hindu; but of their Hindu past the Kashmiris retained no memory. In the mountains there were cave-dwellers, thinly bearded and moustached, handsome, sharp-featured men, descendants, I felt, of Central Asian horsemen; in the summer they came down with their mules among the Kashmiris, who despised them. Of their first arrival in Kashmir there was a folk memory: 'Once, long, long ago they lived beyond the mountains. Then there was a king of Cabul who began killing them, and so they left and walked over the mountains and came here.' But of the conversion of the Valley to Islam there was no memory at all. Aziz, I know, would have been scandalised if it had been suggested to him that his ancestors were Hindus. 'Those?' the engineer said, driving past the Awantipur ruins. 'Hindu ruins.' He was showing me the antiquities of the Valley, and the ruins lay just at the side of the main road; but he didn't slow down or say any more. The eighth-century ruins were contemptible; they formed no part of his past. His history only began with his conquerors; in spite of travel and degrees he remained a medieval convert, forever engaged in the holy war.

Yet the religion as practised in the Valley was not pure. Islam is inconoclastic: the Kashmiris went mad when they saw the hair from the Prophet's beard; and all around the lake were Muslim shrines, lit at night. I know, though, what Aziz would have said if I had told him that good Muslims did not venerate relics. 'They not Muslim.' Should another conversion now occur, should another Law as complete be imposed, in a hundred years there would be no memory of Islam.

It was in politics as it was in religion. The analyses of the Kashmir situation which I had been reading endlessly in newspapers had no relation to the problem as the Kashmiris saw it. The most anti-Indian people in the Valley were Punjabi Muslim settlers, often in high positions; to them Kashmiris were 'cowardly', 'greedy'; and they often came to the hotel with rumours of troop movements, mutinies and disasters on the frontier. To their politics the Kashmiris brought not self-interest but their gifts of myth and wonder; and their myths centred on one man, Sheikh Abdullah, the Lion of Kashmir, as Mr Nehru had called him. He had made the Kashmiris free; he was their leader; he had been friendly to India but had ceased to be friendly, and since 1953 had been, except for a few months, in jail. From Kashmiris I could get no more; I could get no glimpse of the leader's achievements, personality or appeal. Over and over I was told, as if in explanation of everything, that when he came out of prison in 1958 there were crowds along the road from Kud to Srinagar, and red carpets everywhere.

'Listen,' said the college student, 'and I will tell you how Sheikh Abdullah won freedom for the people of Kashmir. For many, many years Sheikh Abdullah had been fighting for the freedom of the people. And then one day the Maharaja became *very* frightened and sent for Sheikh Abdullah. He said to Sheikh Abdullah, "I will give you anything, even up to half my kingdom, if only you let me keep my throne." Sheikh Abdullah refused. The Maharaja became *very* angry and said, "I will throw you in oil and make it hot." And you know what the result of that would be. That only a heap of ashes would remain. But Sheikh Abdullah said, "All right, boil me in oil. But I tell you that out of every drop of my blood will grow another Sheikh Abdullah." When the Maharaja heard this he was *very* frightened, and he gave up the throne. That was how Sheikh Abdullah won the freedom for the people of Kashmir.'

I objected. I said that people didn't behave like that in real life.

'But it's true. Ask any Kashmiri.'

It was an account of the events of 1947 that ignored Congress, Gandhi, the British, the Pakistan invasion. And this was at the high level of literacy in English. Below this there were people like Aziz, who almost daily regretted the Maharaja's repressive rule because things were so much cheaper then. Recent history was already sinking into medieval legend. Aziz and the *khansamah* had served the British; they knew them as people of certain tastes, skills and language ('padre' for priest, and to Aziz 'bugger' was an affectionate word for a dog) who had departed as unaccountably as they had come. But there had grown up a generation of students who had learned of the British only from their history books, and to them the British intervention was as remote as the Mogul glory.

Bashir told me one day that the 'East India Company went away in 1947'; and this, in our political discussions, was his sole reference to the British. Bashir was nineteen, college-educated. 'I am *best* sportsman,' he had said, introducing himself to me. 'I am *best* swimmer. I know *all* chemistry and *all* physics.' He detested the Kashmiri and Indian habit of wearing pyjamas in public; and he told me he never spat in the street. He regarded himself as educated and emancipated: he 'inter-dined' (one of the English locutions of the subcontinent) with everyone, regardless of religion or sect. He wore western-style suits, and he spoke English as well as he did because 'I come from an unusually intelligent family'.

It might be that Bashir's ignorance of history was due to his stupidity, or to his education in a language he did not fully understand (when he said *best* he only meant 'very good'), or to bad teachers and bad textbooks. (I examined one of his history books later. It was a typical Indian textbook; it was in question-and-answer form and gave the preservation of purity as one of the virtues of the caste system and gave miscegenation as one of the reasons for the decline of Portuguese power in India.) Or it might simply have been that Bashir and his friends took no interest in politics; and indeed, without news-papers and the radio, it was possible to be in Kashmir for weeks without realising that there was a Kashmir problem. But Kashmir was being talked about on every side. All-India Radio was carrying detailed reports of the annual United Nations debate; Radio Pakistan tirelessly warned that in Kashmir as in the rest of India Islam was in danger, and Radio Kashmir as tirelessly retaliated. Mr Nehru came to Srinagar, and Radio Pakistan reported that a public meeting he addressed broke up in disorder. (He was in fact convalescing after an illness.) Whatever might be said, Bashir's ignorance of the recent history and situation of his country was startling. And he was privileged. Below him were the grimy, barefooted, undernourished primary-school boys in blue shirts who had no chance of going to college; below them were those who didn't go to school at all.

I was in bed one afternoon with an inflamed throat when Bashir brought Kadir to see me. Kadir was seventeen, small, with soft brown eyes in a square gentle face; he was studying engineering but wanted to be a writer.

'He is *best* poet,' Bashir said, interrupting his prowling about the room, sinking across my feet on the bed, and grabbing my cigarettes. He had brought Kadir to see me; but his purpose was also to show me off to Kadir, and this he could do only by this hearty familiarity which he had never before attempted with me. He could not be rebuffed. I merely wiggled my toes below his back.

'When Bashir told me I was going to meet a writer,' Kadir said, 'Of course I had to come.'

'*Best* poet,' Bashir said, lifting himself off my feet and supporting himself on his elbows.

The poet's shirt, open at the neck, was dirty; there was a hole at the top of his pullover. He was small and sensitive and shabby: I yielded to him.

'He is *great* drinker,' Bashir said. '*Too* much of whisky.'

This was a proof of his talent. In India poets and musicians are required to live the part: it is necessary to be sad and alcoholic.

But Kadir looked so young and poor.

'Do you really drink?' I asked him.

He said simply, 'Yes.'

'Recite,' Bashir ordered.

'But he wouldn't understand Urdu.'

'Recite. I will translate. It is not easy, you understand. But I will translate.'

Kadir recited.

'He says,' Bashir said, 'and he is talking of a poor boatman's daughter, you understand—he says in his poem that she gives colour to the rose. You get it, mister? Another man would say that the *rose* gives her the colour. He says that *she* gives colour to the rose.'

'Very beautiful,' I said.

Kadir said wearily, 'Kashmir has beauty and nothing else.'

Then Bashir, his large eyes shining, recited a couplet which, he said, I would find in some Mogul building in Delhi. He became sentimental. 'An Englishman went walking in the hills one day, you know,' he said. 'And he saw a Gujjar girl sitting under a tree. She was *very* beautiful. And she was reading Koran. The Englishman went up to her and said, "Will you marry me?" She looked up from Koran and said, "Of course I will marry you. But first you must give up your religion for mine." The Englishman said, "Of course I will change my religion. I love you more than anything in the world." So he changed his religion and they were married. They were *very* happy. They had four children. One became a colonel in the army, one became a contractor, and the girl married Sheikh Abdullah. The Englishman was *very* rich. *Too* much of money. He owned Nedou's Hotel. You know Nedou's Hotel? Best hotel in Srinagar.'

'Oberoi Palace is best,' Kadir said.

'Nedou's is best. *Best* hotel. So you see, she is English.'

'Who?'

'Sheikh Abdullah's wife. *Pure* English.'

'She couldn't be pure English,' Kadir said.

'*Pure* English. Her father was an Englishman. He owned Nedou's Hotel.'

So, often and in this manner of legend, the talk turned to Sheikh Abdullah. Why had Sheikh Abdullah fallen out with New Delhi? One man said that the Indian Government had wanted to buy over the Post Office but Sheikh Abdullah wouldn't sell. The implication was clear: there had been a tussle over a demand for greater autonomy. To my informant, however, the Post Office was the post office on the Bund, a type of super-shop, doing brisk business every day, which the Indian Government wanted to steal from Kashmir. He was an educated man; and doubtless the fact of a demand for greater autonomy had undergone further distortion and simplification before it had passed down to the peasants. Propaganda needs to find its level; and medieval propaganda was as simple-clever and as fearful as any technique of hidden persuasion. Radio Pakistan could claim that the large sums of money being spent on education in Kashmir were a means of undermining Islam and the Law; and it was more effective propaganda than the Kashmir Government's boards giving development facts and figures.

'But Sheikh Abdullah was Prime Minister for more than five years. What did he do?'

'Ah, that is the beauty. He did nothing. He wouldn't take help from anyone. He wanted the people of Kashmir to learn to stand on their own feet.'

'But if he did nothing in five years, why do you think he is great? Give me an example of his greatness.'

'I will give you an example. One year, you know, the rice crop failed and the people were starving. They went to Sheikh Abdullah and said to him, "Sheikh Abdullah, we have no rice and we are starving. Give us rice." And you know what he said to them? He said, "Eat potatoes".'

Humour was not intended, and the advice was sound. Indians are willing to eat only what they have always eaten; and staples vary from province to province. In the Punjab they ate wheat. In Kashmir, as in the South, they ate rice. It was rice alone, enormous platefuls of it, moistened perhaps with a little tomato sauce, which energised Aziz's active little body. When there was no rice the Kashmiris starved; they might have potatoes, but potatoes were not food. In this lay the point of Sheikh Abdullah's advice. Needless to say, it had gone unheeded and had instead been transformed into a piece of almost prophetic wisdom, to be relished and passed on as such. *Once there was no food in the land, and the people went to the leader and said, 'We have no food. We are starving.' The leader said, 'You might think you have no food. But you have. You have potatoes. And potatoes are food.'*

Regularly white jeeps and station-wagons raced along the roads. In the afternoons they appeared to carry picnic parties

of women and children in straw hats; in the evenings, bridge
parties. The jeeps and station-wagons were marked U.N. in
thin, square letters; they watched over the ceasefire line. In
Kashmir they seemed as anachronistic as the clock in *Julius
Caesar*.

But there was money in Kashmir, more than there had ever
been. In 1947, I was told, there were fifty-two private cars in
the entire state; now there were nearly eight thousand. In
1947 a carpenter earned two or three rupees a day; now he
could get eleven rupees. The new wealth showed in the in-
creased number of veiled women: for people like tonga-
wallahs and fuel-vendors a new, veiled wife was a symbol of
status. It is estimated that in Kashmir, as in the rest of India,
one-third of development funds drains away in corruption
and the exchanging of gifts. No disgrace attaches to this.
The Kashmiri tailor spoke with envious admiration of his
patwari friend, a surveyor and type of records-keeper, who in
one day might collect as much as a hundred rupees; a lorry-
driver had a similar admiration for a traffic inspector he knew
who received monthly protection money from various lorry-
drivers. From time to time there was an outburst in the
press and Parliament about corruption, and here and there
frenzied action might instantly be taken. In one state a minister
had his doorman charged with corrupt practices: the doorman
had bowed to him too low and too often, and by this had shown
that he expected a tip. An architect in Delhi told me that even
such token attempts to 'stamp out' corruption could be
demoralising and dangerous: the system was necessary and in
India it was the only system that could work.

From the engineer I learned how the system worked in
Kashmir. A contractor dug, say, one hundred cubic feet of
earth. He sent in a bill for two hundred. Now it was precisely
to frustrate such adventurousness that the Indian Civil Service
method of checking and counter-checking had been devised.
The contractor's claim had to be verified; the verification had
to be endorsed; and the endorsement, to be brief, had to be
approved. In the thoroughness of the system lay its equity.

When verification was complete everyone, from top man to messenger, was in the know, and everyone had to be made some offering. The contractor was charged a fixed percentage of his extra profits, and this was divided, again in fixed percentages, among the employees of the department concerned. It was all regulated and above board; everything, the engineer said, smiling as he used the civil service phrase, went 'through proper channel'. It was almost impossible for any government servant to contract out, and no one particularly wanted to. Tipping was expected; the contractor who dug a hundred cubic feet and claimed for a hundred cubic feet was likely to run into trouble; and it had happened that a civil servant who objected to corruption had been transferred or dismissed for corruption. 'Even if the contractor is a relation,' the engineer said, 'he will still have to give something. It's the principle of the thing.' The top man didn't necessarily get the biggest cut of any one levy; but in the long run he made out better than his subordinates because he got a percentage of more levies.

The engineer was in his camp, at the edge of a pine forest, chill when the sun went down. Whitewashed stones lined the path to his tent. In another tent some distance away his subordinates were preparing their evening meal. There had been some trouble with them when he first came on this job, the engineer said. His predecessor had not distributed the levies fairly, and the men were rebellious. His first act had been to renounce his percentage; he had also managed to get them certain stores to which they were not entitled. This had calmed them. The engineer said he himself was against the system. If the system was worked fairly, however, it made for efficiency. It gave the men an interest in their work. Take telegraph poles. They were required to be thirty-four feet tall, to be of a certain girth; and they had to be buried five feet in the ground. Assuming that a pole of thirty-two feet was accepted—and it was only on such sub-standard poles that worthwhile tipping could reasonably be expected—it was important that the pole should be put up quickly. And who was to tell then that it was only three feet in the ground?

There was no means of checking the engineer's account.

But I felt that it partly explained the illicit felling which was stripping Kashmir of its accessible forests. (To this the Kashmiris attributed the hotness of their recent summers.) And certainly the wires hung dangerously low from many of the telegraph poles in Srinagar.

We seemed to be in danger of losing the hotel garden altogether. First there had come the digging for the ugly telegraph pole to carry the electric wires. And now there came the digging for the poles of the awning, which was put up like lightning with the rough-and-ready carpentry of the lake, and the irruption into the hotel garden of dozens of the lake folk, variously clad in pyjamas or flapping trousers, offering advice, help or simply interest. The awning was an appanage of the houseboat; this was the reason for its appearance in the garden, where it served no purpose. It provided little shade and much heat when the sun was out, and it was taken down whenever rain threatened. It had scalloped edges, trimmed with black, and was exactly like every other houseboat awning in the area. These awnings were all made in the single-roomed tailor's shack on the water highway, where everyone, flower-sellers, grocers, red-turbanned policemen, appeared to stop for a chat and a pull at the hookah

A day or so later Mr Butt was painting the poles of the awning a light green, and I went down to watch him. He looked up and smiled, and went on with his painting. When he looked up again he wasn't smiling.

'Sir, you ask Mr Madan to tea?'

'Mr Butt, no.'

The summer had seemed endless. We had put off the ruins: the Palace of the Fairies, which we could see low on the hills beyond the lake; Akbar's lake fort, Hari Parbat; the temple at Pandrethan; the sun temple at Martand; the temple at Awanti-pur. Now we did them all at once.

It was a cool day when we went to Awantipur, the dry

fields a warm brown against the dark grey-blue mountains. We could make little of the ruins, the massive central platform, the anvil-shaped fonts of solid stone that lay among the rubble, the carvings; and the villager who attached himself to us didn't help. 'It *all* fell down,' he said in Hindustani, waving a hand. '*All*?' '*All*.' It was a type of North Indian dialogue, made possible by the stresses of the language, which I had grown to enjoy. He showed the base of a column and indicated by gestures that it was the bottom stone of a quern. That was the limit of his knowledge. No tip for him; and we walked down to the village to wait for the bus.

The blue-shirted boys had just been released from school; down a side lane we saw the young Sikh teacher organising a ball game in the schoolyard. The boys gathered around us; they all carried enormous bundles of books wrapped in grubby, inky cloths. We made one boy take out his English book. He opened it at a page headed 'Our Pets', read out: 'Our Body', and began reeling off a text which, after a search, we found on another page. And what book was this? Urdu? They became helpless with laughter: it was Pharsi, Persian, as any child could tell. The crowd had now grown. We broke out of it, saying we wanted to get back to Srinagar; and they all then began waving down buses for us. Many buses passed, full; then one shot past, hesitated, stopped. A Kashmiri attempted to get on but was repelled by the conductor, who made room for us.

We sat in the back among some sensationally unwashed people, their cotton dhotis brown with dirt, and many Dalda tins. The man next to me was stretched out on the seat, clearly unwell, his eyes without expression, the pestilential Indian flies undisturbed on his lips and cheeks; from time to time he gave a theatrical groan, to which no one in the chattering bus paid the slightest attention. We saw that we were in a bus of 'lower-income' tourists and that we were sitting with their servants.

At the ruins the bus stopped and the khaki-clad moustached driver turned around and tried to persuade his passengers to go out and have a look. No one moved. The driver spoke again, and at length one elderly man, whom we had already recognised as the wit and leader of the bus, heaved himself up with a sigh and went out. He wore a black Indian jacket, and his top-knot proclaimed him a brahmin. The others followed.

From nowhere children appeared: '*Paisa, sahib, paisa.*' 'Oh,' said the leader in Hindi. 'You want money? Now what does a little child like you want money for?' '*Roti, roti,*' they chanted. 'Bread, bread.' 'Bread, eh?' He was only teasing. He gave; the others gave.

The leader climbed to the top of the stone steps and regarded the ruins with patronage. He made a witticism; he lectured. The others idled about dutifully, looking without interest where he looked.

A sixteen-year-old boy in white flannel trousers hurried over to me and said, 'This is Pandavas' fort.'

I said, 'This is not a fort.'

'It is Pandavas' fort.'

'No.'

He waved hesitantly towards the leader. 'He says it's Pandavas' fort.'

'You tell him no. He doesn't know what he's talking about.'

The boy looked shocked, as though I had offered him violence. He edged away from me, turned and fled to the group around the leader.

We were all back in the bus and about to start when the leader suggested food. The conductor threw open the door again and an especially grimy manservant, old and toothless, came to life. Briskly, proprietorially, he shoved the Dalda tins along the dusty floor and lifted them out on to the verge. I began to protest at the delay; the boy in white flannels looked at me in terror; and I realised that we had fallen among a family, that the bus was chartered, that we had been offered a lift out of charity. The bus again emptied. We remained helpless in our seats, while Srinagar-bound passenger buses, visibly holding spare seats, went past.

They were a brahmin family and their vegetarian food was served according to established form. No one was allowed to touch it except the dirty old servant who, at the mention of food, had been kindled into such important activity. With the very fingers that a moment before had been rolling a crinkled cigarette and had then seized the dusty Dalda tins from off the dusty bus floor, he now—using only the right hand, of course—distributed puris from one tin, scooped out curried potatoes from another, and from a third secured dripping fingerfuls of chutney. He was of the right caste; nothing served by the fingers of his right hand could be unclean; and the eaters ate with relish. The verge had been deserted; now, in the twinkling of an eye, the eaters were surrounded by villagers and long-haired Kashmiri dogs. The dogs kept their distance; they stood still, their tails low and alert, the fields stretching out behind them to the mountains. The villagers, men and children, stood right over the squatting eaters who, like celebrities in the midst of an admiring crowd, slightly adjusted their behaviour. They ate with noisier relish; just perceptibly they raised their voices, heightened and lengthened out their laughter. The servant, busier than ever, frowned as if made impatient by his responsibilities. His lips disappeared between his toothless gums.

The leader spoke to the servant, and the servant came to where we were. Busily, like a man with little time to waste, he slapped two puris into our hands, plastered the puris with potatoes, leaked chutney on the potatoes, and withdrew, hugging his tins, leaving us with committed right hands.

A family spokesman came to the door of the bus. 'Just *taste* our food.'

We tasted. We felt the eyes of the villagers on us. We felt the eyes of the family on us. We smiled, and ate.

The leader made overtures of friendship; he sought to include us in his conversation. We smiled; and now it was the turn of the boy in white flannels to look hostile. Still, all the way into Srinagar we smiled.

In India I had so far felt myself a visitor. Its size, its temperatures, its crowds: I had prepared myself for these, but in its very extremes the country was alien. Looking for the familiar,

I had again, in spite of myself, become an islander: I was looking for the small and manageable. From the day of my arrival I had learned that racial similarities meant little. The people I had met, in Delhi clubs and Bombay flats, the villagers and officials in country 'districts', were strangers whose backgrounds I could not read. They were at once narrower and grander. Their choice in almost everything seemed more restricted than mine; yet they were clearly inhabitants of a big country; they had an easy, unromantic comprehension of size. The landscape was harsh and wrong. I could not relate it to myself: I was looking for the balanced rural landscapes of Indian Trinidad. Once, near Agra, I had seen or made myself see such a landscape; but the forlorn wasted figures reclining on string beds in the foreground were not right. In all the striking detail of India there was nothing which I could link with my own experience of India in a small town in Trinidad.

And now, unexpectedly in Kashmir, this encounter with the tourist family answered. The brief visit to the fort of the Pandavas, the gaiety of the excursion party, the giving of small coins to the begging children, the food, the rough manner of its distribution which yet concealed the observance of so many forms: I might have known that family, I could have assessed the relationships, could have spotted the powerful, the weak, the intriguing. The three generations which separated me from them shrank to one.

The encounter had done more than dislodge a childhood memory; it awakened a superseded consciousness. That food should be served in certain strict ways I at once understood. Equally I understood the mixture of strictness and dirt, the overdone casualness with which the puris and potatoes had been slapped into hands. It was partly a type of inverted asceticism, by which a necessary pleasure is heightened; it was partly the conviction, perhaps derived from a rural society poor in implements, perhaps derived from religion, that greater elaboration was unnecessary, pretentious and absurd.*

---

* Luxury, with Indians, and especially Hindus, always seems contrived and strenuous. No people are so little interested in interiors. This lack of interest appears to be historical. The *Kama Sutra*, after laying down that the man of

It was above all a respect for the forms, for the way things had always been done.

Yet three generations and a lost language lay between us. This is Pandavas' fort, the boy had said. The Pandavas were the heroes of the *Mahabharata*, one of the two Hindu epics which are universally known and have something of the sanctity of holy books; the Gita is embedded in the *Mahabharata*. The *Mahabharata* is placed by some in the fourth century BC; the events it describes are put at 1500 BC. Yet the ruins of what was so obviously a four-walled building, exposed on all sides, that could by no stretch of the imagination be the fort of five warrior princes, were the ruins of the fort of the Pandavas. It was not that forts were unknown; in Srinagar itself there was one which nobody could miss. The tourists in the bus went against the evidence of their eyes not because they were eager for marvels but because, living with marvels, they had no sense of the marvellous. It was with reluctance that they had got out of the bus. They had known and accepted the story of the *Mahabharata* from childhood. It was part of them. They were indifferent to its confirmation in rocks and stones, fallen into ruin and become material commonplaces which could only be viewed literally. So this was the fort of the Pandavas, this rubble, no longer of use to anyone. Well, it was time to eat, time for the puris and the potatoes. The

fashion 'should reside where he has a good chance of earning riches but should for preference select a city, a metropolis or a big or small town', prescribes the furnishings of a drawing-room: 'This outer room should contain a bed, richly mattressed, and somewhat depressed in the middle. It should have pillows at the head and the bottom and should be covered with a perfectly white clean sheet. Near this bed there should be a small couch on which the sexual act should be performed so as not to soil the bed. Over the head of the bed there should be fixed on the wall a lotus-shaped bracket on which a coloured portrait or an image of one's favourite deity should be placed. Beneath this bracket should be placed a small table, one cubit in breadth, set against the wall. On this table the following articles, required for the night's enjoyments, should be arranged: balms and perfumed unguents, garlands, coloured waxen vessels, pots for holding perfumes, pomegranate rinds and prepared betels. There should be a spittoon on the floor near the bed; a lute, a drawing slab, a pot with colours and brushes, a few books and wreaths of flowers, too, hung from elephants' tusks let into the wall. Near the bed upon the floor should be placed a circular chair with a back for resting the head on. Boards for the games of dice and chess should be placed against the wall. In a gallery outside the room cages for pet birds should be hung from ivory tusks fixed into the wall.' (Translated by B. N. Basu.)

true wonder of the Pandavas and the *Mahabharata* they carried in their hearts.

Some miles nearer Srinagar, at Pandrethan, in the middle of the army camp a tiny, single-chambered temple, set in a hollow and shaded by a great tree, stood a little crookedly in the centre of a small artificial pool. The water was stale, leaf-littered; and the heavy, inelegant stonework of the temple was roughly patched with new concrete. The temple was in the style of the Awantipur ruin, the 'fort of the Pandavas'; but it was still in use, and it was this, rather than its age, which gave it greater meaning. Romance arose out of a sense of more than physical loss; and here, for Muslim as well as Hindu, nothing had been lost. A building might collapse or be destroyed or cease to be of use; another would take its place, of lesser or greater size or beauty. On the eastern side of Akbar's lake fort an exquisite building lay in ruin. It might have been a mauso-leum. Two towers stood at one end of a small cool quadrangle whose walls were faced with black marble. The towers were broken, the flat brick dome pierced; the elegantly proportioned Mogul arches had been filled in with mud bricks, now partly disintegrated; rubble blocked the entrances and littered the high-stepped Mogul staircases which led to low dusty cham-bers where the fine stone grilling of the windows was broken or lost. But decay, spectacular as it was, lay only in the eye of the visitor. More important than the ruin were the corrugated-iron latrines and washing places which had been built there for the use of those who came to pray at the nearby mosque.

The Mogul gardens remained beautiful because they were still gardens; they still worked. The mausoleum, of the same period, had ceased to be of use; latrines could be set in its ruins. Out of this unexamined sense of flow and continuity the Valley was being disfigured; for if decay lay in the eye of the visitor, so too did beauty. The gardens were clearly meant by their builders to stand alone in the parkland sur-rounding the lake. But on one side of the green pagoda-like roof of the pavilion that rose above the trees of the Chasmashahi Gardens there now stood, totally exposed, ten new 'tourist huts', six in one straight line, four in another. On the other side was the government Guest House, where Mr Nehru had stayed; next to this was a Milk Pasteurisation and Bottling Plant; and next to this, logically enough, was the complex of a government farm. Sheep, I believe, were bred there. Their tracks scored the hillside all the way up to the eighteenth-century Pari Mahal, the Palace of Fairies—a library perhaps it had been, or an observatory, already absorbed, whatever it was, into myth—the flattened, overgrown terraces of which, sweet with wild white roses and dangerous with bees, were littered with sheep droppings. Through receding arches, cracked plaster revealing brick, the lake could be seen. And on the lake, to the delight of all the lake folk, there now increasingly appeared motorboats. They tainted the air and water; their stutter carried far; their propellers whipped up eddies of mud; and long after they had passed, the water remained disturbed, slapping against the floating gardens, washing down their edges, rocking and swamping the *shikaras*. And this was only the beginning.

The medieval mind, which saw only continuity, seemed so unassailable. It existed in a world which, with all its ups and downs, remained harmoniously ordered and could be taken for granted. It had not developed a sense of history, which is a sense of loss; it had developed no true sense of beauty, which is a gift of assessment. While it was enclosed, this made it secure. Exposed, its world became a fairyland, exceedingly fragile. It was one step from the Kashmiri devotional songs to the commercial jingles of Radio Ceylon; it was one step from the roses of Kashmir to a potful of plastic daisies.

It was under the houseboat-style awning in the garden that Mr Butt ceremoniously received his guests, lake folk or tourists. And it was there one very hot Sunday morning that, looking out of my window, I saw a neatly dressed young man, pink from the awning's concentrated heat, sitting alone and selfconsciously sipping tea, the hotel's best china arrayed on a metal tray in front of him.

Brisk feet pattered up the steps. There was a knock on my

door. It was Aziz, breathless, grave, a serving towel or rag
thrown over his left shoulder.

'Sahib, you come have tea.'

I had just had coffee.

'Sahib, you come have tea.' He was panting. 'Mr Butt he
say. Not *your* tea.'

I went down to the young man. I had often been called upon
to handle difficult 'customers' and sometimes to encourage
acceptance of a price more realistic than that mentioned by
Ali Mohammed at the Tourist Reception Centre.

The young man put down his cup with some awkwardness,
stood up and looked at me uncertainly. I sat down in one of
the hotel's weatherbeaten, shredding wicker chairs and
invited him to resume his tea. Aziz, seconds before the urgent
administrator, now the self-effacing, characterless servitor,
deferentially poured for me and withdrew, never looking back,
yet somehow—in spite of his loose flapping trousers, his tilted
fur cap, the serving rag thrown rakishly over one shoulder,
the soles of his bare feet flapping hard, black and cracked—
communicating total alertness.

It was hot, I said to the young man; and he agreed. But it
would soon cool down, I said; you had these changes of
temperature in Srinagar. The lake was certainly cooler than
the city, and the hotel was cooler than any houseboat.

'So you are enjoying?'

'Yes,' I said, 'I am enjoying very much.'

He had given me an opening and I made use of it. But he
was not with me; he did not lose his look of embarrassment.
I decided he was one of my failures.

'Where do you come from?' I put the Indian question.

'Oh, I come from Srinagar. I work in the Tourist Office. I
have been seeing you around for *months*.'

There was nothing more to say. We stewed in the heat of the
awning and sipped tea.

Where I and my typewriter had failed, Mr Butt and Aziz
had succeeded. But Aziz did not behave as though I had failed.
He said that the kitchen was pleased with my handling of the
young man, and a few days later he announced, as though I

alone was responsible for it, that Mr Kak, Mr Madan's deputy, was coming soon to the hotel, to inspect and possibly to have tea.

Mr Kak came. I saw his *shikara* glide up to the landing stage and I decided to hide. I locked myself in the bathroom. But no feet came tripping up the steps. No summons came. No mention of Mr Kak's visit was made that day or on subsequent days; and I learned of the outcome of his visit only when Mr Butt, accompanied by the secretary of the All Shikara Workers Union, came into my room one morning to ask me to type out the 'particulars' of the hotel for inclusion in the Tourist Office's register of hotels. I had failed; even my final cowardice was irrelevant. Mr Butt was smiling; he was a happy man. Dutifully, I began to type.

'Hotel,' said the secretary, looking over my shoulder, 'is Western style.'

'Yes, yes,' Mr Butt said. 'Western style.'

'I can't type that,' I said. 'Hotel is not Western style.'

'Flush system,' Mr Butt said. 'English food. Western style.'

I got up and pointed through the open window to a little roofed box next to the kitchen hut.

The box was perhaps six feet long, four feet wide and five feet high. And it was inhabited. By a thin, sour middle-aged couple whom we had christened the Borrowers. They were Jains. They had brought their pots and pans to Kashmir; they cooked for themselves; they washed up for themselves, scouring their vessels with mud, of which there was now a plentiful supply around the garden tap. They had at first been simple tourists, occupying one of the lower rooms. But they had a transistor radio; and often I saw them sitting under the awning with Mr Butt, all three concentrating on the transistor which, aerial up, volume up, stood on the table between them. We heard from Aziz that a sale was being negotiated; and it must have been during the negotiations that we saw one morning a brisk, brief transferring of pots and pans, bed and bedding, stool and chair, from the hotel room to the tiny box, which that evening appeared to shiver with light, escaping through cracks and gaps, and with music from the transistor.

There was a window, one foot square, Kashmiri-carpentered, crookedly hinged. Through this I tried to get a glimpse of the arrangements inside. I was spotted. A woman's hand pulled the tiny, sagging window to, and closed it with a proprietorial, offended bang.

To this box I now pointed.

The secretary giggled and Mr Butt smiled. 'Sir, sir,' he said, laying his hand on his heart. 'Forgive, forgive.'

Srinagar was hot, and the tourists now went higher up, to Pahalgam, which we were told was 'Indian taste', and Gulmarg, which was 'English'. Presently we had the hotel to ourselves again, as it had been in the early spring. There was no washing on the lawn; no cooking parties in the broom-cupboard below the steps. The mud around the garden tap dried to black, caked earth; and in the garden the sunflowers were indeed like emblematic whirls of colour. Even the tradesmen grew torpid. Maulana Worthwhile, who sold shawls, called to ask if I had any English shoe polish, the only thing, according to him, which was good for his ringworm. The regional court held new elections under the awning and we celebrated with cake and tea. Aziz daily dropped hints about Gulmarg. 'When you going Gulmarg, sir?' He wanted us to take him there, and it was only during these slack weeks that he could leave the hotel. But we put off Gulmarg from day to day, becalmed in the summer stillness of the lake.

Then all at once stillness and peace vanished.

There was a holy man in Delhi. It happened this year that there came to Delhi from East Africa a pious family of wealthy Indian merchants. They met the holy man. He liked them; and they were so taken with him they thought they would devote their holiday to his service. The monsoon was delayed that year and, sitting in Delhi, the holy man said, 'I feel an urge to go now to Kashmir, the holy land of Hindus, the land of the holy cave of Amarnath, the purifying icy Lake of the Thousand Serpents, and the plain where Lord Shiva danced.' The merchants at once packed their American limousines with all that was necessary. 'I fear the journey will be too much for

me,' the holy man said. 'You go by motorcar. I will follow by
Viscount aeroplane.' They made the arrangements and then
drove north for a day and a night until they came to the holy
city of Srinagar. It was nearly midnight when they arrived.
But the news of the arrival of twenty pilgrims spread rapidly
from houseboat to empty houseboat, and wherever they went
they were followed by shrieking men anxious to give them
lodging. When they came to a small hotel on a plot of ground
in the lake they said, 'This is what we have been looking for.
We will stay here and await our holy man.' Still, through the
night the houseboat men came, trying to get them on to their
vessels, and there were many disputes.

This was Ali Mohammed's story.

'But they say,' he told us at breakfast, "We don't want
houseboat, we want here".'

It was the hotel's biggest kill, and Ali Mohammed was
pleased. He was not Aziz; he could not sympathise with us.
Nor could Aziz. He, as if recognising the hopelessness of the
situation, stayed away from us altogether.

They had come equipped for holiness. In their limousines,
the wonder of the lake folk, they had brought bundles of
especially holy leaves, off which they were to eat, like the sages
in the days before plates were plentiful. They did not trust
tap-water; they had brought special containers and early in
the morning they went off to Chasmashahi, the Royal Spring,
to get pure spring water. They had of course to cook for
themselves; and the cooking was done, on stones placed on the
lawn, by four epicene saffron-robed young men who, when
their duties were done, simply idled: they had a fantastic
capacity for inactivity. Holiness meant simplicity of this sort:
cooking on stones, eating off leaves, fetching water from the
spring. It also meant casualness and disorder. Rugs were
rolled up in the hotel rooms, curtains hooked up high, furniture disarranged. Simplicity and the possession of a holy man
induced arrogance. The men among the pilgrims strutted
about the lawn, reducing Ali and Aziz and even Mr Butt to
tiptoeing insignificance. They spoke loudly. They hawked
loudly and spat with noisy repeated relish everywhere but more

especially on the water-lilies, plants which had been introduced to Kashmir from England by the last maharaja and were without the religious associations of the lotus. After their meal, eaten off leaves on the very lawn on which they had been spitting, they belched. They belched thunderously but always with control: it was possible to tell, from the belches alone, who was the leader of the party. He was about forty, tall and fat; a singular element of his holy dress was the multi-coloured towel he wore wrapped around his head. The young men did press-ups and other exercises. They had all lived well; this was a pious boy-scout interlude; and the Liward was their camp.

It seemed that no definite message had come from the holy man about the time of his arrival. The pilgrims took no chances. They drove off to meet every aeroplane from Delhi, leaving behind the epicene young men in saffron robes who, fatigued at last by their idleness, began to indulge in what I at first regarded as a type of child's play. Gathering whatever material they could find, they constructed, with slow, silent intensity, a rough barricade around the cooking stones on the lawn. But they were not playing: they were protecting their food from the gaze of the unclean. This was not all. The turf had been trodden on by numberless unclean people: the turf had therefore to be torn up. And it was this that the squatting saffron-robed vandals were now silently doing.

I sent for Aziz. Since the arrival of the pilgrims we had not had a confrontation. His face was small. He had seen. He had done more: he had provided a plank which the saffron robes, following a logic of their own, had laid over the mud they had instantly created. What could he do? He spoke of Mr Butt's need for money; he said that God sent customers. He said that they were a holy group and that the holy man, who was expected any day, was almost a saint.

The pilgrims brought the holy man back that afternoon; and the atmosphere of arrogant, belching disorder was replaced by one of silent, self-important servitude, brisk scuttlings-about here, conspiratorial whispers there. The holy man sat in a chair below the awning. From time to time women, as though unable to hold themselves in any longer, ran to the holy man and flung themselves before his chair. The holy man barely acknowledged them. But most of the pilgrims simply sat and stared. He was, in truth, finer than any of his admirers. His saffron robe revealed a well-built body of a smooth, warm brown; there was no touch of sensuality in his firm, regular face, which might have been that of a business executive.

Behind their barricade the saffron-robed disciples were preparing their master's meal. When this was eaten, and when the pilgrims, sitting in two silent rows on the lawn, had eaten, it was dusk, and the holy man led them all in devotional song. Two men washed the holy man's robe; then, holding two corners each, they waved it in the air until it was dry.

I went over to the kitchen, for comfort, and found them all huddled and subdued around the hookah.

'To them we are all unclean,' a boatman said. 'Isn't it a cruel religion?'

I recognised the Radio Pakistan phrase. But even the boatman clearly held the holy man in awe and didn't speak above a whisper.

In the morning the lawn had been dug up some more; the area of mud had spread; and the pilgrims, blither than ever, were shelling peas and cooking and belching and spitting toothpaste on the water-lilies and bathing and washing clothes and running up and down the steps.

At breakfast I asked Ali Mohammed, 'When are they leaving?'

He misunderstood my reason for asking. He smiled, baring his ill-fitting dentures, and said, 'Big sadhu say last night, "I like this place. I *feel* I like this place. I stay here five days. I stay here five weeks. I don't know. I feel I like this place".'

'Call Aziz.'

Aziz came, limply carrying his serving rag. The rag was unclean; he was unclean; we were, indeed, all unclean together.

'Aziz, you tell Mr Butt. Either these people go or we go.'

Mr Butt came. He looked down at his shoes.

'Hotel is not Western style, Mr Butt. Not Liward Hotel

now. Liward Mandir, Liward Temple. I am going to invite
Mr Madan to tea *today*.'

Aziz knew an empty threat when he heard one. That last
sentence had betrayed my helplessness. He at once brightened,
flicked his rag about the dining table and said, 'When you
going Gulmarg, sir?'

'Yes, yes,' Mr Butt said. 'Gulmarg. You take Aziz with.'

So we compromised. We would go to Gulmarg for a few
days.

'But, Mr Butt, if they are still here when we get back, we go
for good.'

'That is good, sir.'

Yet I had it in my power to send the pilgrims and the holy
man scuttling out of the hotel in five minutes. I could have
revealed to them that that part of the lawn they had dug up
for the sake of cleanliness and converted into their kitchen
and barricaded lay directly over the hotel's septic tank.

'Hadn't we better find out about the times of the Gulmarg
buses, Aziz?'

'O no, sahib. *Too* much bus.'

We got to the bus station just after eight. Aziz, unfamiliar
in big brown shoes (Mr Butt's), went to buy the tickets.

'We miss eight o'clock bus,' he said, coming back.

'When is the next one?'

'Twelve o'clock.'

'What are we going to do, Aziz?'

'What we do? We wait.'

It was a new bus station. Kashmiris, emerging from
the gentlemen's lavatory, wiped their hands on the curtains,
which were of a contemporary fabric. A well-dressed beggar
woman distributed printed leaflets which told of her tragedy.
We waited.

What was it about Gulmarg that attracted Aziz? It was a
holiday settlement of unpainted wooden huts about a small
green meadow set in the mountains some three thousand feet
above the Valley. On one side the meadow fell away to the
Valley through pine forests; on the other it was bounded by

higher mountains in the interstices of which, even in August, snow lay in brown drifts. We arrived in rain. At the bungalow of the friends with whom we were going to stay Aziz was at once sent off to the servants' quarters, and we saw him again only when the rain was over. He was walking back down the muddy road from such centre as the settlement had. His gait was made unusual by the weight of Mr Butt's shoes. (Mr Butt later reported, almost with emotion, that Aziz had ruined his shoes on this visit.) His smile and greeting were of pure friendliness. 'How you liking Gulmarg, sir?'

So far we had seen little. We had seen the mountains lost in black cloud; we had seen the purple flowers on the wet green meadow. We had seen the buildings and foundations of buildings looted and burned by the Pakistanis in 1947: one grand wooden building cracked open from the roof, like a toy, and left derelict, still, with its broken coloured panes and all its noises, a setting for nightmare.

Had Aziz seen more? Was there an especial friend in Gulmarg? Was there a woman? His moods had been so varied that day. In the morning he had been the efficient hotel servant. At the bus station, settling down for the long wait, he had wiped anticipation off his face, which had grown blank, almost stupefied. In the bus at last, clutching the sandwich basket, he had shown a subdued sociability. Then, as soon as he had got on to the pony for the ride through the pines up to Gulmarg, he had become animated and mischievous, bobbing up and down in his saddle, twirling the reins, making clucking noises, racing ahead, riding back, surprising the other ponies into trots. I think it was the ponies of Gulmarg he looked forward to; somewhere in him there must have been the blood of horsemen. On a pony, and even with his shoes on, he ceased to be comic; the loose tapering trousers were right; they were the trousers of a horseman. On our excursions on the following days he never walked when he could ride, even on the steepest, rockiest, nastiest paths; and as long as he was on the back of a pony he remained animated, crying out delightedly when the pony slipped, '*Oash! Oash!* Easy, easy.' He became talkative. He spoke of the events of 1947 and told of raiders who were so ignorant they took brass for gold. And he told us why he was reluctant to walk. One winter, he said, he had left the service of an employer beyond the Valley; he was without money and had had to cross the snow-covered Banihal Pass on foot. He had fallen ill, and the doctor had forbidden him ever to walk again.

He seemed to be so many persons. It was especially interesting to watch him at work on our friends, to see applied to others that process of assessment through service to which, in the early days, we ourselves had been subjected. They had servants of their own; nothing bound Aziz to them. Yet he was already taking possession of them; and already he was binding them to himself. He had nothing to gain; he was only obeying an instinct. He could not read or write. People were his material, his profession and no doubt his diversion; his world was made up of these encounters and managed relationships. His responses were acute. (How easily, how 'officially', understanding our sentimentality, he had managed the dismissal of the *khansamah*: 'This is happy for him', the *khansamah* raging impotently behind his back.) He had picked up his English by ear; he therefore avoided Indian eye-pronunciations and spoke the words he knew with a better accent than many college-educated Indians. Even his errors ('any' for 'some': 'anybody don't like ice') showed his grasp of a language only occasionally heard; and it was astonishing to hear a word or phrase I had used coming back, days later, with my very intonations. Would he have gone far if he had learned to read and write? Wasn't it his illiteracy which sharpened his perception? He was a handler of people, as in their greater ways rulers of this region, also illiterate, had been: Ranjit Singh of the Sikhs, Gulab Singh, founder of the Jammu and Kashmir State. To us illiteracy is like a missing sense. But to the intelligent illiterate in a simpler world mightn't literacy be an irrelevance, a dissipation of sensibility, the mercenary skill of the scribe?

On the way back to Srinagar I watched him prepare a face for Mr Butt. He ceased to be animated; he became morose and harassed; he unnecessarily loaded himself in the bus with bags and baskets and made himself as uncomfortable as he could. When we got off the bus his expression would have convinced anyone that Gulmarg, so far from being a holiday from hotel work, had been tedious and exhausting. He subtly overdid his glum attentions to us, as though convincing himself that we had been a great strain. It was possible, too, that he shared our anxieties about the holy man and the pilgrims and was being defensive in advance. When we were driving in the tonga along the lake boulevard he said, 'Mr Butt he say you not pay for me as guide.'

Guide! Had he been our guide? Hadn't he persuaded us to take him to Gulmarg, hadn't he dropped daily reminders? Hadn't we paid for his pony rides?

'Yesterday big sadhu say, "I *feel* I go Pahalgam today".'

So Ali Mohammed reported. And they had gone, leaving only the ruined lawn, mud-splashed walls and a few lentils, already sprouting in the mud, to speak of their passing. In the garden the first canna had opened, bright yellow with spots of the purest red.

I showed the sprouting lentils to Mr Butt.

'O sir,' he said. 'My shame! My shame!'

And, as if to underline this, he came to me on the following day with Aziz, and through Aziz he said, 'Sir, you ask Maharaja Karan Singh to tea. Maharaja Karan Singh come to tea here, I take down hotel sign, I sack customer, I close hotel.'

7. PILGRIMAGE

It was Karan Singh, the young Maharaja of Kashmir, now the elected Head of the Jammu and Kashmir State, who encouraged us to join the pilgrimage to the Cave of Amarnath, the Eternal Lord. The cave lies thirteen thousand feet up the eighteen-thousand-foot Amarnath Mountain, some ninety miles northeast of Srinagar, and is made holy by the five-foot ice *lingam*, symbol of Shiva, which forms there during the summer months. The *lingam*, it is believed, waxes and wanes with the moon and reaches its greatest height on the day of the August full moon: on this day the pilgrimage arrives. It was a mystery, like Delphi, of the older world. It had survived because it was of India and Hinduism which, without beginning, without end, scarcely a religion, continued as a repository and living record of man's religious consciousness.

Karan Singh had gone to the cave some years before, though not with the traditional pilgrimage, and he had published a vivid account of the journey. I could not share his religious fervour, but I relished his exact descriptions of snowclad mountains, icy green lakes and changing weather. To me the true mystery of the cave lay in its situation. It was at the end of a twenty-mile track, a journey of two days, from Chandanwari, which was as far as the jeep-road went. For many months of the year this track disappeared under Himalayan snow and the cave was inaccessible; and in summer, in spite of the annual efforts of the Public Works Department, the track was difficult and in bad weather dangerous. It zigzagged up a two-thousand-foot drop; it led over a pass fifteen thousand feet high; it was a narrow ledge on a bare, curving mountainside. Beyond the tree-line breathing was not easy, and the nights were very cold. The snow never completely melted. It remained hard in sheltered gullies and canyons; it formed solid bridges over summer-slackened streams, bridges which on the surface were as brown and gritty as the surrounding land but which several feet below, just above the water, were scooped out into low, ice-blue caverns.

How had the cave been discovered? How had its mystery been established? The land was bare; it offered no fuel or food. The Himalayan summer was short, its weather treacherous. Every exploration, like every pilgrimage even today, had to be swift. And how had this mystery, so much of ice and snow, so briefly glimpsed each year, penetrated to every corner of ancient India? Himalayas, 'abode of snow': how could they be related to the burning North Indian plain and the palm-fringed beaches of the South? But they had been charted, their mysteries unearthed. Beyond the Amarnath Cave was the mountain of Kailas and beyond that the lake of Manasarovar. And legends attached to every stage of the Amarnath pilgrimage. These rocks were what remained of defeated demons; out of that lake Lord Vishnu arose on the back of a thousand-headed serpent; on this plain Lord Shiva once did the cosmic dance of destruction and his locks, becoming undone, created these five streams: wonders revealed only for a few months each year before disappearing again below the other, encompassing mystery of snow. And these mountains, lakes and streams were indeed apt for legend. Even while they were about you they had only a qualified reality. They could never become familiar; what was seen was not their truth; they were only temporarily unveiled. They might be subject to minute man-made disturbances—a stone dislodged into a stream, a path churned to dust, skirting snow—but as soon as, on that hurried return journey, they had been left behind they became remote again. Millions had made the journey, but the naked land carried few signs of their passage. Each year the snows came and obliterated their tracks, and each year in the cave the ice *lingam* formed. The mystery was forever new.

And in the cave, the god: the massive ice phallus. Hindu

speculation soared so high; its ritual remained so elemental. Between the conception of the world as illusion and the veneration of the phallus there was no link; they derived from different strata of responses. But Hinduism discarded nothing; and it was perhaps right not to. The phallus endured, unrecognised as such, recognised only as Shiva, as continuity: it was doubly the symbol of India. So often on journeys through the derelict Indian countryside it had seemed that the generative force alone remained potent, separate from its instruments and victims, men. To those whom it degraded and deformed its symbol remained, what it had always been, a symbol of joy. The pilgrimage was appropriate in every way.

'You want cook,' Aziz said. 'You want one man for help me. You want coolie. You want sweeper. You want seven pony.'

Each pony came with its owner. This would make fourteen of us altogether, not counting animals, with Aziz in charge.

I began pruning. 'No cook.'

'He not only cook, sahib. He guide.'

'There are going to be twenty thousand pilgrims. We don't want a guide.'

The cook was Aziz's protégé. He was fat and jolly and I would have liked to take him. But he had revealed, through Aziz, that he shared Aziz's disability: he too had been advised not to walk and he too required a pony for himself. Then he had sent word from the kitchen, through Aziz again, that he required a new pair of shoes for the journey. I couldn't afford him. I decided, too, that the coolie was unnecessary; and the sweeper was to be replaced by a small spade.

Aziz, defeated, suffered. He had known glorious establishments and he had no doubt visualised an expedition in the old style. He must have seen himself jacketed, trousered and furcapped, trotting about on his pony and superintending. Now he saw only five days of labour. But he had never been to Amarnath and he was excited. He told us that the Muslims had been there first and that the cave, *lingam* and all, used to be a Muslim 'temple'.

He reported to Mr Butt. Mr Butt summoned an English-

knowing lake scribe and a few days later, when I was in bed
with yet another cold, sent in his estimate:

From Srinagar to Palguime Boy Bus Rotin	30.0.0.
3 Roding Poine Rotine	150.0.0.
2 Pakige Poine Rotine	100.0.0.
Tente a Kachen	25.0.0.
Tabel a chare Bed	15.0.0.
one colie	30.0.0.
	350.0.0.
Sweper	20.0.0.
Extre loding and Noey Loding colie	20.0.0.
	390.0.0.
From 11 august up to 17 august	
7 day conteri Food	161.0.0.
	Rs551.0.0.

If you going Bus for Imri Nath then is last 100 Rs.

It was a remarkable document: an unfamiliar language, an
unfamiliar script, and most of its approximations understandable. Too understandable: I was being overcharged. I was
bitterly disappointed. I had known them for four months; I
had declared my affection for them; I had done what I could for
the hotel; I had given them a party. It must have been the
depth of this disappointment; or it might have been my two
days in bed. I jumped up, pushed Aziz aside, ran to the window,
threw it open and heard myself shouting to Mr Butt in a
strange insincere-sincere voice, the result perhaps of remembering, even while I shouted, that I had to speak clearly, as to a
child, and to use words which he would understand: 'This is
not *good*, Mr Butt. Butt Sahib, this is not *honest*. Mr Butt, do
you know what you have done? You have *hurt* me.'

He was standing in the garden with some boatmen. He
looked up, startled and uncomprehending. Then his face, still
turned up to me, went blank. He said nothing.

In the silence that followed my words I felt foolish and not a little uneasy. I closed the window and quietly got back into bed. India, it was said, brought out concealed elements of the personality. Was this me? Was this the effect of India?

Whatever it was, it alarmed them at the hotel; and when, after giving me time to cool down, they gathered around my bed to discuss the estimate, they were solicitous, as though I was ill with more than a cold. Their manner also held reproach: it was as if, during all the weeks I had been with them, I had concealed my emotionalism, thereby encouraging an approach for which they could not, with justice, be blamed.

In the end many rupees were knocked off the estimate and we became friends again. Mr Butt seemed happy; he came with us to Pahalgam to see us off. Aziz was happy. He was wearing his fur cap, Ali Mohammed's striped blue suit, sandals (Mr Butt had refused to lend his shoes again), and a pair of my socks. He did not have the retinue he would have liked, but no one else on the pilgrimage appeared to be travelling in comparable style. We did, after all, have a staff; and we had a second tent for the staff. And when, at sunset, we halted at the crowded camp in the smoking woods of Chandanwari, he not only managed by his swift, intelligent arrangements to create something like luxury in the midst of restrictions, but he also managed, by his mixture of bustle, of orders sharply given to the pony men and his assistant, and of reverential, exaggerated attentions to us, to hedge us around with dignity. The camp was a chaos of tents and guy-ropes and cooking stones and pilgrims defecating behind every bush. The woods were already littered with uncovered excrement; hanks and twists of excrement crowned every accessible boulder of the Lidder river, beside which we had camped. But Aziz made us feel apart; he put us on show. This was his craft, his pride. And just as that morning when we set out from the hotel for Gulmarg he could not hide his pleasure, but had to tell everyone he passed on the lake that he was off to Gulmarg, so now, pouring warm water for me to wash my hands, he said, 'Everybody asking me, "*Who* is your sahib?"' It was less a tribute to me than to himself.

His troubles began the next day. For half a mile out of Chandanwari the path ran easily between rock and the boulder-stewn Lidder river until it came to the almost vertical two-thousand-foot wall of Pissu Ghati. Here the path narrowed and zigzagged up and up between rocks, the slain demons of one legend, for two miles. The pilgrims queued for the climb, and the queue moved slowly. At Chandanwari it did not move at all. It was hours before we could get going, and then we discovered that during our morning's stupor one of our pony-men had absconded. So Aziz's torment began. The ponies had to be urged up Pissu Ghati, their loads held in place—we could hear the pony men's cries all the way up and the occasional crash of tumbling loads—and there was nothing Aziz could do but to get off his pony and start pushing the abandoned, tent-laden pony up the steep path: he in his striped blue suit, his fur cap, his terylene socks, he who had been forbidden to walk. Dignity abandoned him. He complained like a child; he cursed in Kashmiri; he swore to get vengeance; he asked me to write to Mr Madan. His whip hand flashed again and again. 'Bloody swine man!' he shouted in English, and the terylene socks sagged down his stamping, sandalled feet. His cries grew fainter as we went ahead on our ponies. Looking down, we glimpsed him from time to time negotiating a hairpin bend, angrily dodging the tent-poles, and each time he looked tinier, dustier, more crumpled and more enraged.

We got to the top and waited for him. We waited a long time, and when at last he appeared, shouting behind his still re-calcitrant pony, he was a picture of outraged misery. Ali Mohammed's blue suit had been discoloured by dust to the fawn of my terylene socks, the tops of which had now worked their way down to his heels. Dust stuck to his small sweating face; even through his crumpled clothes I could feel the fragility of his suffering legs. My delight in his discomfiture, his abrupt transformation from majordomo to Kashmiri *ghora-wallah*, pony man, now felt like malice.

'Poor Aziz,' I said. 'Bloody *ghora-wallah*.'

This encouragement was a mistake. From now on he talked of nothing but the renegade *ghora-wallah*. 'You dock his pay, sahib.' 'You write Mr Madan Touriasm.' 'You complain Government, they take away his permit.' And he made up for his walk up Pissu Ghati by staying on his pony all the way to Sheshnag. We shouted to him to get off, to give his assistant a rest. He never heard; it was we who got off our ponies, to give the chance of a ride to the assistant, excessively burdened by Aziz after Pissu Ghati. Breathing was not easy; walking was painful, even up the gentlest slope. Aziz rode serenely on now. A pony had been provided for him; that was part of the contract. Dignity gradually returned to him. He became once again the majordomo, importantly slung with an *English* vacuum flask, which he had insisted on carrying. ('This is *beautiful* thermos,' he had said, passing a sensuous hand over it, and throwing one of our own words back at us.) From time to time he halted and waited for us; and as soon as we caught up with him it was: 'You go see Government. They take away *ghora-wallah* permit.' He was out for blood; I had never seen him so determined.

In front and behind the pilgrimage stretched in a thin irrelevant line of movement which appeared to have no beginning or end, which gave scale to the mountains and emphasised their stillness. The path had been trampled into dust, inches thick, that rose at every step. It was important not to overtake or be overtaken. Dust overcame the dampness below wet rock; dust powdered the hard snow in gullies. Over one such gully a skullcapped Kashmiri had made himself the harassed master. He had a spade and feverishly dug up snow, which he offered, for a few coins, to pilgrims. The pilgrims, continually pressed from behind, could not stop. Nor could the Kashmiri: he frantically dug, ran with extended spade after the pilgrims already departing, did a lightning haggle, took his coins, ran back, dug again. He was all motion: it was a one-day-a-year trade.

We had passed the tree-line and now we came into sight of the milky green lake of Sheshnag and the glacier that fed it. From Karan Singh's essay I had learned that the icy waters of Sheshnag were auspicious. Some members of his party had gone down the half a mile or so to the lake, to have a lucky dip. But he had made a compromise: 'I have to admit that I used the less orthodox, though certainly more convenient, method of getting water from the lake carried up and warming it for my bath.' It would have been pleasant to dawdle here, to go down to the lake. But the pilgrimage pressed us on, and Aziz was anxious to camp.

He was right to be anxious. The camping ground, when we got to it, was crowded; the rocky banks of the turbulent mountain river was already lined with defecating pilgrims, and soon it would have been difficult to find an accessible washing spot that was unsullied. Hundreds of ponies, freed of their burdens, had been hobbled and turned loose on the mountainside, browsing on what they could find; some were to die on this journey. The evening light fell golden on the three snowy peaks above Sheshnag; it shot through the smoke which, rising above the camp, converted the tents into an extensive miniature mountain range, peak beyond white peak dissolving in evening mist; it fell on the two long rows of sadhus, more brilliant splashes of saffron and scarlet, who were being fed, at the Kashmir Government's expense, in an open area that had been spared impurity. These sadhus had been gathered from every corner of India, and their feeding, I believe, was part of the Tourist Department's public relations: officially we were all 'tourists-cum-pilgrims'.

Aziz did not cease to complain about the runaway *ghora-wallah*. I knew that he had chosen me as the instrument of his vengeance and I cannot understand why I did not rebel. His complaint and pleas wore me down; and after dinner I allowed myself to be led through the dark, cold camp, past ropes and glinting rivulets and heaven knows what other dangers, to the tent of one of the government officials accompanying the pilgrimage. I had met him the previous evening at Chandanwari, and now he greeted me warmly. I was glad for Aziz's sake and my own at this proof of my influence. Aziz behaved like a man already satisfied. He was no longer the leader; he was only my deferential servant. By his behaviour, his interruptions, he presented me as the aggrieved party, a duped tourist; then he withdrew, leaving me to get out of the situation as best I could. My complaint was halfhearted. The

official made notes. We talked about the difficulties of organising such a pilgrimage, and he offered me a cup of coffee with
the compliments of the Indian Coffee Board.

I was in the Coffee Board's tent, sipping coffee, when a tall
white girl of striking appearance came in.

'Hi,' she said, sitting beside me. 'I'm Laraine.'

She was American; she was thrilled by the *yatra*, the pilgrimage. Her speech abounded in Hindi words.

She attracted me. But I had grown tired of meeting young
Americans in unlikely places. It was amusing, and charitable,
to think that some of them were spies for the CIA or whatever
it was. But there were too many of them. It seemed more
likely that they were a new type of American whose privilege
it was to go slumming about the world and sometimes scroung-
ing, exacting a personal repayment for a national generosity.
I had met the type in Egypt, looking for Lawrence Durrell's
Alexandria, living on a few piastres a day, eating *foul* and willing
to accept any Eastern hospitality that was going. In Greece
for one day I had had to feed an unashamed beggar, a 'teacher',
who said he never went to restaurants or hotels: 'As long as
there are doors to knack on, I knack.' (He was almost certainly
a spy, and he thought I was one too. 'Why is it,' he said, 'that
every goddam outa-the-way place I go, I meet Indians?') In
New Delhi I had met the type in its most developed form:
this was a 'research student', of ineradicable grossness, who
had billeted himself for six weeks in the house of a stranger,
casually encountered at a wedding party. India, the world's
largest slum, had an added attraction: 'cultural' humility was
sweet, but 'spiritual' humility was sweeter.

So: No, I said, I wasn't thrilled by the *yatra*. I thought the
yatris had no idea of sanitation; they polluted every river we
came to; I wished they would follow Gandhi's advice about
the need for a little spade.

'Then you shouldn't have come.'

It was the only reply, and it was unanswerable. My resentment had made me speak foolishly. I sought to work the
conversation back to a more normal give-and-take and tried
to get her to tell me about herself.

She had come to India, she said, for two weeks, and had already stayed six months. She was attracted to Hindu philosophy; when she left the *yatra* she was going to spend some time in an ashram. She was a seeker.

Her cheekbones were high; her neck was slender. But her leanness was of the sort which holds fleshy surprises; her breasts were good and full. I did not think it was the body of someone who would be allowed to remain a seeker for long. Yet in the light of the pressure lamp her eyes conveyed uncertainty. I thought they hinted at family problems and childhood distress. This, and a certain coarseness of her skin, added a disturbing edge to her good looks.

I would have liked to see more of her. But though we promised to look out for one another, we never met again during the pilgrimage.

That, however, was not the last of Laraine.

Ridiculously, the next morning I allowed Aziz to persuade me to complain to the government official again about the missing *ghora-wallah*. Aziz wanted blood, and his faith in the power of officials was boundless. He was almost triumphant when we started out. We had gone less than a mile, however, Aziz serene on his pony, when our bedding bundle rolled off the untended pony and tumbled down a precipice. Our cavalcade had to stop; Aziz had to walk the pony back and then down; the pony had to be reloaded and urged up again. He was raging when, half an hour later, he rejoined us. 'Swine!' he said. 'Bloody swine man!' And all the way to Panchtarni he alternately brooded and raged.

At Sheshag we had been at an altitude of thirteen thousand feet. A gradual climb of two thousand feet brought us to the Mahagunas Pass, and a world of bleached grey stone: the snows were only temporarily absent. The mountains were grained like wood; and each mountain was grained at a different angle. From here it was an easy descent to the Panchtarni Plain, an abrupt, unbroken levelling-out between the mountains, a mile long, a quarter of a mile wide, down which a keen wind blew and shallow streams raged, white over grey rocks. Colour had grown austere and arctic, and the word 'plain' was like a definition of lunar geography.

At the edge of the wet, pale plain, and unprotected from the wind, an unburdened, unhobbled pony stood shivering to death, his Kashmiri master standing sad-eyed beside him, doing nothing, offering only his presence, both removed from the bustle of the camp, the last full camp of the pilgrimage. The talk among porters and pony men was already of the swift journey back, and even Aziz, infected in spite of his brooding, was saying like an old Amarnath hand, 'Tomorrow I go *straight* back to Chandanwari.' In that 'I' he included us all.

It was mid-afternoon when we pitched our tents. After Aziz had given us tea he left us, saying he was going to have a look round. Something was on his mind. When he returned, less than half an hour later, his look of preoccupation had disappeared; he was all smiles.

'How you liking, sir?'

'I am liking very much.'

'Pony dead.'

'Pony dead!'

'Sweeper come just now take him away.' At twelve thousand feet, and from a devout Muslim, caste. 'Why you not write Mr Butt letter, sir? Tell him how much you like. Post Office here with *yatra*. You post letter here.'

'No paper, no envelope.'

'I buy.'

He had already bought: it was an Inland Letter form that he was pulling out from one of the pockets of Ali Mohammed's jacket.

I wrote to Mr Butt, postcard sentiments. I was about to seal the letter when Aziz said, 'You put this in, sir.' It was a dirty scrap of paper, possibly an envelope flap, on which one sentence of Urdu had been written with a ballpoint pen.

'You can't put anything inside these letters, Aziz.'

At once he tore the Urdu note into tiny pieces, which he let fall to the ground, and he referred no more to it. I don't believe he posted the letter I wrote; at least Mr Butt never received it. The note was secret, that was clear. It would have been less secret if the Urdu writer had known the name of the person to whom it was addressed; the addressing was therefore my job. This must have been the plan he had been devising all day. Yet he had abandoned it so easily. Was it only a taste for mystification? Even if it was, it had very nearly enabled Aziz, an illiterate, to send a secret message to someone ninety miles away. I was disturbed. Did I fully know Aziz? Did he respond to affection like mine, or was his loyalty only to an employer?

The pilgrims, when they were on the march, could have formed a line ten to fifteen miles long. For hours, then, the line must have moved, unbroken, from camp to camp. Even as the sun was going down over the grey, whistling plain where a pony had died, where ponies every year died, the pilgrims continued to come down the mountains and across the plain, a thin wriggling line of colour rapidly merging into the darkness there, here in the lights of the camp revealed as a slow, silent march of Kashmiri pony men, skull-capped, with dusty feet in disintegrating straw sandals, Gujjars whose studded leather shoes, curiously small and elegant, curling back at the tips, matched the sharpness of their fine features, and ladies riding side-saddle, muffled against the dust during the day, now muffled against the cold.

They came into a camp where the tension of adventure, so high only that morning, had already slackened. The adventure was nearly over; the restlessness was the restlessness of anticipated breaking-up and return. Many of the pilgrims had turned in early; they wished to be up for the four o'clock dash to the cave the next morning. The posters in the tent of the Indian Coffee Board were tarnished: they would be needed for only a few hours more. There were fewer wanderers about the camp than at Sheshnag or Chandanwari. No one gazed at the silver rods which for a century had been sent on the pilgrimage by the Kashmir royal house and were displayed in a lighted tent at the head of the camp; that wonder had been seen before. The crowd around the pundit in the second tent was small and settled, a sifting of the crowds of the two previous nights.

From Karan Singh's essay, I imagine that during our night halts he had been reciting from the *Amarkatha*, a Sanskrit account of the pilgrimage 'believed to have been related by Lord Shiva himself to his consort Parvati in the Amarnath Cave'. He was a man of ferocious, magazine-illustration handsomeness, exactly filling his role: he had a wavy black beard, long hair, large bright eyes, and remained bare-shouldered even in the bitter cold. Tonight in his windy tent he was chanting, his eyes closed, his fingers delicately bunched on his knees. Just beyond the yellow of his pressure lamp, light was silver: the moon, almost full. Rock was as white as raging water; the wind blew; the camp went stiller.

The path to the cave was a narrow ledge cut diagonally, ever rising, ever curving, into the mountains beyond Panchtarni. Pilgrims were already returned from the cave when we started in bright sunlight the next morning; and men with red Public Works Department armbands stood at dangerous corners, controlling the two-way traffic. The foreheads of the returning pilgrims were marked with sandalwood paste. Their faces were bright with ecstasy. They had seen the god; they were exuberant and aggressive. They were unwilling to give way. They shouted, '*Jai Shiva Shankar!*' and the cave-bound pilgrims, as subdued as a cinema queue when the earlier, fulfilled audience streams out, replied softly, '*Jai Shiva Shankar!*'

'You!' a sandalwood-smeared young man shouted to me in English. 'You say, "*Jai Shiva Shankar!*" '

'*Jai Shiva Shankar!*'

My promptness confused him. All right. Good.' And he passed on. '*Jai Shiva Shankar!*'

Down the steep mountainside yellow flowers presently appeared in profusion, and everyone was reminded that fresh flowers were an acceptable offering to the god. Since four o'clock that morning, though, pilgrims had been passing this way: few flowers remained within easy reach, and it seemed that for many the faded flowers bought from the camp bazaar would have to serve. Then we came upon Kashmiris squatting in safe recesses before bunches of the yellow flowers, which silently, with averted eyes, they offered for sale.

We began to descend again, and from bright sunlight we turned off into the cold shadow of a long narrow valley. The valley might have been the bed of a recent river. Its base was littered with brown rubble and its sides, curving steeply, carried what looked like black tidemarks. But this was not rubble or grey shingle; this was old snow, gone the colour and texture of earth. Down one side of the valley the line of pilgrims, going and coming, stretched; and there, far away, they were crossing the ice bed, mere specks, robbed of all but the brightest colour, distinguishable only by their movement from the rubbled surface of the snow. Here was a mountain, there a valley and a river: the geography of these ranges was simple, easily grasped. But one had brought to them the scale of a smaller, managed world, and it was only at times like these, seeing a line of men swiftly diminished within what seemed a small space, that one realised what distances these Himalayas held.

Now indeed, in that valley, India had become all symbol. We on the path rode on ponies. But there, on the brown snow below, in the shadow of mountains that denied life, walked pilgrims from the plains, supporting themselves on staffs (bought from Kashmiri roadside vendors at Pahalgam): a broken line merging at the end of the valley into that other line which, across the snow-bed, no goal in sight, disappeared into the grey-brown mountains and became of their texture. The god existed: the faces and cries of the returning pilgrims carried this reassurance. I wished I was of their spirit. I wished that something of their joy awaited me at the end.

Yet a special joy had been with me throughout the pilgrimage and during all my time in Kashmir. It was the joy of being among mountains; it was the special joy of being among the Himalayas. I felt linked to them; I liked speaking the name. India, the Himalayas: they went together. In so many of the brightly coloured religious pictures in my grandmother's house I had seen these mountains, cones of white against simple, cold blue. They had become part of the India of my fantasy. It would have astonished me then, in a Trinidad achingly remote from places that seemed worthwhile and real because fully known, to be told that one day I would walk among the originals of those mountains. The pictures I knew to be wrong; their message was no message to me; but in that corner of the mind which continues child-like their truth remained a possibility. And it was partly with that sense of the unattainable given by those pictures, such as, after a lifetime it seemed, I had seen again in Indian bazaars and among the dusty stock of pavement booksellers, that I looked upon these mountains. To be among them was fleetingly, and with a truer sense of their unattainability, to claim them again. To reject the legend of the thousand-headed Sheshnag was easy. But the fact of the legend established the lake as mine. It was mine, but it was something I had lost, something on which I would soon have to turn my back again. Was it fanciful to think of these Himalayas, so well charted and perhaps once better known, as the Indian symbol of loss, mountains to which, on their burning plains, they looked back with yearning, and to which they could now return only in pilgrimages, legends and pictures?

At the end of the valley, where the ice, less protected, was partly broken, one remembered picture came to life: a sadhu, wearing only a leopard skin, walking barefooted on Himalayan snow, almost in sight of the god he sought. He held his trident like a spear, and from the trident a gauze-like pennant fluttered. He walked apart, like one to whom the journey was familiar. He was a young man of complete, disquieting beauty. His skin had been burned black and was smeared with white ash; his hair was reddish-blond; but this only made unnatural the perfection of his features, the tilt of head, the fineness of his limbs, the light assurance of his walk, the delicate play of muscles down his back and abdomen. Some days before the pilgrimage I had seen him in Srinagar, resting in the shade of a chenar, languid genitals arrogantly exposed. He had seemed out of place, an idler, an aboriginal come to town. His ash-smeared nudity, implying an indifference to the body, had made his beauty sinister. Now he lent his nobility to all the pilgrims: his goal was theirs.

Out of the shadow of the valley the broad pyramidal slope

of Amarnath burst upon us, rock-strewn, quivering white in sunlight; and the cave to which it led rose black and still, taller and wider than I had imagined it, yet now, after so much expectation, oddly obvious, like a cave in a simple religious picture. It dwarfed the pilgrims seething at its mouth; again men were needed to give scale to a too simple geography. At the foot of the slope pilgrims, preparing for the final ascent, bathed in the clear, holy waters of the Amarvati stream and rubbed their bodies with its sand. On his own pilgrimage Karan Singh had compromised here, as he had done at Sheshnag: 'Here again I adopted the unorthodox course of getting the water carried in buckets to the tent, but this time I did not get it warmed up and bathed with the ice cold water. It was clear and warm, however, so the cold bath did not cause any inconvenience.'

Sunlight, white rock, water, bare bodies, brilliant garments: it was a scene of pastoral at thirteen thousand feet. Just above, however, was turmoil. Beyond the stream there were few restraining khaki-clad policemen, few men with red Public Works Department armbands; and after their placid ablutions the pilgrims scrambled up to the cave and joined the purified, frenzied crowd fighting to get a view of the god and to make their offerings. The cave was about a hundred-and-twenty feet wide, a hundred feet high, and a hundred feet deep. It was not big enough. Within the cave, damp and dripping, a steep ramp led to the inner sanctum, the abode of the god. This was protected by a tall iron railing, with a gate that opened outwards. The crowd pressed forward; the gate could hardly be opened; whenever it was, the whole ramp seethed and there were cries from those who feared they might be pushed off the ramp: it was a long drop from the gloom of the cave to the white sunlit slope up which more and more pilgrims were coming. The newcomers, barefooted, carrying fresh or faded flowers, wedged themselves into the crowd and hoped to be taken forward by the general movement. Individual advance or retreat was impossible; a woman was sobbing with terror. I climbed up and held on to the iron railing: I could see only crowd and a low rock vault blackened by damp or incense.

I climbed down again. Up the slope and from far down the ice-bed of the valley pilgrims steadily approached. They were like pebbles, they were like sand: a stippling of colour which, receding, grew finer. For hours, perhaps for all that day, there would be no slackening of the throng on the ramp.

No sight of the god, then, for me: I would sit it out. Not so Aziz. He was a Muslim, an iconoclast; but his devoutness as a Muslim could not overcome his curiosity as a Kashmiri. He joined the crowd and instantly vanished, his fur cap alone revealing his progress. I squatted on the wet ground, in a litter of paper and wrappings and cigarette packets, beside a grimy skullcapped Kashmiri Muslim who was guarding the shoes of the Hindu devout at four annas a pair. He was doing good business. Slowly Aziz progressed. Now, at the gates, he was squeezed out of the crowd, like a pip out of an orange: fur cap, bewildered but determined face, Ali Mohammed's striped blue jacket, hands clawing at the rails. Somehow, hands working, unseen legs no doubt also working, he managed to be squeezed through the narrow opening of the gate, and then disappeared, fur cap and all, once again.

I waited a long time for him, in a ringing cave which in a few hours had been turned into a busy Indian bazaar. A bazaar: at this moment of climax there came the flatness I had all along feared. And it was like the flatness, equally expected, equally feared, of my first day in Bombay. Pilgrimages were only for the devout. I concentrated on the Kashmiri's shoes, the coins on his scrap of newspaper.

When Aziz reappeared, tarnished but awed, he reported with contradictory satisfaction, which yet held nothing of surprise— he was, after all, a Muslim—that there was no *lingam*. Perhaps none had formed this time; perhaps it had melted in the rush. Where the *lingam* ought to have been there were only offerings of flowers and money. But the pilgrims streaming through the exit were as ecstatic as any we had met on the morning's march.

'You don't come for the *lingam*,' one man said. 'It's the spirit of the thing.'

The spirit of the thing! Squatting in the cave, which rang

continuously with shouts and shuffling, concentrating on the
bazaar litter on the wet floor, glimpsing out of the corner of
my eye the ever ascending crowd whose numbers I could less
easily grasp than I could the size of the mountains and the
valleys, I had grown light-headed. A physical growth, because
it was extraordinary, was a spiritual symbol. The growth failed;
it became the symbol of a symbol. In this spiralling, deliques-
cing logic I felt I might drown. I went outside into the light.
Pilgrims, their offerings made, were looking up for the two
rock pigeons, followers of Lord Shiva once, before they were
turned into pigeons by the anger of their Lord and doomed
forever to live near Him in His cave. I did not look up. I went
on down the white slope, hopping from rock to rock, and did
not stop until I came to the clear stream.

Our return was to be swift. At Panchtarni, where the camp of
the morning had already almost ceased to exist, our bundles
were packed and the ponies were waiting. Aziz spoke of going
straight on to Chandanwari; he wanted to be back in Srinagar
on the following day, to be in time for another religious
occasion: the display of the hair from the beard of the Prophet
at Hazratbal Mosque. I would have preferred to remain a little
longer in the mountains. But no; we had to hurry; all about us
there was the atmosphere of haste, almost of flight. Later, I
thought. Later we would come back and spend an entire
summer among these mountains. We would experience their
weather—that morning in the camp at Sheshnag mist had
suddenly swirled down the snowcapped mountains, adding
ominousness to beauty, and had as suddenly lifted, revealing
the bright sky. And in the afternoons we would have the
streams to ourselves. But 'later' is always part of these moments.
Already, in fact, the desolate camp at Panchtarni had affected
me. The pilgrimage was over, our path was known; the journey
had grown stale.

Some time in the afternoon a Kashmiri in a green cap joined
our party, and a quarrel instantly blew up between him and
Aziz. I was on foot; from afar I could see the gesticulating
figures; and when I drew near I recognised the man in the green

cap as the missing *ghora-wallah*. He was attempting to take charge of the pony he had abandoned two days before; there was nothing to stop him, but at every shout from Aziz he behaved like a man who was being restrained by physical force. Vengeance was now Aziz's; this was the moment he had been waiting for; and his anger and contempt were frightening, except perhaps to another Kashmiri. For all its passion, in fact, the exchange had something of play. The *ghora-wallah* pleaded, but he seemed untouched by Aziz's abuse. He wept. Aziz, astride his shabby little pony, his socked, sandalled feet hanging very low, refused to be mollified. Suddenly, no longer weeping, the *ghora-wallah* ran to the abandoned pony and made as if to seize the reins. Aziz screamed; the *ghora-wallah* stopped short, as though he had been surprised in a furtive act and struck a heavy blow on the head. Finally he ceased to weep or plead; he blustered; he became abusive; and Aziz replied. He hung back; he ran forward; he hung back again. Then he didn't run forward, and gradually dwindled in the distance, a still, standing figure occasionally roused to frenzy, shaking a fist against the Himalayan skyline.

'When we reach Pahalgam you report Touriasm Office,' Aziz, perfectly calm, said to me. 'They take away his permit.'

Sheshnag camp was almost deserted; it looked trampled over and unsavoury. We passed it by and at dusk pitched our tents at a small encampment a few miles on. For hours afterwards lights came twinkling down the mountain, and went past: pilgrims hastened back to Chandanwari, puffs of dust in the light of the full moon.

The journey that remained was easy. We ourselves were in the woods of Chandanwari early next morning and by midday we were in sight of Pahalgam, back in a green world of fields and trees and earth. It was all downhill now. I got off my pony and scrambled down, avoiding the lengthy twists and turns of the jeep-track, and soon was far ahead of Aziz and the others. Aziz made no attempt to catch up with me; and even when, together again, we were on the metalled road and passing the bus station and the Tourist Office, he said not a word about the missing *ghora-wallah*. I did not remind him. He jumped off his pony to take an uninvited, and unresented, pull at someone's hookah: he had abandoned the role of the aloof majordomo. Momentarily we lost him, and when he reappeared he was carrying a quantity of peas in his shirt, the front of which was knotted to form something like a tray, which he did not need to support. The transformation from majordomo to hotel servant was complete. He was even without the vacuum flask; that, like Mr Butt's shoes, he had destroyed.

At our base, a tent in the shade of a tree, the *ghora-wallah* in the green cap was waiting for us. As soon as he caught sight of me he began to wail and weep: a formal self-abasement, a formal weeping, dry and scraping, without a hint of real distress. He ran to me, dropped to his knees and grabbed my legs with his powerful hands. The pony men gathered round with looks of satisfaction. Aziz, his shirtful of peas before him, was openly smiling down at the *ghora-wallah*.

'He is poor man, sahib.'

What was this? After all that I had heard from him about the *ghora-wallah*, could this be Aziz?

The *ghora-wallah* wept more loudly.

'He have wife,' Aziz said. 'He have children. You not report Touriasm, sahib.'

The *ghora-wallah* ran his hands down my legs and banged his forehead on my shoes.

'He very poor man, sahib. You not dock his pay. You not take away his permit.'

Holding my knees firmly, the *ghora-wallah* rubbed his forehead against them.

'He not honest man, sahib. He bloody swine. But he poor. You not report Touriasm.'

The ritual went on, without any reference, it seemed, to me.

'All right, all right,' I said. 'I not report.'

Instantly the *ghora-wallah* was up, not a trace of anxiety or relief on his broad peasant's face: he had simply been working. He dusted the knees of his trousers in a businesslike way, took out some rupee notes from a pocket, counted five and, even as I looked, gave them to Aziz.

This was the price of Aziz's intercession. Had they come to

some arrangement the previous afternoon? Had it been planned days before? Had Aziz intended all his groans and complaints to lead to this, an extra five rupees? It seemed unlikely—that labour up Pissu Ghati had been real—but with Aziz I could no longer be sure. He seemed surer of me: he had taken a gift— in the long run my money—in my presence. Throughout the journey he had promoted my dignity; he must have frightened the *ghora-wallah* with my importance. But this true assessment was plain. I was harmless. Faced with this assessment, I felt my will weaken. No, I wouldn't, simply for the sake of my pride, make a scene; when all was said and done, Aziz was my servant. It would be less troublesome to preserve my character, as he had read it, until we got back to Srinagar.

The five rupees, checked, disappeared into one of Aziz's pockets. The moment for reprimand passed. I said nothing. His assessment had, after all, proved correct.

Then the *ghora-wallah*, leading his pony by the reins, came up to me again.

'*Bakshish?*' he said, and stretched out one hand.

The sunflowers in the garden faded and were like emblems of dying suns, their tongues of fire limp and shrivelled. My work was almost done; it would soon be time to go. Farewell visits had to be made. We went first to our friends at Gulmarg.

'We've been having our adventures too,' Ishmael said.

They always had. They attracted drama. They were interested in the arts and their house was always full of writers and musicians.

'You didn't by any chance meet a girl called Laraine on your pilgrimage?'

'An American girl?'

'She said she was going to Amarnath.'

'But how extraordinary! Was she staying here too?'

'She and Rafiq nearly drove us mad.'

This adventure (Ishmael said) had begun in Srinagar, in the Indian Coffee House on Residency Road. There one morning Ishmael met Rafiq. Rafiq was a musician. He played the sitar. The apprenticeship of a musician in India is long and severe. And though Rafiq was nearly thirty and though, according to Ishmael, he was very good, he had not yet made a name; he was just beginning to give recitals on local radio stations. It was in order to relax before one such recital that Rafiq had come to Kashmir for a fortnight. He had little money. Ishmael, generous and impulsive as always, invited Rafiq, whom he had met that morning for the first time, to stay at his bungalow in Gulmarg. Rafiq took his sitar and went.

The arrangement worked well. Rafiq found himself with a couple who understood the artistic temperament. His music delighted them; he could never practise enough. The routine of the house was also congenial. Dinner was at midnight, after music, talk and drink. Breakfast was at midday. Then perhaps the masseur called, carrying his equipment in a small black box marked with his name. Afterwards, if it was not raining, there was a walk through the pines. Sometimes they collected mushrooms; sometimes they collected cones for the fire, to give a quick aromatic blaze.

Then one afternoon all this changed.

They were having coffee on the sunlit lawn when on the path below there appeared a white girl. She was arguing with a Kashmiri *ghora-wallah*: she had no companion and was clearly in some trouble. Ishmael sent Rafiq down to see what he could do. In that moment Rafiq's holiday was ruined; in that moment he was lost. When, a minute or so later, he returned, his hosts could scarcely recognise him as the mild, courteous sitar-player they had picked mushrooms with. He was like a man possessed. In that short time, during which he had also settled with the *ghora-wallah*, he had conquered and had surrendered: a relationship had been decided and had become explosive. Rafiq did not return alone. He had the girl, Laraine, with him. She was going to stay with them, he said. Did they mind? Could they make the necessary arrangements?

Stunned, they agreed. Later that afternoon they suggested a walk: they would show their new guest the peak of Nanga Parbat, forty miles away, on which the snow glistened like oil paint. Rafiq and Laraine soon fell behind, then disappeared. Ishmael and his wife were a little aggrieved. Selfconsciously and silently, like guests rather than hosts, they continued on their walk, pausing here and there to admire the view. In time they were rejoined by Rafiq and Laraine. No fulfilment on their faces, no fatigue: they were both hysterical. They were quarrelling and their rage was real. Presently they exchanged blows. The faces of both were already marked. She kicked him. He groaned, and slapped her. She cried out, swung her bag at him, kicked him again, and he tumbled down the brambly slope. Torn, bleeding, he came bellowing up, snatched her bag and threw it far down into a valley, where it would remain until the snows came and washed it away. At this she sat down and wept like a child. His rage vanished; he went to her; she yielded to him.

He took it out of the sitar when they got back to the bungalow. He practised like a man gone mad; the sitar whined and whined. That night they had another fight. Their shouts and screams brought the police, ever on the alert for Pakistani raiders, who had made a swift looting expedition on the slopes of Khilanmarg the previous year.

Now they were both damaged and scarred; it seemed dangerous for them to be alone together. Laraine, intermittently lucid, left the bungalow more than once. Sometimes Rafiq fetched her back; sometimes she returned while he was still making the sitar cry out. For Ishmael and his wife it was too much. On the second night, during one of Laraine's absences, they asked Rafiq to leave. He put his sitar on his head and prepared to leave. His docility then, a reminder of the old Rafiq, and the sight of the musician carrying away his instrument, softened them; they asked him to stay. He stayed; Laraine returned; it began all over again.

In the end it was Laraine, bruised, fatigued, lucid and desperate, who cracked. After three days—which to Ishmael and his wife seemed like three weeks and which to Laraine and Rafiq must have seemed as long as life itself—she said she couldn't stand it; she had to get away. She would go on the pilgrimage to Amarnath; then she would go to an ashram. She was a woman and an American: her will endured long enough for her to make her escape.

'*Laraine! Laraine!*' Rafiq bellowed through the bungalow when she had gone, the name strange in his Indian mouth.

He would be practising. Suddenly he would stop and scream out: 'I must have Laraine!'

He had known passion. He was to be envied; he was also to be pitied. How often, and with what pain, he would relive not perhaps those three days but that first moment: that going down to the strange girl and that first glimpse of her answering, disturbed eyes, which would never speak in quite the same way to any other man. And it might have been while he was bellowing her name one evening in Gulmarg that I was studying her eyes in the cold tent of the Indian Coffee Board at Sheshnag, and reading in them a broken family and a distressed childhood. I was partly right, as it turned out. But I had missed the greater turmoil.

When Rafiq left Gulmarg it was with the intention of finding her. She had said she was going to an ashram. But India abounded in ashrams. Where was he to look?

He didn't have to look far.

I was at the blue table in my room one afternoon when I heard an American woman's voice in the garden. I looked out. It was Laraine; and before I pulled my head in I caught sight of the back of a man's head above sturdy fawn-jacketed shoulders. So she had surrendered; she had ceased to seek. They had come to the hotel for tea. I also heard them inquiring about rooms, and later heard them inspecting.

'Everything *thik?*' she asked, mispronouncing the Hindi *th*, still game for India, still spattering her speech with Hindi. 'Everything all right?'

There was a muffled male rumble as they went down the steps.

They moved in the next day. I never saw them. They remained in their room all day, and occasionally the hotel quivered with sitar music.

'I think,' Aziz said at dinner, 'that the sahib and the memsahib getting married today.'

I was awakened that night by activity in the hotel, and

when Aziz came in with coffee in the morning I questioned him.

'The sahib married the memsahib last night,' he whispered. 'They mealing at one o'clock.'

'No!'

'Mr Butt and Ali Mohammed take them Mufti. She turn Muslim, get Muslim name. They get married. They mealing at *one* o'clock last night.' The lateness of the meal had impressed him almost as much as the marriage.

And now from the bridal chamber, silence: not even the sitar. No wedding breakfast, no coming out to look at the view. All morning the room remained closed, as though they were both hiding inside, awed at what had happened. After lunch they slipped out. I did not see them go.

It was not until the late afternoon, when I was having tea on the lawn, that I saw Laraine returning alone across the lake to the hotel. She was wearing a blue cotton frock; she looked cool; and she was carrying a paperback. She might have been a simple tourist.

'Hi!'

'Is it true what I hear? That you're married?'

'You know me. Impulsive.'

'Congratulations.'

'Thank you.'

She sat down; she was a little frightened; she wanted to talk.

'But isn't it crazy? Me with all this interest in Hinduism'— she showed the paperback she was carrying: it was Mr Rajagopalachari's retelling of the *Mahabharata*—'and now overnight I'm a Muslim and everything.'

'What is your new name?'

'Zenobia. Don't you think it's pretty?'

It was a pretty name, but it had brought problems. She didn't know whether she had lost her American nationality as a result of her marriage, and she wasn't sure whether she would be allowed to work in India. She had some idea that she was now very poor and would have to live in straitened circum-stances—not, I felt, fully visualised—in some Indian town. But already she was speaking of 'my husband' as though she had used the words all her life; already she was concerned about 'my husband's work' and 'my husband's career' and 'my husband's recital'.

They were poorer than she had perhaps imagined. Even the Liward was too expensive for them. They were to move elsewhere the following day, and trouble about their hotel bill blew up in the morning.

Aziz reported, 'He say I overcharge. He say, "Why you tell other sahib I married?" I say, "Why you want secret? Man get married. This is for good. He give party. He invite. He not hide. And why I not tell? You wake up my sahib and he complain".'

'Are you sure you are not overcharging them, Aziz?'

'O no, sahib.'

'But he doesn't have a lot of money, Aziz. He wasn't expecting to get married when he came to Kashmir. How much did they spend on their marriage?'

'O sahib, how much they spend? Some people give Mufti five, some give fifteen, some give fifty.'

'How much did they give?'

'A hundred.'

'You are a brute. You shouldn't have let him. He couldn't afford a hundred rupees. No wonder he can't pay you now.'

'But this is for good, sahib. You get married American memsahib, you give big party. You give Pharsi *khana*, *bangola* fireworks. You not hide. They not give party, they not give nothing.'

'The memsahib is American, but they don't have money.'

'No, sahib. They hide. Lotta people come Kashmir, feel what do here not matter. They feel Kashmir wedding not matter. But wedding paper get show in court, sahib.'

And Ali Mohammed came up with a copy of the marriage certificate, on which I saw the signatures of Zenobia, Rafiq and Mr Butt.

'They not hide, sahib,' Aziz said. 'They married good.'

It wasn't only money. They had been hurt in their pride as Kashmiris and Muslims. They had welcomed a convert; now they feared they were being made fools of.

'He not pay,' Aziz said, 'I take away sitar.'

But Rafiq chased through Srinagar and borrowed the necessary rupees. By midday he and Zenobia were ready to leave. We were having lunch when Zenobia came in to say goodbye. A man hovered behind the door curtain.

'Rafiq.'

He came in and stood a few paces behind her.

Self-possession momentarily deserted her. She knew that we knew the Gulmarg story.

'This,' she said, with acute embarrassment, 'is my husband'.

I had expected someone more tormented, more wasted-looking. He was of medium height and powerfully built, with a round, blunt-featured face. I had expected someone wild-eyed, defiant. He was dreadfully shy, with sleepy eyes; it was as if he had been caught smoking and was trying to hide the burning cigarette behind his back and to swallow the smoke without coughing. He was a musician and an Indian: I had expected long hair and a wide-sleeved white tunic, not an army-style haircut and an Indian-tailored fawn suit.

He was not the man I had imagined who would make his sitar cry out his anguish; he was only the man who would object to his marriage being known. Poor Rafiq! He had come to Kashmir for a holiday; he was going back exhausted, broke, married. I had thought of passion as a gift, a faculty with which human beings were unequally endowed. Now I felt that it was something which, in a complex conjunction of circumstances, might overtake us all.

He gave me a military handshake. He pulled out an un-impressive fountain pen from his inside pocket and in a flowing, clerk-like hand wrote down his address, now Laraine's, now Zenobia's.

'You must come and see us,' she said. 'You must come and have dinner one evening.'

Then they went through the curtained doorway, and I never saw Rafiq again.

It was time for us, too, to pack up and go, to say goodbye to the mountains and the room with the two views. The reeds had turned brown; in the afternoons *shikara*-loads of cut reeds went down the water highways. The sunflower plants—so thick their stalks now, and the birds pecked at the seeds in the black, burnt-out flowers—were all cut down in one afternoon and thrown in a bundle outside the kitchen. The garden seemed exposed and ravaged, the sunflower stumps showing as white as wood.

Aziz gave us dinner one evening at his tall brick house in the lake, paddling us there himself (together with a napkin-covered pitcher of tap-water from the hotel). Night, a lantern in the *shikara*, silence, the house approached down a willow-hung water alley, and Aziz behaving with an ancient courtesy. Details were obscured; it might have been the beginning of a Venetian entertainment. We ate sitting on the floor of an upper room that had been cleared of all furniture and people, whose presence we could yet detect in close whispers and the sounds of movement; and Aziz knelt before us, talking, no longer a hotel servant but our host, grave, independent, a man of substance, a man of views and, when the women and the babies flooded in, a responsible family man. The walls were thick, comfortingly grimed, full of arched recesses; windows were small. The room promised idleness and the warmth of charcoal braziers in winter, when the lake would freeze so hard a jeep could be driven over it: we would follow the weather in Srinagar.

After our last dinner in the hotel Mr Butt assembled the servants for the tipping ceremony: Aziz, Ali Mohammed, the cook, the gardener, the odd-job boy. They had been disappointed in a wedding; I hoped I wasn't going to disappoint them further: their smiling faces carried the conviction that the age of style was not yet over. They acknowledged my gifts and typewritten testimonials with graceful Muslim gestures; they continued to smile. Perhaps they were merely being courteous; perhaps they had learned to accommodate themselves to the lesser age. But Aziz was pleased. I could tell that from the indifferent manner with which, after a lightning assessment, he thrust the money into his pocket. He became morose, active, a man harassed by duties that were never done: money was not as important to him at that moment as setting the dining room to rights. He would relax as soon as he left the room; they would all relax. And going to the kitchen later that evening for a last pull at the hookah, I surprised them giggling over the testimonial I had written, with some care, for the odd-job boy.

We left early in the morning. Mr Butt paddled us over to the lake boulevard. It was not yet light. The water was still; on the boulevard the tonga waited. We went past the closed house-boats, the lotus beds. On the balustrade of the boulevard a man was exercising. The tonga roof sloped low: we had to lean forward to see the lake and the mountains. The town was awakening from minute to minute, and the Tourist Reception Centre, when we got to it, was infernally alive.

'Three rupees,' the tonga-wallah said.

In four months I had established among the lakeside tongas that I never paid more than one and a quarter rupees for the ride into town. But the circumstances were extraordinary. I offered two. The tonga-wallah refused to touch the notes. I offered no more. He threatened me with his whip; and I found, to my surprise—it must have been the earliness of the hour—that I had seized him by the throat.

Aziz intervened. 'He not tourist.'

'Oh,' the tonga-wallah said.

He dropped his whip hand, and I released him.

Our seats on the bus had been booked, but it was necessary to scramble, to fight, to shout. Aziz and Ali Mohammed scrambled and shouted for us, and we withdrew to the edge of the crowd.

Then we saw Laraine, Zenobia.

She was alone, and was peering shortsightedly at buses. She wore a chocolate skirt and a cream-coloured blouse. She looked thinner. She was not happy to meet us and had little news to give. She was off to her Hindu ashram after all; later she would be joining her husband. Now she was busy: she had to find her bus. It was a bus of the Radhakishun service. She turned this name to the more familiar 'Radha Krishna': her mind still ran on the Hindu legends. Krishna was the dark god, Radha the fair milkmaid with whom he sported.

And, asking for Radha Krishna, peering at the number plates on buses, she disappeared into the crowd.

Our own seats had now been secured, our bags placed below the tarpaulin on the roof of the bus. We shook hands with Aziz and Ali and went inside.

'You don't worry about tonga-wallah,' Aziz said. 'I settle.' There were tears in his eyes.

The engine started.

'Tonga-wallah?'

'You don't worry, sahib. Correct fare three rupees. I pay.'

The driver was blowing his horn.

'Correct fare?'

'Morning fare, sahib.'

He was right; I knew that.

'Two rupees, three rupees, what different? Goodbye, goodbye. You don't worry.'

I dug into my pockets.

'Don't worry, sahib. Goodbye.'

Through the window I pushed out some rupee notes.

He took them. Tears were running down his cheeks. Even at that moment I could not be sure that he had ever been mine.

She wore a chocolate skirt and a cream-coloured blouse. Rafiq would remember those garments; perhaps he had seen her lay them out the previous evening. He never saw her after that morning. She went to her ashram; and then she left India. He wrote; she replied; then his letters were returned unopened. Her parents had been separated and lived in different countries. He was supported by one, rejected by the other. Still he wrote; and months later he was still grieving.

But I heard this in another season. And in the Poste Restante of another town this letter awaited me:

HOTEL LIWARD
Advance Arrangements for
Trecking, Shooting, Fishing,
Gulmarg Hut & Pahalgam Experienced Guide
Prop: M. S. Butt

My dear Sir,

I beg to acknowledge your kind favour of the 7th inst. and find that you had to face a lot of trouble en route to your destination, since the bus in which you were travelling broke. However I am pleased to find that you have reached safely your destination by His Grace.

I quite realise how the Kashmir view and other things of this place don't go out of your memory. I wish you to be here again and thus give me a chance to serve you.

In your room there was one client from Bombay and other from Delhi.

The whole family of ours send their best compliments to you.

Hoping this would find you in the best of health and cheerful spirits.

Thanking you in anticipation,
Yours sincerely,
M. S. Butt
(Mohd. Sidiq Butt).

Part III

8. FANTASY AND RUINS

The British had possessed the country so completely. Their withdrawal was so irrevocable. And to me even after many months something of fantasy remained attached to all the reminders of their presence. I had grown up in a British colony and it might have been expected that much would have been familiar to me. But England was at least as many-faceted as India. England, as it expressed itself in Trinidad, was not the England I had lived in; and neither of these countries could be related to the England that was the source of so much that I now saw about me.

This England had disturbed me from the first, when, sitting in the launch, I had seen the English names on the cranes of the Bombay docks. It was partly the disturbance we feel—the abrupt moment of unreality in which fleetingly we lose our powers of assessment—at the confirmation of a bizarre but well-established fact. It was also for me a little more. This confirmation laid bare a small area of self-deception which, below knowledge and self-knowledge, had survived in that part of my mind which held as a possibility the existence of the white Himalayan cones against a cold blue sky, as in the religious pictures in my grandmother's house. For in the India of my childhood, the land which in my imagination was an extension, separate from the alienness by which we ourselves were surrounded, of my grandmother's house, there was no alien presence. How could such a thing be conceived? Our own world, though clearly fading, was still separate; and an involvement with the English, of whom on the island we knew little, would have seemed a more unlikely violation than an

involvement with the Chinese or the Africans, of whom we knew
more. Into this alienness we daily ventured, and at length we
were absorbed into it. But we knew there had been change,
gain, loss. We knew that something which was once whole
had been washed away. What was whole was the idea of
India.

To preserve this conception of India as a country still
whole, historical facts had not been suppressed. They had been
acknowledged and ignored; and it was only in India that I
was able to see this as part of the Indian ability to retreat, the
ability genuinely not to see what was obvious: with others a
foundation of neurosis, but with Indians only part of a greater
philosophy of despair, leading to passivity, detachment,
acceptance. It is only now, as the impatience of the observer
is dissipated in the processes of writing and self-inquiry, that
I see how much this philosophy had also been mine. It had
enabled me, through the stresses of a long residence in England,
to withdraw completely from nationality and loyalties except
to persons; it had made me content to be myself alone, my
work, my name (the last two so different from the first); it
had convinced me that every man was an island, and taught
me to shield all that I knew to be good and pure within myself
from the corruption of causes.

Before the reminders of this England of India, then, I ought
to have been calm. But they revealed one type of self-deception
as self-deception; and though this was lodged in that part of the
mind where fantasy was permissible, the revelation was painful. It was an encounter with a humiliation I had never before
experienced, and perhaps more so to me than to those Indians
who hurried about streets with unlikely English names, in the
shadow of imperial-grand houses, as others might have felt for
me the colonial humiliation I did not feel in Trinidad.

Colonial India I could not link with colonial Trinidad.
Trinidad was a British colony; but every child knew that we
were only a dot on the map of the world, and it was therefore
important to be British: that at least anchored us within a wider
system. It was a system which we did not feel to be oppressive;
and though British, in institutions and education as well as in

political fact, we were in the New World, our population was greatly mixed, English people were few and kept themselves to themselves, and England was as a result only one of the countries of which we were aware.

It was a country to a large extent unknown; a taste for English things was something a cultivated islander might affect. To the majority America was more important. The English made good tiny cars for careful drivers. The Americans made the real automobiles, as they made the real films and produced the best singers and the best bands. Their films spoke universal sentiments and their humour was immediately comprehensible. American radio was modern and marvellous and at least you could understand the accent; you could listen to fifteen minutes of news on the BBC and not understand a word. The American soldiers loved a fat back-street whore, the blacker the better; they packed them into their jeeps and raced from club to club, throwing their money about; and they could always be enticed into unequal brawls. They were people with whom communication was possible. Beside them the British soldiers were like foreigners. In Trinidad they were incapable of hitting the right note. They were either too loud or too withdrawn; they spoke this strange English; they referred to themselves as 'blokes' (this was once the subject of a news-item in the *Trinidad Guardian*), not knowing that in Trinidad a bloke was a term of abuse; their uniforms, their shorts in particular, were ugly. They had little money and little sense of propriety: they could be seen in the Syrian shops buying cheap women's underwear. This was the England of popular conception. There was of course the other England —the source of governors and senior civil servants—but this was too remote to be real.

We were colonials in a special position. The British Empire in the West Indies was old. It was an empire of the sea and apart from a square here and a harbour there it had left few monuments; and because we were in the New World— Trinidad was virtually without a population in 1800—these monuments appeared to belong to our prehistory. By its very age the Empire had ceased to be incongruous. It required some detachment to see that our institutions and our language were the results of empire.

The England of India was totally different. It remained an incongruous imposition. Fort St George, grey and massive and of an eighteenth-century English taste known from day trips, could not be related to the Madras landscape; in Calcutta the wide-fronted, pillared house, pointed out as Clive's, on the choked road to Dum Dum airport, appeared to require a less exotic setting. And because it was incongruous, its age, which was less than the age of the empire in the West Indies, came as a surprise: these eighteenth-century monuments ought to have appeared superficial, but now one saw that they had become part of this country of alien ruins. This was one aspect of Indian England; it belonged to the history of India; it was dead.

Distinct from this was the England of the Raj. This still lived. It lived in the division of country towns into 'cantonments', 'civil lines' and bazaars. It lived in army officers' messes, in the silver so frequently given, so reverentially polished and displayed, in uniforms and moustaches and swagger sticks and mannerisms and jargon. It lived in the collectorates, in the neat fading handwriting of those settlements which add up to a domesday book of a continent: suggesting endless days in the sun on horseback, with many servants but few real comforts, and evenings of patient effort. ('The effort exhausted them,' a young IAS officer said to me. 'After this they just couldn't move on to anything else.') It lived in the clubs, the Sunday morning bingo, the yellow-covered overseas edition of the *Daily Mirror* in the manicured hands of middle-class Indian ladies; it lived in the dance-floors of city restaurants. It was an England more full-blooded than anyone coming from Trinidad might have thought possible. It was grander, more creative and more vulgar.

Yet it did not ring true. It had never rung true to me in Kipling and other writers; and it did not ring true now. Was it the mixture of England and India? Was it my colonial, Trinidad-American, English-speaking prejudice which could not quite accept as real this imposition, without apparent competition, of one culture on another? With one part of myself I felt the coming together of England and India as a violation; with the other I saw it as ridiculous, resulting in a comic mixture of costumes and the widespread use of an imperfectly understood language. But there was something else, something at which the architecture of the Raj hinted: those collectorates, in whose vaults lay the fruits of an immense endeavour, those clubs, those circuit houses, those inspection houses, those first-class railway waiting rooms. Their grounds were a little too spacious, their ceilings a little too high, their columns and arches and pediments a little too rhetorical; they were neither of England nor India; they were a little too grand for their purpose, too grand for the puniness, poverty and defeat in which they were set. They were appropriate to a conception of endeavour rather than to endeavour. They insisted on being alien and were indeed more alien than the earlier British buildings, many of which might have been transported whole from England. They led to the humourlessness of the Victoria Memorial in Calcutta and Lord Curzon's gifts to the Taj Mahal: a humourlessness which knew it was inviting ridicule but which derived from a confidence that could support such ridicule. It was embarrassing to be in these buildings; they still appeared to strive to impose attitudes on those within and those without.

It was all there in Kipling, barring the epilogue of the Indian inheritance. A journey to India was not really necessary. No writer was more honest or accurate; no writer was more revealing of himself and his society. He has left us Anglo-India; to people these relics of the Raj we have only to read him. We find a people conscious of their roles, conscious of their power and separateness, yet at the same time fearful of expressing their delight at their situation: they are all burdened by responsibilities. The responsibilities are real; but the total effect is that of a people at play. They are all actors; they know what is expected of them; no one will give the game away. The Kipling administrator, perpetually sahib-ed and huzoor-ed, hedged around by fabulous state, is yet an exile, harassed, persecuted, misunderstood by his superiors and the natives he strives to elevate; and on his behalf Kipling can rise to towering heights of mock-anger and can achieve a mock-aggressive self-pity: play within play.

At home they, the other men, our equals, have at their disposal all that town can supply—the roar of the streets, the lights, the pleasant faces, the millions of their own kind, and a wilderness of pretty, fresh-coloured Englishwomen . . . We have been deprived of our inheritance. The men at home are enjoying it all, not knowing how fair and rich it is.

Self-congratulation coquettishly concealed by complaint to be the better revealed: it is the feminine note of the club writer who has accepted the values of the club and genuinely sees the members as they see themselves. It is the tone exactly described by Ada Leverson in her novel, *Tenterhooks*, published in 1912:

'I feel all the time as if he [Kipling] were calling me by my Christian name without an introduction, or as if he wanted me to exchange hats with him . . . He's so fearfully familiar with his readers.'
'But you think he keeps at a respectful distance from his characters?'

To say that Kipling is a club writer is of course to use a loaded word. The club is one of the symbols of Anglo-India. In *Something of Myself* Kipling tells how every evening in Lahore he went to dine at the club and there met people who had just been reading what he had written the day before. He regarded this as a valuable discipline. The approbation of the club was important to him: he wrote about the club for the club. In this lies his peculiar honesty, his value as a poetic chronicler of Anglo-India. But in this also lies his special vulnerability, for by applying to the club only the values of the club he has exposed both the club and himself.

His work is of a piece with the architecture of the Raj; and within the imperial shell we find, not billiard room cartoons or a suburban taste in novels, as in the district clubs, but Mrs Hauksbee, the wit, the queen, the manipulator and card of

Simla. How she suffers from the very generosity which sought
to bestow on her the attributes she desired! Her wit is no wit;
and to us today the susceptibility of her admirers is a little
provincial, a little sad. Yet the circle—queen, courtiers, jester
—is so complete; something, whether we approve of it or not,
has been created by which men can live in special circumstances;
and it seems an intolerable cruelty to point to its falseness. A
response to Kipling cannot but be personal and on this level.
He is too honest and generous; he is too simple; he is too gifted.
His vulnerability is an embarrassment; the criticism he invites
can only seem a type of brutality. Mr Somerset Maugham has
already disposed of the pretensions of Mrs Hauksbee. She
once said of the voice of another woman that it was like the
screech of the brakes of an underground train as it came into
Earl's Court station. If Mrs Hauksbee were what she claimed
to be, Mr Maugham commented, she had no business to be in
Earl's Court; and she certainly oughtn't to have gone there by
underground. There is much in Kipling that can be dealt with
in this way. He genuinely saw people bigger than they were;
they, perhaps less securely, saw themselves bigger than they
were. They reacted one on the other; fantasy hardened into
conviction. And to us they are now all betrayed.

There is a night train from Delhi to Kalka; from Kalka you
continue to Simla by road or by the narrow-gauge, toy railroad that winds up the mountains. I went by road, in the
company of a young IAS officer, encountered on the train to
Kalka. He spoke sadly of the decay of the town since 1947.
To him, as to all Indians, the myth was real. The glory of
Simla was part of the Indian inheritance, which was being
squandered: there were now *pan*-shops in the town. While we
talked rustles came from the back of the van from the officer's
pet weaver-birds. They were in a large covered cage, and when
the rustles appeared to be reaching a pitch of frenzy the officer
clucked and cooed and spoke soothingly to the cage. From time
to time we had a glimpse of the toy train going into or coming
out of a toy tunnel. It was mid-January, the air frosty,
but the shirtsleeved passengers leaned passively out of open

windows as though, this being India, it was always summer.

And at first it seemed that the officer was right, that Kipling's city had altogether decayed. It was wet and cold; the narrow streets were muddy; barefooted stunted men stamped uphill with heavy loads strapped to their backs; their caps recalled Kashmir and those ragged porters who ran shouting after every arriving bus at village resorts. Could glamour ever have been found here? But so it was with every Indian landscape known from books. Deception, one thought; and then, decay. But it was only that the figures in the foreground had to make their impact before fading from a vision grown as selective as when, in a dark room full of familiar objects, one's eyes have grown accustomed to the dark.

Vision contracted: Simla outlined itself: a town built on a series of ridges, a network of switchback lanes in which it was easy to get lost. In my imagination the Mall was broad and straight; it turned out to be narrow and winding. Every few yards notices warned against spitting; but the *pan*-shops were there, as the IAS man had said, and the streets were stained red with betel-juice. The photographers' windows carried faded photographs of Englishwomen in styles of the thirties. They were not relics; the shops were busy. But in India everything is inherited, nothing is abolished; everything grows out of something else, and now the Mall was given over to the offices, clamantly labelled, of the Himachal Pradesh administration, whose officers drove about the narrow lanes in green Chevrolets of the late nineteen-forties: decay upon decay. The sun sank behind the mountains; the cold grew intense. The unsettling figures disappeared, the bazaar impression faded. The ridge sparkled with electric light, and in the lamplit darkness the town centre defined itself more clearly: an English country town of fairyland, of mock mock-styles, the great ecclesiastical building asserting the alien faith, the mean-fronted shops, ornately gabled, out of which nightcapped, nightgowned men might have appeared, holding lanterns or candles: a grandiloquent assertion of a smallness and cosiness that never were. A fabulous creation, of fantasy supported by a confidence which it was impossible not to admire. But it was

not what I had expected. My disappointment was the disappointment we momentarily feel when, after reading of the
house at Combray, we see the photograph of the house at Illiers
The vision is correct; but it is a child's myth-creating vision.
No city or landscape is truly real unless it has been given the
quality of myth by writer, painter or by its association with
great events. Simla will never cease to be Kipling's city: a
child's vision of Home, doubly a fairyland. India distorts and
enlarges; with the Raj it enlarged upon what was already a
fantasy. This is what Kipling caught; this is his uniqueness.

During the night it snowed, the first snow of the winter.
In the morning the hotel servant, like a magician, announced:
'Barf! Snow.' He pulled the curtains to one side and I saw the
valley white and wet with mist. After breakfast the mist
cleared. The roofs dripped; the crows cawed, flapping from
pine to pine, shaking down snow; the dogs barked far below
and there was a sound as of revelry. On the government
boards marked 'Himachal Pradesh'—sweet name: the Snow
State—snow lay emblematically, as in a Christmas poster. The
Mall was busy with holidaymakers, doing the morning
promenade. For a long way down the snow was still thick.
As we left Simla farther and farther behind, high up in the
sky, the snow thinned, became like scattered cakings of salt on
hard ground, then disappeared; and it was through a thick and
very white Punjab fog, which delayed trains and grounded
aircraft, that we crawled all the way to Delhi.

To understand the eighteenth-century England that one
saw in India, it was necessary to see it as part of India. Warren
Hastings can only with difficulty be read as an Englishman;
as an Indian, he fits. But the Raj, though so completely of
India, is part of nineteenth-century England.

Consider Adela and Ronny in *A Passage to India*. The sun is
going down over the Chandrapore *maidan*; and they, turning
their backs on the polo game, walk to a distant seat, to talk.
He apologises for his bad temper earlier in the day. She cuts
into his apologies and says: 'I've finally decided we are not
going to be married, my dear boy.' They are both disturbed.

But they remain controlled; nothing passionate or profound is
said; and the moment passes. Then Adela says:

> 'We've been awfully British over it, but I suppose that's
> all right.'
> 'As we are British, I suppose it is.'

It is an amusing exchange, still fresh after forty years. It might
be said that 'British', as Adela uses it, is given point by the
imperial Indian background; but the word might have been
used by many of Forster's characters and its intention would
have been the same. To Forster's characters their Englishness
is like an extra quality which challenges, and is challenged by,
all that is alien. It is a formulated ideal; it needs no elucidation.
The word British, as used by Adela, can almost be spelt with
a small *b*. It is difficult to imagine the word being so used in
Jane Austen. In *Pride and Prejudice* it occurs once, when Mr
Collins, on his first visit to Longbourn, is speaking of the
virtues of his patroness's daughter, Miss de Bourgh:

> 'Her indifferent state of health unhappily prevents her being
> in town; and by that means, as I told Lady Catherine myself
> one day, has deprived the British court of its brightest
> ornament.'

For Jane Austen and Mr Collins the word is geographical; it
is entirely different from Adela's 'British'.

Between the two uses of the word lie a hundred years of
industrial and imperial power. In the beginning of this period
we can sense the swiftness of change, from stage-coach to
railway, from the essays of Hazlitt to those of Macaulay, from
the *Pickwick Papers* to *Our Mutual Friend*. In painting it is like
a second springtime: Constable discovering the sky, Bonington
discovering the glory of light, of sand and sea: youth and delight that can communicate themselves to us even today. It is a
period of newness and self-discovery: Dickens discovering
England, London, discovering the novel; newness even in
Keats and Shelley. It is a period of vigour and expectation.

And then, abruptly, there come fulfilment and middle-age. The process of self-discovery is over; the English national myth appears, complete. The reasons are well known: the narcissism was justifiable. But with this there was loss. A way of looking was weakened. What was English was settled; by this the world was to be assessed, and in the travel-writing of the century we can observe a progressive deterioration, from Darwin (1832) to Trollope (1859) to Kingsley (1870) to Froude (1887). More and more these writers are reporting not on themselves but on their Englishness.

At the beginning of this period Hazlitt can dismiss the English writings of Washington Irving with scorn because Irving insisted on finding Sir Roger de Coverleys and Will Wimbles in a country that had moved on since the days of *The Spectator*. Hazlitt's myth-rejecting attitude is like the attitude of those today who object to British travel advertising in the United States. ('Loverly Way to London,' says the advertisement in *Holiday* in 1962. 'Fly Sabena to Manchester. Drive right off past thatch-roofed cottages and start wending your way to London. Gradually. Beautifully.') But soon the myth becomes important; and in the new narcissism class consciousness as well as race consciousness are heightened. Punch in the 1880s has Cockneys talking in the vanished accents of Sam Weller. The consciousness of class in Forster is altogether different from the knowledge of class as an almost elemental division in Jane Austen. In a country as fragmented by class as England the stereotype might be considered necessary if only as an aid to communication. But, excessively cherished, it limits vision and inquiry; it occasionally even rejects the truth.

To this dependence on the established and reassuring might be traced the singular omissions of English writing in the last hundred years. No monumental writer succeeded Dickens. In the English conditions the very magnitude of his vision, its absorption into myth, precluded as grand an attempt. London remains Dickens's city—how few writers since appear to have *looked* at the city! There have been novels about Chelsea and Bloomsbury and Earl's Court; but on the modern mechanised city, its pressures and frustrations, English writers have remained silent. It is precisely this, on the other hand, which is one of the recurring themes of American writers. It is the theme, in the words of the novelist Peter de Vries, of city people who live and die without roots, suspended, 'like the fabled mistletoe, between the twin oaks of home and office'. It is an important theme, and not specifically of America; but in England, where narcissism applies to country, class and self, it has been reduced to the image of the bank clerk, always precise, always punctual, who farcically erupts into mis- demeanour.

When such a theme is ignored it is not surprising that there exists no great English novel in which the growth of national of imperial consciousness is chronicled. (It is useless to look for this in the work of historians. They, more than novelists, work within the values of their society; they serve those values. It is undeniable that the possession of an empire greatly influenced British attitudes in the nineteenth century; yet G. M. Trevelyan in his *English Social History*—regarded, I believe, as a classic—devotes exactly one page and a half to 'Overseas Influences', and in this vein: '. . . the postage stamp kept the cottage at home in touch with the son who had "gone to the colonies", and often he would return on a visit with money in his pocket, and tales of new lands of equality . . . .') An early novel by Somerset Maugham, *Mrs Craddock*, attempted the theme in a small way; this is the story of a farmer who strives, by a superior nationalism, to establish his claim to the superior class into which he has married. For the rest, we are presented with *stages* in the transformation, which can thus best be charted through individual books.

Osborne in *Vanity Fair* sees himself as a solid British mer- chant. But 'British' here is only contrasted with, say, 'French' It is no more than the patriotism of someone like de Quincey. Thackeray's solid British merchant would dearly have liked his son to marry Miss Swartz, the West Indian Negro heiress. Mr Bumble and Mr Squeers are English; but that is not their most important feature. Twenty years later, however, what different characters begin to appear in Dickens! There is Mr Podsnap of *Our Mutual Friend*; he knows foreigners and is proud to be British. John Halifax is only a gentleman; Rider Haggard dedicates one of his books to his son in the hope that he will become an Englishman and a gentleman; it was with a similar hope that Tom Brown was sent off by his father to Rugby. By the time we get to *Howards End* even Leonard Bast can be found saying 'I am an Englishman', and meaning by this more than de Quincey ever meant; now the word is loaded indeed.

Writers cannot be blamed for being of their society; and in the novel, then, interest shifts from human behaviour to the Englishness of behaviour, Englishness held up for approval or dissection: a shift of interest reflected in the difference between the inns of the early Dickens and Simpson's Restaurant in the Strand just seventy-five years later, of which Forster in *Howards End* (1910) says:

> Her eyes surveyed the restaurant, and admired its well-calculated tributes to the solidity of our past. Though no more Old English than the works of Kipling, it had selected its reminiscences so adroitly that her criticism was lulled, and the guests whom it was nourishing for imperial purposes bore the outer semblance of Parson Adams and Tom Jones. Scraps of talk jarred oddly on the ear.
> 'Right you are! I'll cable out to Uganda this evening ....'

Forster has made his point exactly. He has pointed at the contradiction in the myth of a people overtaken by industrial and imperial power. Between the possession of Uganda and the conscious possession of Tom Jones there is as little connection as there is between the stories of Kipling and the novels of his contemporary, Hardy. So, at the height of their power, the British gave the impression of a people at play, a people playing at being English, playing at being English of a certain class. The reality conceals the play; the play conceals the reality.

This endears them to some and exposes them to the charge of hypocrisy from others. And in this imperialist period, when the pink spreads like a rash on the map of the world, the

English myth is like a developing language. Quantities alter; new elements are added; codification, repeatedly attempted, cannot keep pace with change; and always between the projected, adjustable myth—Parson Adams in Simpson's, the harassed empire-builder in Uganda or India—and the reality there is some distance. It is long after Waterloo, in a period which begins with the disasters of the Crimea and ends with the humiliations of South Africa, that we have a period of jingoistic militarism. It is after the empire has been built that the concept arises of the merchant and administrator as an empire-builder; and, sternly, Kipling summons the rulers of the world to their pleasant duties. It is the play of puritans. At Home it creates Simpson's in the Strand. In India it creates Simla, the summer seat of the Raj where, as Philip Woodruff tells us in *The Guardians*, the 'affectation' existed among officials, at about the same time, 'of being very English, of knowing nothing at all about India, of eschewing Indian words and customs'.

Half-way across the world was Trinidad, a truly imperial creation. There people of many races accepted English rule, English institutions and the English language without questioning; yet England and Englishness, as displayed in India, were absent. And to me this remained the peculiar quality of the Raj: this affectation of being very English, this sense of a nation at play, acting out a fantasy. It was there in all the architecture of the Raj and especially in its faintly ridiculous monuments: the Victoria Memorial in Calcutta, the India Gate in New Delhi. They were not monuments worthy of the power they celebrated; they were without the integrity of the earlier British buildings and the even earlier Portuguese cathedrals in Goa.

In *The Men Who Ruled India* Philip Woodruff has written with sad, Roman piety of the British achievement. It was a tremendous achievement; it deserved this piety. But Woodruff's Raj is far from the Raj of the popular English imagination: the sun-helmet (which Gandhi thought sensible but which, for reasons of national pride, he could not wear), the innumerable

salaaming, sahib-ing and memsahib-ing servants, and
Englishman as superman, the native as wog and servant and
clerk, specimens of whose imperfect English can be gathered
into little books (still found in secondhand bookstalls) for the
amusement of those who know the language well: a Raj that can
be found in a thousand English books on India, particularly
in children's books with an Indian setting, and can be found
even in Vincent Smith's annotations, for the Oxford University
Press, on the writings of the great Sleeman.

To Woodruff this side of the Raj, however established and
real, is an embarrassment; it does not represent the truth of the
British endeavour. But so it is with all who wish to see purpose,
creative or negative, in the Raj, be it Woodruff or be it an
Indian like K. M. Munshi, author of a 1946 pamphlet whose
title, *The Ruin That Britain Wrought*, makes description unnecessary. There is always an embarrassment, of racial arrogance on the one hand and of genuine endeavour of the other.
Which is the reality? They both are; and there is no contradiction. Racial arrogance was part of the Simpson's-in-the-
Strand fantasy, inevitably heightened in the puniness of the
Indian setting, the completeness of the Indian subjection.
Equally heightened, and part of the same fantasy, was the
spirit of service. They both issued out of people who knew
their roles and knew what was expected of their Englishness.
As Woodruff himself says, there is something un-English,
something too premeditated about the administration of the
Raj. It could not have been otherwise. To be English in India
was to be larger than life.

The newspaperman in Madras presses me to attend his
lecture on 'The Shakespearean Hero in Crisis'. The business
executive in Calcutta, explaining why he feels he must join
the army to fight the Chinese, begins solemnly, 'I feel I am
defending my right—my right to—' and ends hurriedly, with
a self-deprecating laugh, 'play a game of golf when I want to.'
Almost the last true Englishmen, Malcolm Muggeridge wrote
some time ago, are Indians. It is a statement that has point only
because it recognises the English 'character' as a creation of
fantasy. In India the Moguls were also foreigners, with

fantasies as heady; they ruled as foreigners; but they were finally absorbed into India. The English, as Indians say again and again, did not become part of India; and in the end they escaped back to England. They left no noble monuments behind and no religion save a concept of Englishness as a desirable code of behaviour—of chivalry, it might be described, tempered by legalism—which in Indian minds can be dissociated from the fact of English rule, the vulgarities of racial arrogance or the position of England today. The Madras brahmin was reading O'Hara's *From the Terrace* and loathing it: 'You wouldn't get a well-bred Englishman writing this sort of tosh.' It is a remarkable distinction for a former subject people to make; it is a remarkable thing for a ruling nation to have left behind. This concept of Englishness will survive because it was the product of fantasy, a work of national art; it will outlast England. It explains why withdrawal was easy, why there is no nostalgia such as the Dutch still have for Java, why there was no Algeria, and why after less than twenty years India has almost faded out of the British consciousness: the Raj was an expression of the English involvement with themselves rather than with the country they ruled. It is not, properly, an imperialist attitude. It points, not to the good or evil of British rule in India, but to its failure.

It is well that Indians are unable to look at their country directly, for the distress they would see would drive them mad. And it is well that they have no sense of history, for how then would they be able to continue to squat amid their ruins, and which Indian would be able to read the history of his country for the last thousand years without anger and pain? It is better to retreat into fantasy and fatalism, to trust to the stars in which the fortunes of all are written—there are lecturers in astrology in some universities—and to regard the progress of the rest of the world with the tired tolerance of one who has been through it all before. The aeroplane was known to ancient India, and the telephone, and the atom bomb: there is evidence in the Indian epics. Surgery was highly developed in ancient India: here, in an important national newspaper, is the text of a

lecture proving it. Indian shipbuilding was the wonder of the
world. And democracy flourished in ancient India. Every
village was a republic, self-sufficient, ordered, controlling its
own affairs; the village council could hang an offending villager
or chop off his hand. This is what must be recreated, this
idyllic ancient India; and when *panchayati raj*, a type of village
self-rule, is introduced in 1962 there will be so much talk of the
glories of ancient India, so much talk by enthusiastic politicians
of hands anciently chopped off, that in some villages of the
Madhya Pradesh state hands will be chopped off and people
will be hanged by village councils.

Eighteenth-century India was squalid. It invited conquest.
But not in Indian eyes: before the British came, as every Indian
will tell you, India was rich, on the brink of an industrial
breakthrough; and K. M. Munshi says that every village had
a school. Indian interpretations of their history are almost as
painful as the history itself; and it is especially painful to see the
earlier squalor being repeated today, as it has been in the
creation of Pakistan and the reawakening within India of
disputes about language, religion, caste and region. India, it
seems, will never cease to require the arbitration of a conqueror.
A people with a sense of history might have ordered matters
differently. But this is precisely the saddening element in
Indian history: this absence of growth and development. It is a
history whose only lesson is that life goes on. There is only a
series of beginnings, no final creation.

It is like reading of a land periodically devastated by hordes
of lemmings or locusts; it is like turning from the history of a
coral reef, in which every act and every death is a foundation,
to the depressing chronicle of a succession of castles built
on the waste sand of the sea-shore.

This is Woodruff on the difference between European history
and Indian history. He has chosen his images well. But the
sandcastle is not quite exact. The sandcastle is flattened by the
tide and leaves no trace, and India is above all the land of ruins.

From the south Delhi is approached through a wilderness of

ruins that extend for forty-five square miles. Twelve miles away from the modern city are the ruins of the mightily walled town of Tughlakabad, abandoned for lack of water. Near Agra is the still complete city of Fatehpur Sikri, abandoned for the same reason. ('Why do you want to go to Fatehpur Sikri?' asked the travel agent in the foyer of the Delhi hotel. 'There is *nothing* there.') And listen to the guide at the Taj, talking to a party of Australians: 'So when she died he said, "I can't live here any more". So he went to Delhi and he built a *big* city there.' To the Indian, surrounded by ruins, this is a sufficient explanation of creation and decay. Consider these extracts from the first ten pages of Route 1 in the Pakistan section of Murray's *Handbook:*

Tatta, now small, but as late as 1739 a great city of 60,000 inhabitants .... The most remarkable sight in Tatta is the great mosque, 600 ft by 90 ft with 100 domes, begun by Shah Jahan in 1647 and finished by Aurangzeb, though now much decayed ....

$1\frac{1}{2}$m farther N. .... is the tomb of the famous Nizam-ud-din ... which some have thought was built from the remains of a Hindu temple.

Excursion to Arore—formerly the very ancient Alor (Alor, Uch and Hyderabad are believed to have been the sites of three of many Alexandrias) ... A ridge of ruins runs N.E. Reti station ... 4m S. are the vast ruins of *Vijnot*, a leading city before the Muslim conquest: there is nothing to be seen but debris.

Multan ... of great antiquity, and supposed to be the capital of the Malli mentioned in Alexander's time .... The original temple stood in the middle of the fort and was destroyed by Aurangzeb, while the mosque built upon its site was totally blown up in the siege of 1848.

During the reign of Shah Beg Argun the fortifications were rebuilt, the fort of Alor, 6m away, being destroyed to supply material.

Sukkur, pop. 77,000, was formerly famous for its pearl

trade and gold embroidery. A large biscuit factory has recently been started.

Mosque on temple: ruin on ruin. This is in the North. In the South there is the great city of Vijayanagar. In the early sixteenth century it was twenty-four miles round. Today, four hundred years after its total sacking, even its ruins are few and scattered, scarcely noticeable at first against the surrealist brown rock formations of which they seem to form part. The surrounding villages are broken down and dusty; the physique of the people is poor. Then, abruptly, grandeur: the road from Kampli goes straight through some of the old buildings and leads to the main street, very wide, very long, still impressive, a flight of stone steps at one end, the towering *gopuram* of the temple, alive with sculpture, at the other. The square-pillared lower storeys of the stone buildings still stand; in the doorways are carvings of dancers with raised legs. And, inside, the inheritors of this greatness: men and women and children, thin as crickets, like lizards among the stones.

A child was squatting in the mud of the street; the hairless, pink-skinned dog waited for the excrement. The child, big-bellied, rose; the dog ate. Outside the temple there were two wooden juggernauts decorated with erotic carvings: couples engaged in copulation and fellatio: passionless, stylised. They were my first glimpse of Indian erotic carving, which I had been longing to see; but after the first excitement came depression. Sex as pain, creation its own decay: Shiva, god of the phallus, performing the dance of life and the dance of death: what a concept he is, how entirely of India! The ruins were inhabited. Set among the buildings of the main street was a brand-new whitewashed temple, pennants flying; and at the end of the street the old temple was still in use, still marked with the alternating vertical stripes of white and rust. One noticeboard about six feet high gave a list of fees for various services. Another, of the same size, gave the history of Vijayanagar: once, after the Raja had prayed, there was 'rain of gold': this, in India, was history.

Rain, not of gold, swept suddenly across the Tungabhadra

river and over the city. We took shelter up a rock slope behind
the main street, in the recesses of an unfinished gateway of
rough-hewn stone. A very thin man followed us there. He was
wrapped in a thin white cotton sheet, dappled with wet. He
let the sheet fall off his chest to show us that he was all skin
and bones, and he made the gestures of eating. I paid no
attention. He looked away. He coughed; it was the cough of a
sick man. His staff slipped from his hand and fell with a clatter
on the stone floor down which water was now streaming. He
hoisted himself on to a stone platform and let his staff lie where
it had fallen. He withdrew into the angle of platform and wall
and was unwilling to make any motion, to do anything that
might draw attention to himself. The dark gateway framed
light: rain was grey over the pagoda-ed city of stone. On the
grey hillside, shining with water, there were the marks of
quarryings. When the rain was over the man climbed down,
picked up his wet staff, wrapped his sheet about him and made
as if to go. I had converted fear and distaste into anger and
contempt; it plagued me like a wound. I went to him and
gave him some money. How easy it was to feel power in India!
He, earning his money, took us out into the open, led us up
the washed rock slope and pointed silently to buildings. Here
was the hill of rock. Here were the buildings. Here the five-
hundred-year-old marks of chisels. An abandoned, unfinished
labour, like some of the rock caves at Ellora, which remain as
the workmen left them one particular day.

All creation in India hints at the imminence of interruption
and destruction. Building is like an elemental urge, like the
act of sex among the starved. It is building for the sake of
building, creation for the sake of creation; and each creation
is separate, a beginning and an end in itself. 'Castles built on
the waste sand of the sea-shore': not quite exact, but at
Mahabalipuram near Madras, on the waste sand of the sea
shore, stands the abandoned Shore Temple, its carvings worn
smooth after twelve centuries of rain and salt and wind.

At Mahabalipuram and elsewhere in the South the ruins have
a unity. They speak of the continuity and flow of Hindu India,
ever shrinking. In the North the ruins speak of waste and

failure, and the very grandeur of the Mogul buildings is oppressive. Europe has its monuments of sun-kings, its Louvres and Versailles. But they are part of the development of a country's spirit; they express the refining of a nation's sensibility; they add to the common, growing stock. In India these endless mosques and rhetorical mausolea, these great palaces speak only of a personal plunder and a country with an infinite capacity for being plundered. The Mogul owned everything in his dominions; and this is the message of Mogul architecture. I know only one building in England with this quality of dead-end personal extravagance, and that is Blenheim. Imagine England a country of Blenheims, continually built, destroyed and rebuilt over five hundred years, each a gift of the nation and seldom for services rendered, all adding up to nothing, leaving at the end no vigorous or even created nation, no principle beyond that of personal despotism. The Taj Mahal is exquisite. Transported slab by slab to the United States and re-erected, it might be wholly admirable. But in India it is a building wastefully without a function; it is only a despot's monument to a woman, not of India, who bore a child every year for fifteen years. It took twenty-two years to build; and the guide will tell you how many millions it cost. You can get to the Taj from the centre of Agra by cycle-rickshaw; all the way there and all the way back you can study the thin, shining, straining limbs of the rickshawman. India was not conquered, the British realist said, for the benefit of the Indians. But then it never had been: this is what all the ruins of the North say.

At one time the British held dances on the platform before the Taj Mahal. To Woodruff and to others this is a regrettable vulgarity. But it is in the Indian tradition. Respect for the past is new in Europe; and it was Europe that revealed India's past to India and made its veneration part of Indian nationalism. It is still through European eyes that India looks at her ruins and her art. Nearly every Indian who writes on Indian art feels bound to quote from the writings of European admirers. Indian art has still to be compared with European; and the British accusation that no Indian could have built the Taj

Mahal has still to be rejected as a slander. Where there has been
no European admiration there is neglect. The buildings of
Lucknow and Fyzabad still suffer from the contemptuous
political attitudes of the British towards its decadent rulers.
Yearly the great Imambara in Lucknow crumbles into ruin.
The detail on the stonework of the mausolea in Fyzabad has
almost disappeared under heavy coats of what looks like
PWD whitewash; elsewhere metalwork is preserved by a good
deal of bright blue paint; in the centre of one garden a white
Ashoka pillar, destroying symmetry and obscuring the view
through the arched entrance, has been put up by an IAS officer
to commemorate the abolition of *zemindari*. But of what
Europe has discovered not enough care can be taken. This has
become India's Ancient Culture. It is there in the comic little
cupolas of the Ashoka Hotel in New Delhi, the comic little
cupolas of the radio station in Calcutta, the little pillars with
wheels and elephants and other devices of Indian culture that
have been scattered about the zoological gardens of Lucknow,
in the mock-Vijayanagar stone brackets of the Gandhi Mandap
in Madras.

The architecture of nationalist India comes close in spirit to
the architecture of the Raj: they are both the work of people
consciously seeking to express ideas of themselves. It is comic
and it is also sad. It is not of India, this reverence for the past,
this attempt to proclaim it. It does not speak of vigour. It
speaks as much as any ruin of exhaustion and people who have
lost their way. It is as though, after all these endless separate
creations, the vital sap has at last failed. Since the schools of
Kangra and Basohli, Indian art has been all confusion. There
is an idea of the behaviour required in the new world, but the
new world is still bewildering. At Amritsar the monument
honouring those who fell in the massacre is a pathetic affair of
flames cut into heavy red stone. At Lucknow the British
memorial of the Mutiny is the ruined Residency, preserved by
Indians with a love the visitor must find strange; and just
across the road is the rival Indian memorial, a white marble
pillar of inelegant proportions capped by a comic little dome
which might, again, represent a flame. It is like seeing Indians

on a dance floor: they are attempting attitudes which do not become them. I did not see a Buddhist site that had not been disfigured by attempts to recreate India's ancient culture. Near Gorakhpur, for instance, there now stands amid the ruins of an old monastery a reconstructed temple of the period. On the flat wasteland of Kurukshetra, the scene of the Gita dialogue between Arjuna and Krishna, his charioteer, there is a new temple, and in its garden there is a representation in marble of the scene. It is less than bazaar art. That chariot will never move; the horses are dead, stiff, heavy. And this is the work of people whose sculpture is worth all the sculpture of the rest of the world, who in the South, at Vijayanagar, could create a whole 'Horse Court' of horses rampant.

Somewhere something has snapped. Where does one begin to look for this failure? One begins with that Kurkshetra temple. On it there is a plaque which says this exactly:

THIS TEMPAL HAS BEEN BUILT THROUGH THE CHARITY OF RAJA SETH BALDEO DASS BIRLA AND HAS BEEN DEDICATED OF SHREE ARYA DHARMA SEVA SANGH IN NEW DELHI. HINDU PILGRIMS OF ALL SECTS E.G. SANATANISTS, ARYA SAMAJISTS, JAINS, SIKHS AND BUDDHISTS ETC WILL BE ENTERTAINED PROVIDED THEY ARE MORALLY AND PHYSICALLY PURE AND CLEAN
NOTE PERSONS SUFFERING FROM INFECTIOUS OR CONTAGIOUS DISEASES WILL NOT BE ADMITTED

The crudity of the language is matched by the crudity of the self-appraisal. India may be poor, the plaque says in effect, but spiritually she is rich; and her people are morally and physically pure and clean. Self-appraisal, the crudity of the stonework and marblework, the imperfect use of the foreign language: they are all related.

Some Indians denied that the Indian plastic sense had decayed. Those who thought it had, rejected the view that the Moguls were partly responsible—for the quantity and extravagance of their building: Akbar exhausting experimentation, his successors taking decoration to its limit—and blamed it on the British intervention. The British pillaged the country thoroughly; during their rule manufactures and crafts declined. This has to be accepted, and set against the achievements listed by Woodruff: a biscuit factory is a poor exchange for gold embroidery. The country had been pillaged before. But continuity had been maintained. With the British, continuity was broken. And perhaps the British are responsible for this Indian artistic failure, which is part of the general Indian bewilderment, in the way that the Spaniards were responsible for the stupefaction of the Mexicans and the Peruvians. It was a clash between a positive principle and a negative; and nothing more negative can be imagined than the conjunction in the eighteenth century of a static Islam and a decadent Hinduism. In any clash between post-Renaissance Europe and India, India was bound to lose.*

The stupefaction of peoples is one of our mysteries. At school in Trinidad we were taught that the aboriginal inhabitants of the West Indies 'sickened and died' when the Spaniards came. In Grenada, the spice island, there is a cliff with the terrible name of Sauteurs: here the Amerindians committed mass suicide, leaping down into the sea. Stupefied communities of other, later races survive. There are the degraded Hindus of Martinique and Jamaica, swamped by Africa; and it is hard to associate the dispirited Javanese of

* If I had read Camus's *The Rebel* before writing this chapter, I might have used his terminology. Where Camus might have said 'capable of rebellion' I have said 'positive' and 'capable of self-assessment'; and it is interesting that Camus gives, as examples of people incapable of rebellion, the Hindus and the Incas. 'The problem of rebellion . . . has no meaning except within our Western society . . . Thanks to the theory of political freedom, there is, in the very heart of our society, an increasing awareness in man of the idea of man and, thanks to the application of this theory of freedom, a corresponding dissatisfaction . . . . What is at stake is humanity's gradually increasing self-awareness as it pursues its course. In fact, for the Inca and the [Hindu] pariah the problem never arises, because for them it had been solved by a tradition, even before they had had time to raise it—the answer being that tradition is sacred. If in a world where things are held sacred the problem of rebellion does not arise, it is because no real problems are to be found in such a world, all the answers having been given simultaneously. Metaphysic is replaced by myth. There are no more questions, only eternal answers and commentaries, which may be metaphysical.' (Translated by Anthony Bower.)

Surinam in South America, objects of local ridicule, with the rioters and embassy-burners of Djakarta. India did not wither, like Peru and Mexico, at the touch of Europe. If she were wholly Muslim she might have done. But her Hindu experience of conquerors was great; Hindu India met conquerors half-way and had always been able to absorb them. And it is interesting, and now a little sad, to see Indians, above all in Bengal, reacting to the British as they might have done to any other conqueror, Indian or Asiatic.

The attempt at a half-way meeting is there in an early English-inspired reformer like Ram Mohun Roy, who is buried in Bristol. It is there, generations later, in the upbringing of Sri Aurobindo, the revolutionary turned mystic, whose father, sending him as a boy of seven to be educated in England, required his English guardians to shield him from all Indian contacts. It is there, a little later still, but now pathetically, in the Mullick Palace in Calcutta. Decaying already, since this is India, with servants cooking in the marble galleries, the Palace is like a film set. As we go through the tall gateway we feel that this is how a film might begin; the camera will advance with us, will pause here on this broken masonry, there on this faded decoration; there will be silence, and then the voices will come through the echo chamber, the sound of carriages on the crescent-shaped drive: for Mullick's entertainments were fabulous. Great columns of the Calcutta Corinthian style dominate the façade; fountains imported from Europe still play in its grounds; statues representing the four continents stand in the corners of the marble patio where the family now keep birds in cages; on the lower floor a large room is made small by a colossal statue of Queen Victoria; and elsewhere, below excessively chandeliered ceilings, dust has gathered on what looks like the jumble of a hundred English antique shops: a collector's zeal turned to mania: the Bengali landowner displaying his appreciation of European culture to the super-cilious European. Nothing here is Indian, save perhaps the portrait of the owner; but already we can sense the Anglo-Bengali encounter going sour.

Englishness, unlike the faith of other conquerors, required

no converts; and for the Bengali, who was most susceptible to Englishness, the English in India reserved a special scorn. An imperial ideal, well on the way to a necessarily delayed realisation, was foundering on the imperialist myth, equally delayed, of the empire-builder, on the English fantasy of Englishness, 'the cherished conviction,' as one English official wrote in 1883, 'which was shared by every Englishman in India, from the highest to the lowest, by the planter's assistant in his lowly bungalow ... to the Viceroy on his throne ... that he belongs to a race whom God has destined to govern and subdue'. The mock-imperial rhetoric of the dedication of Nirad Chaudhuri's *Autobiography of an Unknown Indian* might serve as an epitaph on this unfulfilled imperial encounter. Translated into Latin, it might be carved in Trajan lettering on the India Gate in New Delhi: 'To the memory of the British Empire in India, which conferred subjecthood on us but withheld citizenship, to which yet every one of us threw out the challenge *Civis Britannicus sum*, because all that was good and living within us was made, shaped, and quickened by the same British rule.'

No other country was more fitted to welcome a conqueror; no other conqueror was more welcome than the British. What went wrong? Some say the Mutiny; some say the arrival in India afterwards of white women. It is possible. But the French, with or without their women, might have reacted differently to the francophile Bengali. The cause, I believe, has to be looked for not in India but in England where, at a time we cannot precisely fix, occurred that break in English sensibility as radical and as seemingly abrupt as that which we have witnessed in our time. The civilisation to which the Indians were attracted had been replaced by another. It was confusing —the guests whom Simpson's Restaurant in the Strand was nourishing for imperial purposes continued to bear the outer semblance of Parson Adams and Tom Jones—and many Indians, from Aurobindo to Tagore to Nehru to Chaudhuri, have recorded their bewilderment.

It is perhaps only now that we can see what a clean break with the past the Raj was. The British refused to be absorbed into India; they did not proclaim, like the Mogul, that if there was a paradise on earth, it was this, and it was this, and it was this. While dominating India they expressed their contempt for it, and projected England; and Indians were forced into a nationalism which in the beginning was like a mimicry of the British. To look at themselves, to measure themselves against the new, positive standards of the conqueror, Indians had to step out of themselves. It was an immense self-violation; and in the beginning, in fact, a flattering self-assessment could only be achieved with the help of Europeans like Max Muller and those others who are quoted so profusely in nationalist writings.

It resulted in the conscious possession of spirituality, proclaimed as in the plaque of the Kurukshetra temple. *Spiritualise Science, Says Prasad* is a newspaper headline over a report of one of the late President's almost daily speeches in retirement. It results in this, from the *Times of India*:

A 'RETAILER' OF SPIRITUALITY
Santiniketan, January 16
Acharya Vinoba Bhave yesterday described himself as a 'retailer' with regard to the wealth of spirituality.

He made this remark at a reception here saying that the Buddha, Jesus, Krishna, Tagore, Ramakrishna and Vivekananda were 'wholesalers of spirituality while I myself am a retailer, drawing from that inexhaustible storehouse to supply to the villagers.'—PTI

It resulted in the conscious possession of an ancient culture. At an official reception for the former governor of a state someone called across to me, as we sat silently in deep chairs set against the walls of the room, 'How is Indian culture getting on in your part of the world?' The former governor, a heavily-stockinged veteran of the Independence struggle, leaned forward and noticed me. He was reported to be keen on Indian culture; I was later to read newspaper reports of his speeches on the subject. Wishing to show that I took the question seriously and was anxious to establish a basis for discussion, I shouted back across the large room: 'What do you mean by Indian culture?' My IAS friend, under whose protection I was, closed his eyes in dismay. The former governor leaned back; silence returned to the room.

Spirituality and ancient culture, then, were as consciously possessed as Parson Adams and Tom Jones in Simpson's. But it was inevitable that with this unnatural selfconsciousness a current of genuine feeling should fail. The old world, of ruins which spoke only of continuity and of creation as an elemental repetition, could not survive; and Indians floundered about in a new world whose forms they could see but whose spirit eluded them. In the acquiring of an identity in their own land they became displaced.

They acquired a double standard. Five hundred deaths from cholera in Calcutta are reported in a news-brief in an Indian newspaper. The death of twenty children merely requires to be stated.

POX IN FEROZABAD
'The Times of India' News Service

AGRA, June 1: Small-pox is reported to have broken out in epidemic form in Ferozabad.

Twenty persons, mostly children, are reported to have died in Jaroli Kalan village.

The death of sixteen miners in Belgium, in the same newspaper, is big news. The peasants in the collectorate courts attend with open mouths to the drama of debates in a language they cannot understand, while outside, in an atmosphere of the bazaar, other peasants, with all the time in the world, it seems, lounge about in the dust, and the typists sit with their ancient machines in the faint shade of trees, and the lawyers, startling in their legal subfusc, wait for custom. These collectorate bazaars function within a changed assumption of the value of man that is still only legalistic, confined to the collectorate and the court-house, a type of make-believe, part of the complex ritual which supports the Indian through his dusty existence. Caste, another law, which renders millions faceless, is equally to be cherished.

Mimicry conceals the Indian schizophrenia. India must progress, must stamp out corruption, must catch up with the West. But does it truly matter? Does a little corruption hurt anybody? Is material prosperity all that important? Hasn't India been through it all before—the atom bomb, the aeroplane, the telephone? So in conversation Indians can be elusive and infuriating. Yet I had only to think myself back to my grand-mother's house, to that dim, unexpressed awareness of the world within and the world without, to understand, to see their logic, to understand both their passion and their calm despair, the positive and the negative. But I had learned to see; I could not deny what I saw. They remained in that other world. They did not see the defecating squatters beside the railroad in the mornings; more, they denied their existence. And why should these squatters be noticed anyway? Had I seen the beggars of Cairo or the Negro slums of Rio?

Language is part of the confusion. Every other conqueror bequeathed a language to India. English remains a foreign language. It is the greatest incongruity of British rule. Language is like a sense; and the psychological damage caused by the continued official use of English, which can never be more than a second language, is immense. It is like condemning the council of, say, Barnsley to conduct their affairs in French or Urdu. It makes for inefficiency; it separates the administrator from the villager; it is a barrier to self-knowledge. The clerk using English in a government office is immediately stultified. For him the language is made up of certain imperfectly under-stood incantations, which limit his responses and make him inflexible. So he passes his working life in a sub-world of dim perceptions; yet in his own language he might be quick and inventive. Hindi has been decreed the national language. It is understood by half the country; it can take you from Srinagar to Goa and from Bombay to Calcutta. But many in the North pretend not to understand it. And in the South the nationalist zeal for Hindi, encouraged by Gandhi, has alto-gether died. Hindi, it is said, gives the North an advantage; it is better for North and South to remain illiterate and inefficient, but equal, in English. It is an Indian argument: India will never cease to require the arbitration of a conqueror. And the advocates of Hindi, in their new self-appraising way, seek not to simplify the language but to make it more inaccessible. 'Radio', a universal word, will not do: it has to be rendered into the wampum-and-wigwam quaintness of 'voice from the sky'.

Indian attempts at the novel further reveal the Indian confusion. The novel is of the West. It is part of that Western concern with the condition of men, a response to the here and now. In India thoughtful men have preferred to turn their backs on the here and now and to satisfy what President Radhakrishnan calls 'the basic human hunger for the unseen'. It is not a good qualification for the writing or reading of novels. A basic hunger for the unseen makes many Indians vulnerable to novels like *The Razor's Edge* and *The Devil's Advocate*, whose value as devotional literature is plain. Beyond this there is uncertainty. What does one look for in a novel? Story, 'characterisation', 'art', realism, a moral, a good cry, beautiful writing? The point hasn't been settled. Hence the paperbacked numbers of the Schoolgirl's Own Library in the hands of male university students; the American children's comics in the room of the student at St Stephen's, New Delhi; the row of Denise Robins next to the astrological volumes. Hence Jane Austen offered in an Indian paperback as a writer whose use of simile is especially to be relished.

It is part of the mimicry of the West, the Indian self-violation. It is there in Chandigarh, in that new theatre for plays that are not written, in those endless writers' conferences where writers are urged to work for 'emotional integration' or the five-year plans, and where the problems of the writer are tirelessly discussed. These problems appear to be less those of writing than of translation into English; the feeling is widespread that, whatever English might have done for Tolstoy, it can never do justice to the Indian 'language' writers. This is possible; what little I read of them in translation did not encourage me to read more. Premchand, the great, the beloved, turned out to be a minor fabulist, much preoccupied with social issues like the status of widows or daughters-in-law. Other writers quickly

fatigued me with their assertions that poverty was sad, that
death was sad. I read of poor fishermen, poor peasants, poor
rickshaw-men; innumerable pretty young girls either simply and
suddenly died, or shared the landlord's bed, paid the family's
medical bills and then committed suicide; and many of the
'modern' short stories were only refurbished folk tales. In
Andhra I was given a brochure of a Telugu writers' conference.
The brochure spoke of the heroic struggle of the people to
establish a Telugu state, to me an endeavour of pure frivolity,
listed martyrs, and then gave a brief history of the Telugu
novel. It seems that the Telugu novel began with Telugu
adaptations of *The Vicar of Wakefield* and *East Lynne*. A little
farther south I was told of a writer greatly influenced by
Ernest Hemingway.

The Vicar of Wakefield and *The Old Man and the Sea:* it is
difficult to relate them to the Indian landscape or to Indian
attitudes. The Japanese novel also began as part of the mimicry
of the West. Tanizaki has, I believe, confessed that in his early
work he was too greatly influenced by the Europeans. Even
through the mimicry, however, it can be seen that the Japanese
are possessed of a way of looking. It flavours the early work of
Tanizaki as it flavours the recent novels of Yukio Mishima:
that curious literalness which adds up to a detachment formidable enough to make the writing seem pointless. However odd,
this derives from a hunger for the seen and is an expression of
concern with men. The sweetness and sadness which can be
found in Indian writing and Indian films are a turning away
from a too overwhelming reality; they reduce the horror to a
warm, virtuous emotion. Indian sentimentality is the opposite
of concern.

The virtues of R. K. Narayan are Indian failings magically
transmuted. I say this without disrespect: he is a writer whose
work I admire and enjoy. He seems forever headed for that
aimlessness of Indian fiction—which comes from a profound
doubt about the purpose and value of fiction—but he is forever
rescued by his honesty, his sense of humour and above all by
his attitude of total acceptance. He operates from deep within
his society. Some years ago he told me in London that,

whatever happened, India would go on. He said it casually; it was a conviction so deep it required no stressing. It is a negative attitude, part of that older India which was incapable of self-assessment. It has this result: the India of Narayan's novels is not the India the visitor sees. He tells an Indian truth. Too much that is overwhelming has been left out; too much has been taken for granted. There is a contradiction in Narayan, between his form, which implies concern, and his attitude, which denies it; and in this calm contradiction lies his magic which some have called Tchekovian. He is inimitable, and it cannot be supposed that his is the synthesis at which Indian writing will arrive. The younger writers in English have moved far from Narayan. In those novels which tell of the difficulties of the Europe-returned student they are still only expressing a personal bewilderment; the novels themselves are documents of the Indian confusion. The only writer who, while working from within the society, is yet able to impose on it a vision which is an acceptable type of comment, is R. Prawer Jhabvala. And she is European.*

The Indo-British encounter was abortive; it ended in a double fantasy. Their new self-awareness makes it impossible for Indians to go back; their cherishing of Indianness makes it difficult for them to go ahead. It is possible to find the India that appears not to have changed since Mogul times but has, profoundly; it is possible to find the India whose mimicry of the West is convincing until, sometimes with dismay, sometimes with impatience, one realises that complete communication is not possible, that a gift of vision cannot be shared, that there still survive inaccessible areas of Indian retreat. Both the negative and the positive principles have been diluted; one balances the other. The penetration was not complete; the

---

* 'It is possible to separate the literature of consent, which coincides, by and large, with ancient history and the classical period, from the literature of rebellion, which begins in modern times. We note the scarcity of fiction in the former. When it exists, with very few exceptions, it is not concerned with a story but with fantasy .... These are fairy tales, not novels. In the latter period, on the contrary, the novel form is really developed—a form that has not ceased to thrive and extend its field of activity up to the present day .... The novel is born at the same time as the spirit of rebellion and expresses, on the aesthetic plane, the same ambition.' Camus: *The Rebel*.

attempt at conversion was abandoned. India's strength, her ability to endure, came from the negative principle, her unexamined sense of continuity. It is a principle which, once diluted, loses its virtue. In the concept of Indianness the sense of continuity was bound to be lost. The creative urge failed. Instead of continuity we have the static. It is there in the 'ancient culture' architecture; it is there in the much bewailed loss of drive, which is psychological more than political and economic. It is there in the political gossip of Bunty. It is there in the dead horses and immobile chariot of the Kurukshetra temple. Shiva has ceased to dance.

9. THE GARLAND ON MY PILLOW

'I am sure you will never guess what my duties are.'

He was middle-aged, thin, sharp-featured, with spectacles. His eyes were running and there was a drop of moisture on the tip of his nose. It was a winter's morning and our second-class railway compartment was unheated.

'I will give you a little assistance. I work for the Railways. This is my pass. Have you ever seen one?'

'You are a ticket inspector!'

A smile revealed his missing teeth. 'No, no, my dear sir. They wear a uniform.'

'You are from the Police.'

His smile cracked into a wet laugh. 'I see that you will never guess. Well, I will tell you. I am an Inspector of Forms and Stationery, Northern Railway.'

'Forms and Stationery!'

'Indeed. I travel about, night and day, winter and summer, from railway station to railway station, inspecting forms and stationery.'

'But how did this begin, Mr Inspector?'

'Why do you ask, sir? My life has been a failure.'

'Please don't say that, Mr Inspector.'

'I might have done so much better, sir. You have no doubt observed my English. My teacher was Mr Harding. I was a Bachelor of Arts, you know. When I joined the Service I expected to go far. I was put in Stores. In those days I would take down bundles of forms and stationery from the shelves and hand them to the porter. This was, of course, after the indents had been approved.'

'Of course.'

'From Stores to the office: it was a slow business. Steady. But slow. Somehow I managed. I have remained in Forms and Stationery all my life. I have kept my family. I have given the boys an education. I have married my daughter. One son is in the army and the other is in the air force, an officer.'

'But, Mr Inspector, this is a success story.'

'O sir, do not mock me. It has been a wasted life.'

'Tell me more about your job, Mr Inspector.'

'Secrets, you are after my secrets. Well, I will explain. Let me show you, first of all, an indent.'

'It's like a little book, Mr Inspector. Sixteen pages.'

'It goes to the head of a stationmaster sometimes. Once a year these indents are sent out to our stationmasters. They prepare their indents and submit three copies. What you see now, by the way, is an elementary type of indent. There are others.'

'And when the indents are submitted—'

'Then they come to me, you see. And I pay my little visits. I get off at the station like any other passenger. It sometimes happens that I am insulted by the very stationmaster whose indents I have come to prune. Then I declare myself.'

'You are a wicked man, Mr Inspector.'

'Do you think so, sir? An Inspector of Forms and Stationery gets to know his stationmasters. They show themselves in their indents. You get to recognise them. This might interest you. It was yesterday's work.'

The indent, filled in in black, was heavily annotated in red.

'Turn to page twelve. Do you see? A hundred note-pads were what he required.'

'Goodness! You've only given him two.'

'He has six children, all of school age. Ninety-eight of those pads were for those six children. An Inspector of Forms and Stationery gets to know these things. Well, here we are. I shall get off here. I believe I am going to enjoy myself today. I wish I had the time to show you what *he* has indented for.'

*

'I met one of your Inspectors of Forms and Stationery the other day.'

'You met what?'

'One of your Inspectors of Forms and Stationery.'

'There are no such people.'

'I didn't dream this man up. He had his indènts and everything.'

It was a good word to use.

'It just goes to show. You can work for the Railways for years and not know a thing about it. Me, I'm exhausted by presidential tours. Our former president didn't like travelling by air. Do you know what a presidential tour means for the railway administrator? Altering time-tables. Re-routing. Going over the track inch by inch. For twenty-four hours before having men walking up and down within hailing distance of each other. And then going yourself on a decoy run a quarter of an hour ahead of the president's train. So that you get blown up first.'

'But where in this terrible town of yours can we have coffee?'

'The railway station is the centre of civilisation in these parts. And the coffee isn't bad.'

'We'll go there.'

'Sir?'

'Two coffees.'

'No coffee.'

'Oh. Well, bring a pot of tea for two. And bring the Complaints Book.'

'Sir?'

'Complaints Book.'

'Let me talk to the manager, sir.'

'No, no. You just bring a pot of tea and the Book.

'I am sorry about this. But we don't do the catering here. That's in the hand of a local contractor. We give him coffee and tea of a certain quality. He just sells it to somebody else. We can't do anything about it. Our contractor knows a minister. It's the Indian story. But look. Our friend is coming back.'

'Is he bringing the Complaints Book?'
'No. He's bringing two cups of coffee.'

Indian Railways! They are part of the memory of every traveller, in the north, east, west or south. Yet few have written of the romance of this stupendous organisation which makes the Indian distances shrink and which, out of an immense assurance, proclaims in a faded notice in every railway station: *Trains running late are likely to make up lost time*. And the trains usually do. But does the romance exist? A service so complex and fine deserves a richer country, with shining cities organised for adventure. But it is only distance, or the knowledge of distance, that gives romance to the place-names on the yellow boards on Indian coaches. The locomotive will consume distance and will seem to convert it into waste. And it will do so with a speed that will presently appear as pointless as the poor, repetitive vastness of the pigmy land which, supine below a high sky, will abruptly at railway stations burst into shrill life, as though all energy had been spared for this spot and this moment: the shouts of stunted, sweating porters, over-eager in red turbans and tunics, the cries of tea-vendors with their urns and clay cups (the cups to be broken after use), the cries of *pan*-vendors and the vendors of fried or curried messes (the leaf-plates, pinned together by thin dried twigs, to be thrown afterwards on to the platform or on the tracks, where the pariah dogs, fierce only with their fellows, will fight over them—and one defeated dog will howl and howl), the whole scene—yet animated only in the foreground, for these stations are havens as well as social centres, and the smooth, cool concrete platforms are places where the futile can sleep— the whole scene ceilinged by low fans which spin in empty frenzy. The sun will rise and set, and the racing train, caught in the golden light of dawn or dusk, will throw a perfect elongated shadow from the tops of the coaches to the very rails; and distance will still not have been consumed. The land has become distance. Will the metal not ignite? Will there be no release into a land which is fruitful, where the men grow straight? There is only another station, more shouting, the magenta coaches coated with hot dust, more prostrate bodies, more dogs, the fraudulent comfort of a shower in the first-class waiting room and a meal poisoned by one's own distress and cautiousness. And indeed people are less important to Indian Railways than freight; and less revenue comes from the first class than from the third, the sub-standard for whom there is never enough room, even in their rudimentary coaches. The railway administrator, who knows this, can be forgiven if he fails to see the romance of his service or its brilliance. The Indian railways serve India. They operate punctually and cease-lessly because they must. They reveal more than that 'real' India which Indians believe can only be found in third-class carriages. They reveal India as futility and limitless pain, India as an idea. Their romance is an abstraction.

It was a third-class carriage, but not of the real India. It was airconditioned and fitted out like an aeroplane, with rows of separate seats with high adjustable backs. Curtains were draped over the double windows; the aisle was carpeted. We were on one of the 'prestige' services of Indian Railways. These air-conditioned coaches run between the three major cities and New Delhi; for four pounds you can travel a thousand miles in comfort, at an average speed of thirty-five miles an hour.

We were travelling south, and among the South Indians, small, fine-featured, subdued at the beginning of the long journey, the Sikh was at once noticeable. He was very big; his gestures were large; he required much room. His beard was unusually thin, and his black turban, tight and low, looked like a beret: I had taken him at first for a European artist. In defiance of the many printed notices he swung his suitcase up on to the rack and wedged it into place. The action showed up his tight weightlifter's body. Turning slightly, he took in the other occupants of the carriage, from a great height, and ap-peared to dismiss us; his loose lower lip curled downward. He was four or five rows ahead of me and all I could see when he sat down was the top of his turban. But he had made his effect. My eyes returned to that turban again and again, and before we had travelled an hour I felt his presence as an irritant. I feared—as so often on confined journeys I have feared—that my interest was inviting his own and making inevitable a contact I wished to avoid.

The Sikhs puzzled and attracted me. They were among the few whole men in India, and of all Indians they seemed closest in many ways to the Indians of Trinidad. They had a similar energy and restlessness, which caused a similar resentment. They were proud of their agricultural and mechanical skills, and they had the same passion for driving taxis and lorries. They too were accused of clannishness, while their internal politics were just as cantankerous. But the Sikhs were of India; beyond these similarities they were unreadable. The Sikh's individuality appeared to be muffled by his beard and turban; his eyes were robbed of expression. His reputation in India did not make him easier to understand. There was his military tradition; his ferocity as soldier and policeman was known. Equally established, in spite of his adventurousness and obvious success, was his simpleness. The foolish Sikh is a figure of legend. The turban had something to do with it; it heated the Sikh's uncut hair and softened his brain. That was what the stories said; and Sikh politics—consisting of temple plots, holy men, miraculous fasts, Wild West rivalries punctuated with gunshot on the Delhi-Chandigarh road—certainly seemed both comic and fierce. There was energy, no doubt. But perhaps it was too much for India: against the Indian background the Sikhs were always a little alarming.

There had been an accident to our train the week before, and we were attached to a substitute dining-car. There was no through way from our carriage. We came to a station and I got out to transfer to the dining-car. I was aware of the Sikh getting out after me and dawdling at a bookstall. In the dining-car I sat with my back to the entrance. South Indian languages, excessively vowelled, rattled about me. The South Indians were beginning to unwind; they were lapping up their liquidised foods. Food was a pleasure to their hands. Chewing, sighing with pleasure, they squelched curds and rice between their fingers. They squelched and squelched; then, in one swift

circular action, as though they wished to take their food by
surprise, they gathered some of the mixture into a ball, brought
their dripping palms close to their mouths and—flick!—rice
and curds were shot inside; and the squelching, chattering and
sighing began again.

'You don't mind if I sit with you?'

It was the Sikh. He was carrying the *Illustrated Weekly of
India*. His tight black turban, slightly askew, his tight shirt and
tight belted trousers gave him the appearance of a pirate of
children's books. His English was fluent; it indicated a residence abroad. His mouth now seemed humorous; it curled,
with amusement, I thought, as, squeezing himself between
table and chair, he regarded the squelchers.

'What do you think of the food?' He gave a low, chest-
heaving chuckle. 'You come from London, don't you?'

'In a way.'

'I can spot the accent. I heard you talking to the guard.
You know Hampstead? You know Finchley Road? You know
Fitzjohn's Avenue?'

'I know them. But I don't know them very well.'

'You know the Bambi Coffee House?'

'I don't think so.'

'But if you know Finchley Road you must know the Bambi.
You remember that little fellow with tight trousers, turtle-neck
sweater and a little beard?' The chuckle came again.

'I don't remember him.'

'You must remember him if you remember the Bambi.
Little fellow. Whenever you went to the Bambi—whenever
you went to *any* coffee house in Finchley Road—he was always
there, jumping about.'

'Did he operate the coffee machine?'

'No, no. Nothing like that. I don't think he used to *do*
anything. He was just there. Little beard. Funny little fellow.'

'You miss London?'

His eyes ranged over the squelchers. 'Well, you just look.'

A woman in a sari, with blue tinted spectacles, and a baby
on her knee, was lapping up *sambar*. She splayed out her
fingers, pressed her palm flat on her plate, drew her fingers

together, lifted her palm to her mouth and licked it dry.

The Sikh gave his deep *mm-mm* chuckle.

'At last,' he said, as the train moved off. 'I didn't want any other Sikhs to come in. Have a fag.'

'But Sikhs don't smoke.'

'This one does.'

The woman looked up from her *sambar*. The squelchers paused, looked at us and looked away quickly as if in horror.

'Punks,' the Sikh said. His expression changed. 'You see how these monkeys stare at you?' He leaned forward. 'You know my trouble?'

'Tell me.'

'I'm colour-prejudiced.'

'But how awkward for you.'

'I know. It's just one of those things.'

Enough had already occurred to warn me, but I was misled by my Trinidad training. 'I'm colour-prejudiced.' The abrupt statement was Trinidadian, and of a special sophistication: it was an invitation to semi-serious banter. I had responded, and he appeared to have taken me up neatly. I forgot that English was only his second language; that few Indians dealt in irony; and that, for all his longing for Finchley Road and Fitzjohn's Avenue, he was an Indian to whom the taboos of caste and sect were fundamental. His smoking was a flamboyant defiance, but it was guarded: he did not smoke in the presence of Sikhs. He wore the turban, beard and bracelet which his religion required; and I am sure he also wore the knife and the drawers. So the moment for declaration, and perhaps withdrawal, passed.

Waiting for our food—'No rice,' he had said, as though starting a caste restriction: rice was the staple of the non-aryan South—he turned the pages of the *Illustrated Weekly of India*, wetting his finger on his tongue. 'Look,' he said, pushing the paper towards me. 'See how many of these South Indian monkeys you can find there.' He showed me a feature on the Indian team at the Asian Games in Djakarta. They were nearly all Sikhs, unfamiliar without their turbans, their long hair stooked and tied up with ribbon. '*Indian* team! Tell me how

this country is going to get on without us. If we sit back, the
Pakistanis can just walk in, you know. Give me one Sikh
division, just one, and I will walk through the whole blasted
country. You see any of these punks stopping us?'

Contact had occurred and there could now be no escape. A
journey of twenty-four hours still lay ahead of us. We got out
and walked together on station platforms, enjoying the shock
of heat after the airconditioned carriage. We ate together.
When we smoked I watched for other Sikhs. 'I don't mind,
you understand,' the Sikh said. 'But I don't want to hurt
them.' We talked of London and Trinidad and coffee houses,
India and the Sikhs. We agreed that the Sikhs were the finest
people in India, but it was hard to find anyone among them
whom he admired. I dredged my memory for Sikh notabilities.
I mentioned one Sikh religious leader. 'He's a bloody Hindu,'
the Sikh said. I mentioned another. 'He's a damned Muslim.'
I spoke of politicians. He replied with stories of their crookedness. 'The man had lost the election. And then suddenly you
had these people running up with ballot-boxes and saying,
"Look, look, we forgot to count these".' I spoke of the energy
of the Sikhs and the prosperity of the Punjab. 'Yes,' he said.
'The sweeper class is coming up.' We talked of Sikh writers.
I mentioned Khushwant Singh, whom I knew and liked; he
had spent years working on Sikh scriptures and history.
'Khushwant? He doesn't *know* anything about the Sikhs.' The
only person who had written well about the Sikhs was Cunning-
ham; and he was dead, as all the finest Sikhs were. 'We're a
pretty hopeless bunch today,' the Sikh said.

Many of his stories were overtly humorous, but often, as in
his references to the Sikh religious leaders, I saw humour
where none was intended. Our relationship had begun in
mutual misunderstanding. And so it developed. He grew
more perceptibly bitter as the journey went on, but this answered my own mood. Shrill railway stations, poor fields,
decaying towns, starving cattle, a withered race of men:
because his reactions appeared to be like mine it did not occur
to me that they were unusual in an Indian. As it was, their
violence steadied me; he became my irrational self. He became

more violent and more protective as the land grew poorer; he showed me that tenderness which physically big men can show to the small.

It was nearly midnight when we came to the junction where I had to leave the train. The platforms were like mortuaries. In the dim light prostrate men showed as shrunken white bundles out of which protruded bony Indian arms, shining stringy legs, collapsed grey-stubbled faces. Men slept; dogs slept; and among them, like emanations risen from the sense-less bodies, over which they appeared to trample, other men and other dogs moved. Silent third-class carriages turned out to be packed with dark, waiting, sweating faces; the yellow boards above the grilled windows showed that they were going some-where. The engines hissed. *Trains running late are likely to make up lost time.* The fans spun urgently. From everywhere dogs howled. One hobbled off into the darkness at the end of the platform; its foreleg had been freshly torn off; a raw bloody stump remained.

The Sikh helped me with my luggage. I was grateful to him for his presence, his wholeness. We had already exchanged addresses and arranged when and where we were to meet again. Now we repeated our promises. We would travel over the South. India yet had its pleasures. We would go hunting. He would show me: it was easy, and I would enjoy the ele-phants. Then he returned to his air-conditioned coach, behind the double glass. Whistles blew; the train moved mightily off. Yet the station remained so little changed: so many bodies remained, awaiting transportation.

My own train was due to leave in about two hours; the coaches were waiting. I changed my third-class ticket for a first-class one, picked my way down dim platforms past the bodies of dogs and men, past third-class carriages which were already full and hot. The conductor opened the door of my compartment and I climbed in. I bolted the door, pulled down all the blinds, trying to shut out the howls of dogs, shutting out intruders, all those staring faces and skeletal bodies. I put on no lights. I required darkness.

*

I did not expect it, but we met again as we had planned. It was in a town where the only other person I knew was a prosperous sweetshop-owner. I had learned to fear his hospitality. At every meeting it was necessary to eat a selection of his sweets. They were corrosively sweet; they killed appetite for a day. The Sikh's hospitality was easier. He sought to revive my appetite with drink, and he gave me food. He also gave me much of his time. I felt he was offering more than hospitality: he was offering his friendship, and it embarrassed me that I couldn't respond. But I was calmer now than I had been on the train, and his moods no longer always answered mine.

'They've let this cantonment area go down,' he said. 'In the old days they didn't allow niggers here. Now the blackies are all over the place.'

The anger was plain, and was not tempered by the humour or self-satire I had seen, or made myself see, in his outbursts on the train.

'These people! You have to shout "Boy!" Otherwise they just don't hear you.'

I had noted this. At the hotel I was shouting 'Boy!' with everybody else, but I couldn't manage the correct tone. Both boys and guests wore South Indian dress, and I had already more than once shouted at the wrong man. My shouts therefore always held muted inquiry and apology.

The Sikh was not amused. 'And you know what they answer? You might think you are in some picture with American darkies. They answer, "Yes, master." God!'

In such moods he was now a strain. His rage was like self-torment; he indulged it to the pitch of soliloquy. I had completely misunderstood him. But by this misunderstanding I had encouraged his friendship and trust. We had parted sentimentally and had had a sentimental reunion. I had fallen in with all his plans. He had made arrangements for our hunting-trip. It would have been as difficult to withdraw as to go ahead. I let him talk, and did nothing. And he was more than his rages. He showed me an increasing regard. As a host he was solicitous; he placed me under a growing obligation. He was disappointed and bitter; I also saw that he was lonely. The condition of India was an affront to him; it was to me, too. The days passed, and I did not break away. He was giving me more and more of his time, and I became more and more involved with his bitterness, but passively, uneasily, awaiting release.

We went one day to the ruins of an eighteenth-century palace which had been cleaned up into a picnic spot. Here India was elegance and solidity, the bazaars and railway stations were far away. He knew the ruins well. Walking among them, showing them to me, he was serene, even a little proud. There were older temples in the neighbourhood, but they did not interest him as much as the palace, and I thought I knew why. He had been to Europe, had suffered ridicule if only in his imagination for his turban, beard and uncut hair. He had learned to look at India and himself He knew what Europe required. The palace ruins might have been European, and he was glad to show them to me. We walked in the gardens and he talked again of our hunting trip: I would marvel at the silence of the elephants. We dawdled by the tank, ate our sandwiches and drank our coffee.

On the way back we visited one of the temples. This was at my suggestion. The derelict beggar-priest, barebacked, roused himself from his string-bed and came out to meet us. He spoke no English and welcomed us in dumb show. The Sikh gave his chuckle and became remote. The priest didn't react. He walked ahead of us into the low, dark temple, raising his shrivelled arm and pointing out this and that, earning his fee. Carvings were scarcely visible in the gloom, and to the priest they were not as important as the living shrines, lit by oil lamps, in which there were bright images, gaudily dressed in doll's clothes, of black gods and white gods: India's ancient mixture of aryan and Dravidian.

'This is how the trouble started,' the Sikh said.

The priest, staring at the gods, waiting for our exclamations, nodded.

'You've been to Gilgit? You should go. They're pure aryan up there. Beautiful people. Let a couple of these

Dravidians loose among them, and in no time they spoil the race for you.'

Nodding, the priest led us back into the open and stood beside us while we got into our shoes. I gave him some money and he returned silently to his cell.

'Until we came to India,' the Sikh said sadly, as we drove off, 'we were a good race. *Arya*—a good Sanskrit word. You know the meaning? Noble. You must read some of the old Hindu books. They will tell you. In those days it was unclean to kiss a very black woman on the lips. You think this is just a crazy Sikh talking? You read. This aryan-Dravidian business isn't new. And it's starting up again. You see in the papers that the blackies are asking for their own state? They are asking for another licking. And they are going to get it.'

The land through which we drove was poor and populous. The road was the neatest thing about it. On either side there were small rectangular hollows where peasants had dug clay for their huts. The roots of the great shade trees that lined the road were exposed and here and there a tree had collapsed: pigmy effort, gigantic destruction. There were few vehicles on the road, but many people, heedless of sun, dust and our horn. The women wore recognisable garments of purple, green and gold; the men were in rags.

'They've all got the vote.'

When I looked at the Sikh I saw that his face was set with anger. He was more remote than ever, and his lips were moving silently. In what language was he speaking? Was he speaking a prayer, a charm? The hysteria of the train journey began to touch me again. And now I felt I carried a double responsibility. The Sikh's anger was feeding on everything he saw, and I longed for the land and the people to change. The Sikh's lips still moved. Against his charm I tried to pitch my own. I felt disaster close; I let reason go. I tried to transmit compensating love to every starved man and woman I saw on the road. But I was failing; I knew I was failing. I was yielding to the rage and contempt of the man beside me. Love insensibly turned into a self-lacerating hysteria in which I was longing for greater and greater decay, more rags and filth, more bones, men more starved and grotesque, more spectacularly deformed. I wished to extend myself, to see the limits of human degradation, to take it all in at that moment. For me this was the end, my private failure; even as I wished I knew I would carry the taint of that moment.

On the pedestal of a high white culvert, PWD-trim, a man stood like a statue. Rags hung over his bones, over limbs as thin and brittle-looking as charred sticks.

'Ha! Look at that monkey.' There was a chuckle in his voice, instantly replaced by torment. 'God! Can you call that a man? Even the animals, if they have to live . . . even the animals.' Words were not coming to him. 'Even the animals Man? What does that—that *thing* have? You think he even has instinct? To tell him when to eat?'

He was reacting for me, as he had done on the train. But now I knew my hysteria for what it was. The words were his, not mine. They broke the spell.

Peasants, trees and villages were obliterated by the dust of our car.

At times it seems that to our folly and indecisiveness, and to our dishonesty, there can be no limit. Our relationship ought to have ended at the end of that journey. A declaration would have been painful. But it could have been avoided. I could have changed hotels; I could have disappeared. This was my instinct. But the evening found us drinking together. Peasants and dust were forgotten, black gods and white, aryan and Dravidian. That moment on the road had grown out of a sense of nameless danger, and that had probably been the effect of the heat or my own exhaustion. The leaden Indian beer had its effect, and we talked of London and coffee houses and the 'funny little fellow'.

Dusk turned to night. Now there were three of us at the glass-crowded table. The newcomer was a commercial Englishman, middle-aged, fat and red-faced. He spoke with a North Country accent. From my alcoholic quietude I noted that the talk had turned to Sikh history and Sikh military glory. The Englishman was at first rallying, but presently the smile on his face had grown fixed. I listened. The Sikh was talking of the decline of the Sikhs since Ranjit Singh, of the disaster that had come to them with Partition. But he was also talking of Sikh revenges in 1947 and of Sikh atrocities. Some of the talk of atrocities was, I felt, aimed at me; it carried on from our drive back to the town. It was too calculated; it left me cold.

Dinner, we wanted dinner; and now we were on our way to the restaurant, and the Englishman was no longer with us.

It was very bright in the restaurant.

'They are staring at me!'

The restaurant was bright and noisy, full of people and tables.

'They are staring at me.'

We were in a crowded corner.

I sat down.

Slap!

'These bloody Dravidians are staring at me.'

The man at the next table had been knocked down. He lay on his back, his head on the seat of an empty chair. His eyes were wide with terror, his hands clasped in greeting and supplication.

'Sardarji!' he cried, still lying flat.

'Staring at me. South Indian punk.'

'Sardarji! My friend said, "Look, a sardarji." And I just turned to look. I am not a South Indian. I am a Punjabi. Like you.'

'Punk.'

Something like this I had always feared. This was what my instinct had scented as soon as I had seen him on the train: some men radiate violence and torment, and they are dangerous to those who fear violence. We had met, and there had inevitably been a reassessment. Below all the wrongness and unease of our relationship, however, lay my original alarm. This moment, of fear and self-disgust, was logical. It was also the moment I had been waiting for. I left the restaurant and took a rickshaw to the hotel. The whole city, its streets now silent, had been coloured for me, from the first, by my association with the Sikh; I had assessed it, whether in contempt or straining love, according to the terms of his special racialism. It was as much by this that I was now sickened as by the violence I had witnessed.

I made the rickshaw-man turn and take me back to the restaurant. There was no sign of the Sikh. But the Punjabi, his eyes wild with humiliation and anger, was at the cash-desk with a group who appeared to know him.

'I am going to kill your friend,' he shouted at me. 'I am going to kill that Sikh tomorrow.'

'You are not going to kill anybody.'

'I am going to kill him. I am going to kill you too.'

I went back to the hotel. The telephone rang.

'Hallo, punk.'

'Hello.'

'So you ran out on me when I was in a little trouble. And you call yourself a friend. You know what I think of you? You are a dirty South Indian swine. Don't go to sleep. I am coming over to beat you up.'

He could not have been far away, for in a few minutes he appeared, knocking twice on the door, bowing exaggeratedly, and staggering in theatrically. We were both more lucid than we had been, but our conversation see-sawed drunkenly, and falsely, between reconciliation and recrimination. At any moment we could have become friends again or agreed not to meet; again and again, when we tilted to one of these possibilities, one of us applied a corrective pressure. There still existed concern between us. We drank coffee; our conversation see-sawed more and more falsely; and in the end even this concern had been talked away.

'We were going to go hunting,' the Sikh said, as he left. 'I had *plans* for you.'

It was a good Hollywood exit line. Perhaps it was meant. I couldn't say. The English language in India could be s misleading. Exhaustion overcame me: for all our coffee and playacting talk, the break had been violent. It brough. relief and regret. There had been so much goodwill and generosity there; my misunderstanding had been so great.

In the morning horror was uppermost. I had seen photographs of the Punjab massacres of 1947 and of the Great Calcutta Killing; I had heard of trains—those Indian trains!— ferrying dead bodies across the border; I had seen the burial mounds beside the Punjab roads. Yet until now I had never thought of India as a land of violence. Now violence was something I could smell in the air; the city seemed tainted by the threat of violence and self-torment of the sort I had seen. I wanted to get away at once. But the trains and buses were booked for days ahead.

I went to the sweetshop-owner. He was soft and welcoming. He sat me at a table; one of his waiters brought me a plate of the sweetest sweets; and master and servant watched me eat. Those Indian sweets! 'Serves them in place of flesh': a Kipling phrase, perhaps altered by memory, came and stayed with me; and *flesh* seemed a raw and fearful word. For all that was soft and feeble and sweet-loving in that city I was grateful; and I feared for it.

In the sweetshop the next evening the owner introduced me to a relation of his, who was visiting. The relation started when he heard my name. Could it be true? He was reading one of my books; he had thought of me as someone thousands of miles away; he had never dreamed of finding me eating sweets in the bazaar of an out-of-the-way Indian town. But he had expected someone older. I was a *baccha*, a boy! However, he had met me, and he wished to show his appreciation. Could I tell him where I was staying?

Acrid white smoke billowed out of my hotel room when I opened the door that night. There was no fire. The smoke was incense. To enter, I had to cover my face with a handkerchief. I opened doors and windows, turned the ceiling fan on, and hurried out again to the corridor with streaming eyes. It was minutes before the incense-fog thinned. Great clumps of incense sticks burned like dying brands everywhere; on the floor the ash was like bird droppings. Flowers were strewn over my bed, and there was a garland on my pillow.

10. EMERGENCY

CHINESE LAUNCH MASSIVE, SIMULTANEOUS ATTACKS IN NEFA
AND LADAKH. Newspaper headlines can appear to exult. In
Madras, where I was, the waiters at the hotel read the news
to one another in corridors and on staircase landings; and in
Mount Road the unemployed boys and men who usually stood
outside the Kwality Restaurant, offering to fetch taxis and
scooters for people who had had their lunch, gathered round a
man who was reading aloud from a Tamil newspaper. On the
pavement women dished out cooked meals for labourers at a
few annas a head; in side streets, amid buses and cars, barebacked carters pulled and pushed at their heavy-wheeled carts,
grunting, the carters between the shafts disguising their strain
by a lightfooted, mincing walk. The setting mocked the headlines. India did not qualify for modern warfare. 'She, whose
only peer was the Holy Roman Empire, she shall rank with
Guatemala and Belgium perhaps!' So Forster's Fielding had
mocked forty years before; and after fifteen years of independence India remained in many ways a colonial country.
She continued to produce mainly politicians and speeches. Her
'industrialists' were mainly traders, importers of simple
machinery, manufacturers under licence. Her administration
was still negative. It collected taxes, preserved order; and now
to the passion of an aroused nation it could only respond with
words. The Emergency was a seeking for precedents, the
issuing of a correct Defence of the Realm Act, complete with
instructions about gas masks, incendiary bombs and stirrup
pumps. The Emergency was suspension and cancellation;
censorship which encouraged rumour and panic; slogans in the

newspapers. The Emergency became words, English words. THIS IS TOTAL WAR, the Bombay weekly said on its front page. 'What do I mean by total war?' the IAS candidate said, replying to a question from the examining board. 'It is a war in which the whole world takes part.' The news grew worse. There were rumours of Gurkhas sent up to Ladakh armed only with their knives, and of men flown from the Assam plains to the mountains of NEFA clad only in singlets and tennis shoes. All the swift violence of which the country was capable was gathered into one ball; there was a feeling as of release and revolution. Anything might have happened; if will alone counted, the Chinese would have been pushed back to Lhasa in a week. But from the politicians there came only speeches, and from the administrators correct regulations. The famous Fourth Division was cut to pieces; the humiliation of the Indian Army, India's especial pride, was complete. Independent India was now felt to be a creation of words—'Why didn't we have to *fight* for our freedom?'—and it was collapsing in words. The magic of the leader failed, and presently passion subsided into fatalism.

The Chinese invasion had been with us for a week. In the house of a friend there gathered for dinner a film producer, a script-writer, a journalist and a doctor. Before we went in we sat in the verandah, and even as I listened to the talk I knew I could not convincingly reconstruct it. At times it seemed frivolous and satirical; then despairing; then fantastic. Its moods were always muted. The Chinese would stop at the Brahmaputra, the producer said; they merely wanted to consolidate their occupation of Tibet. He spoke coolly; no one questioned his assumption that India could not be anything but passive. From this the talk slipped to a good-humoured disputation about *karma* and the value of human existence; and before I could work out how it had done so, we were back to the border situation. The country's unpreparedness was ridiculed. No one was blamed, no plans were put forward: a comic situation was merely outlined. And where was this leading? 'A fact many people do not know,' the doctor said, 'is that it is dangerous to have an inoculation against cholera during an epidemic.' The medical analogy was overwhelming: the country had been unprepared and it was foolish, indeed dangerous, to make any preparations now. This was accepted; the film producer repeated his view that the Chinese would stop at the Brahmaputra. Gandhi was mentioned; but how did the doctor move on from this to state his belief in the occult, and why did he throw out, almost as a debating point, that 'the great healers have always used their powers to save themselves'? We remained for some time on the subject of miracles. The Tibetans, I heard, were suffering because they had forgotten the *mantras*, charms, which might have repelled their enemies. I examined the faces of the speakers. They seemed serious. But were they? Mightn't their conversation have been a type of medieval intellectual exercise, the dinnertime recreation of South Indian brahmins? Dinner was announced, and now at last a conclusion was reached. Indians too, it was said, had forgotten the *mantras*, they were powerless against their enemies and there was nothing that could be done. The situation on the border had been talked away. We went in calmly to dinner and talked of other matters.

Indian life, Indian death, went on.

Wanted a Telugu Brahmin Vellanadu non-Kausiga Gotram bride below 22 years for young graduate earning Rs 200 monthly.

On the grass verge outside the hotel, next to the open refuse-heap where women and buffaloes daily rummaged among the used banana food-leaves and the hotel's discarded food, a little brown puppy lay dying. It moved about a small area, as though imprisoned, fading from day to day. One morning it looked dead. But a crow approached; and the puppy's tail lifted and dropped.

Exquisitely beautiful, Enchanting classical Bharatha Natyam dancer, brilliant graduate, aristocratic family, broadminded, delightful temperament, fair, slim, tall, modern outlook, aged 21, wishes to marry a millowner, business magnate, well-to-do landlord, doctor, engineer, or top executive.

Caste, creed, nationality no bar.

The news from New Delhi did not change. But the festival of Deepavali was at hand and the beggars were swarming into Mount Road. This boy did not at first look like a beggar. He was handsome, of a fine brown complexion; he wore red shorts and had a white cloth over his shoulders. He caught sight of me as I came out of the post office; then, behaving as one suddenly reminded of duty, he smiled and lifted the white cloth to reveal a monstrously deformed right arm. It was no arm at all; it was shaped like a woman's breast, ending not in a nipple but in a fingernail on a toy finger.

There was an audience of eight—not counting the secretary and the top-knotted watchman—for the lecture at the Triplicane Theosophical Society on 'Annie Besant, Our Leader'. The speaker was a middle-aged Canadian woman. She came from Vancouver. This was not as odd as it appeared, she said: according to Annie Besant, Vancouver had been a centre of the occult in far-off times. Annie Besant's Irish ancestry doubtless explained her psychic gifts, and much of her character could be explained by what she must have been in former lives. Annie Besant had been, above all, a great leader; and it was the duty of every Theosophist to be a leader, to keep Annie Besant's message alive and her books in circulation. The Theosophical Society was now encountering a certain indifference—the secretary had already said as much—and many people were no doubt asking why, if she was with us again, Annie Besant wasn't in the Theosophical Society. But there was no logic in the question. There was no reason why Annie Besant should be in the Society. Her work for the Society had been done in a previous life; she was now almost certainly, under what name we could not tell, doing equally important work in some other field. Two men in the audience were dozing.

Behind the high, clean walls of the Aurobindo Ashram in Pondicherry, one hundred miles to the south, they were perfectly calm. In 1950, the year of his death, Aurobindo had warned Mr Nehru of the expansionist designs of 'a yellow race'; he had prophesied the Chinese conquest of Tibet and had seen this as the first step in the Chinese attempt to conquer India. It was there in black and white in one of the Ashram's numberous publications, and must have been shown often in the last few days: the receptionist opened the book easily at the correct page.

The Master's raised, flower-strewn *samadhi*, a site now for collective meditation, lay in the cool paved courtyard of the ashram. The Mother was still alive, though now a little withdrawn. She gave *darshan*—made an appearance, offered a sight of herself—only on important anniversaries: the date of Aurobindo's birth, the date of her own arrival in India, and so on. Of Aurobindo I knew a little. He had been educated almost wholly in England; returning to India, he became a revolutionary; escaping arrest, he fled to Pondicherry, a French territory, and there, abandoning politics, he had remained, a revered holy man in a growing ashram. But of the Mother I knew nothing except that she was a Frenchwoman, an associate of Aurobindo's, and that her position in the Ashram was special. For three and a half rupees I bought a book from the Ashram's bookstand, *Letters of Sri Aurobindo on the Mother*.

Q: Am I right in thinking that she as an Individual embodies all the Divine Powers and brings down the Grace more and more to the physical plane? and her embodiment is a chance for the entire physical to change and transform? A: Yes. Her embodiment is a chance for the earth-consciousness to receive the Supramental into it and to undergo first the transformation necessary for that to be possible. Afterwards there will be a further transformation by the Supramental, but the whole consciousness will not be supramentalised—there will be first a new race representing the Supermind, as man represents the mind.

Photographs of the Mother by Henri Cartier Bresson were also on sale. They showed a Frenchwoman of a certain age, with an angular face and large, slightly protruding teeth. She was smiling; her cheeks were full and well defined. An em-

broidered scarf covered her head and came down to just above
her darkened eyes, which held nothing of the good humour of
the lower half of her face. The scarf was tied or pinned at the
back of her head and the ends fell on either side of her neck.

Q: *Pourquoi la Mère s'habille-t-elle avec des vêtements riches et
beaux?*
A: *Avez-vous donc pour conception que le Divin doit être réprésenté
sur terre par la pauvreté et la laideur?*

Both Aurobindo and the Mother had Lights. Aurobindo's had
been pale blue; his body glowed for days after he died. The
Mother's Light was white, sometimes gold.

When we speak of the Mother's Light or my Light in a
special sense, we are speaking of a special occult action—we
are speaking of certain lights that come from the Supermind.
In this action the Mother's is the White Light that purifies,
illumines, brings down the whole essence and power of the
Truth and makes the transformation possible . . . .
  The Mother has certainly no idea of making people see
it—it is of themselves that one after another, some 20 or 30
in the Ashram, I believe, have come to see. It is certainly
one of the signs that the Higher Force (call it supramental
or not) is beginning to influence Matter.

The Mother was also responsible for the organisation of the
Ashram; an occasional impatience in Aurobindo's replies to
inmates hinted at early difficulties.

In the organisation of work there was formerly a formidable
waste due to the workers and *sadhaks* following their own
fancy almost entirely without respect for the Mother's will;
that was largely checked by reorganisation.

It is a mistake to think that the Mother's not smiling
means either displeasure or disapproval of something wrong
in the *sadhak*. It is very often merely a sign of absorption or

of inner concentration. On this occasion the Mother was putting a question to your soul.

Mother did not know at that time of your having spoken to T. So your conjecture of that being the cause of her fancied displeasure is quite groundless. Your idea about Mother's mysterious smile is your own imagination— Mother says that she smiled with the utmost kindness.

It is not because your French is full of mistakes that Mother does not correct it, but because I will not allow her to take more work on herself so far as I can help it. Already she has no time to rest sufficiently at night and most of the night she is working at the books, reports and letters that pour on her in masses. Even so she cannot finish in time in the morning. If she has to correct all the letters of the people who have just begun writing in French as well as the others, it means another hour or two of work—she will be able to finish only at nine in the morning and come down at 10.30. I am therefore trying to stop it.

All bad thoughts upon the Mother or throwing of impurities on her may affect her body, as she has taken the *sadhaks* into her consciousness; nor can she send these things back to them as it might hurt them.

Withdrawn though the Mother now was, her hand could still be seen in the running of the Ashram. The noticeboard carried notices about the cholera outbreak in Madras—inmates were warned against contact with people from that town—and about the annoyance of chatter at the Ashram gates; the notices were signed 'M', in a firm, stylish zigzag. And the Ashram was only part of the Aurobindo Society. Pondicherry had already melted into the rest of southern Indian; even the French language seemed to have disappeared. But the numerous, well-kept buildings of the Society still gave it the feel of a small French town that had been set down on a tropical coast. Walls were shuttered and blank against the light, which was intense above the raging surf; and the Society's walls were painted in the Society's colours. The Society seemed to be the only flourishing thing in Pondicherry. It had its estates outside the town; it had its workshops, its library, its printing press. It was a self-contained organisation, efficiently run by its members. Their number could grow only by recruitment, from India and overseas, for the Mother, I was told, disapproved strongly of three things: politics, tobacco and sex. The children who came into the Ashram with their parents were taught trades as they grew up; the leaders among them wore distinctive uniforms, in the very short shorts of which I thought I could detect a French influence. Work was as important as meditation; the physical was not to be neglected. (I was later told by an Englishman in Madras that, running into a group of oddly dressed elderly Europeans on roller skates one day in Pondicherry, and tracing them to their source, he had come to the Ashram gates. But that might have been only a story. I saw only one European in the Ashram. He was barefooted and very pink; he wore a dhoti and Indian jacket; and his long white hair and beard gave him a resemblance to the dead Master.) By recruiting people from the world, then, the Society never became inbred; and by employing their developed talents it prospered.

The present General Secretary, for instance, was a Bombay businessman before he withdrew to the Ashram and took the name of Navajata, the newborn. His appearance still suggested the businessman. He was holding a briefcase and he seemed pressed for time. But he said he had never been happier.

'Now I must go,' he said. 'I have to go up and see the Mother.'

'Tell me. Has the Mother said anything about the Chinese invasion?'

'1962 is a bad year,' he recited hurriedly. '1963 is going to be a bad year. Things will start getting better in 1964, and India will win through in 1967. Now I must go.'

For weeks I had been seeing this young man. I thought he was a business executive trainee of French or Italian origin. He was tall and thin, wore dark glasses, carried a briefcase, and had a brisk, twiddly walk. He always looked self-assured and purposeful, but it puzzled me that he seemed to have much time on his hands. I saw him at bus stops at odd times of day. I saw him in museums in the afternoons. I saw him at dance performances in the evenings. We often passed one another in the street. Then—one aspect of the mystery solved when, to our mutual astonishment, we saw one another in the corridor on the top floor of the hotel one morning—I discovered that he had the room next to mine.

He puzzled and embarrassed me. But I was causing him distress, and I did not know it. In Madras they don't invite you to their homes; whatever their eminence, they prefer to call on you. So I sat for hours in my hotel room every day, receiving, with the 'boys' continually bringing in coffee for new visitors. I believe it was the convivial sounds of chatter and coffee spoons which made my neighbour break down. We came out of our rooms at the same time one morning. Ignoring one another, we locked our doors. We turned. There was confrontation. And suddenly a torrent of American speech gushed out, brooking no interjection even of greeting.

'How are you? How long are you staying here? I'm in a terrible state. I've been here six months and I've lost sixteen pounds. I felt the call of the East ha-ha and came out to India to study ancient India philosophy and culture. It's driving me mad. What do you think of the hotel? I think it's *creepy*.' He hunched his shoulders. 'It's the food.' Mouth working, he struck his palm against his dark glasses. 'It's sending me *blind*. It's these people. They're *crazy*. They don't accept you. Help me. You have people running in and out of your room all day. You know some English people here. Talk to them about me. Introduce me to them. They might take me in. You must help me.'

I promised to try.

The first person I spoke to said, 'Well, I don't know. Experience tells me that when people are doing inward things like answering the call of the East it is better to stay away.'

I did not try again. And now I feared to meet the young

American. I did not meet him. The trains between Madras and
Calcutta were running again, after the long dislocation caused
by floods and the movement of troops.

Ladies, painted in yellow on some carriages. *Military*, marked
in chalk on many more. It was so unlikely, this train-load of
soldiers moving north through all the distress of India to the
calamity on the frontiers. With their olive-green uniforms, their
good looks and good manners, and their moustached, swagger-
sticked officers, they transformed the railway platforms at
which we stopped: they lent drama and order, and to them how
comforting the familiar, receding squalor must have been!
The plump little major in my compartment, carrying his water
in a champagne bottle, had been so quiet after leaving his wife
and daughter at Madras Central station—the three had simply
sat silently side by side. Now, as the journey lengthened, he
brightened; he asked me the Indian questions: where did I
come from, what did I do? And the soldiers became playful.
Once the train stopped beside a field of sugarcane. A soldier
jumped out and began to cut stalks of cane with his knife.
More soldiers jumped out, more cane was cut. The angry
farmer appeared. Money passed, anger turned to smiles and
waves as we moved off again.

Afternoon now, and the train's shadow racing beside us.
Sunset, evening, night; station after dimly-lit station. It was an
Indian railway journey, but everything that had before seemed
pointless was now threatened and seemed worth cherishing;
and as in the mild sunshine of a winter morning we drew near
to green Bengal, which I had longed to see, my mood towards
India and her people became soft. I had taken so much for
granted. There, among the Bengali passengers who had come
on, was a man who wore a long woollen scarf and a brown
tweed jacket above his Bengali dhoti. The casual elegance of
his dress was matched by his fine features and relaxed posture.
Out of all its squalor and human decay, its eruptions of
butchery, India produced so many people of grace and beauty,
ruled by elaborate courtesy. Producing too much life, it denied
the value of life; yet it permitted a unique human development

to so many. Nowhere were people so heightened, rounded and individualistic; nowhere did they offer themselves so fully and with such assurance. To know Indians was to take a delight in people as people; every encounter was an adventure. I did not want India to sink; the mere thought was painful.

And it was in this mood that I walked about Calcutta, the 'nightmare experience' of Mr Nehru, 'the world's most miserable city', according to an American magazine, 'the pestilential behemoth' of another American writer, the world's last stronghold of Asiatic cholera, according to the World Health Organisation: a city which, built for two million, now accommodated six million on its pavements and in its *bastees*.

'*Chuha*,' the waiter at Howrah station restaurant said affectionately, pointing. 'Look, a rat.' And the pink, depilated creature, barely noticed by the Assamese soldier and his wife, both sucking away at rice and curried fish, sluggishly made its way across the tiled floor and up a pipe. This promised horror. But nothing I had read or heard had prepared me for the red-brick city on the other side of Howrah Bridge which, if one could ignore the stalls and rickshaws and whiteclad hurrying crowds, was at first like another Birmingham; and then, in the centre, at dusk, was like London, with the misty, tree-blobbed Maidan as Hyde Park, Chownringhee as a mixture of Oxford Street, Park Lane and Bayswater Road, with neon invitations, fuzzy in the mist, to bars, coffee houses and air travel, and the Hooghly, a muddier, grander Thames, not far away. On a high floodlit platform in the Maidan General Cariappa, the former commander-in-chief, erect, dark-suited, was addressing a small, relaxed crowd in Sandhurst-accented Hindustani on the Chinese attack. Around and about the prowed, battleship-grey Calcutta trams, bulging at exits and entrances with men in white, tanked away at less than ten miles an hour. Here, unexpectedly and for the first time in India, one was in a big city, the recognisable metropolis, with street names—Elgin, Lindsay, Allenby—oddly unrelated to the people who thronged them: incongruity that deepened as the mist thickened to smog and as, driving out to the suburbs, one saw the chimneys smoking among the palm trees.

This was the city which, according to bazaar rumour, Chou En-Lai had promised the Chinese people as a Christmas present. The Indian Marwari merchants, it was said, were already making inquiries about business prospects under Chinese rule; the same rumour had it that in the South the Madrasis, despite their objection to Hindi, were already learning Chinese. Morale was low; the administration in Assam had collapsed and there were tales of flight and panic. But it was not in this alone that the sadness of the city lay. With or without the Chinese, Calcutta was dead. Partition had deprived it of half its hinterland and burdened it with a vast dispirited refugee population. Even Nature had turned: the Hooghly was silting up. But Calcutta's death was also of the heart. With its thin glitter, its filth and overpopulation, its tainted money, its exhaustion, it held the total Indian tragedy and the terrible British failure. Here the Indo-British encounter had at one time promised to be fruitful. Here the Indian renaissance had begun: so many of the great names of Indian reform are Bengali. But it was here, too, that the encounter had ended in mutual recoil. The cross-fertilisation had not occurred, and Indian energy had turned sour. Once Bengal led India, in ideas and idealism; now, just forty years later, Calcutta, even to Indians, was a word of terror, conveying crowds, cholera and corruption. Its aesthetic impulses had not faded—there was an appealing sensibility in every Bengali souvenir, every over-exploited refugee 'craft' —but they, pathetically, threw into relief the greater decay. Calcutta had no leaders now, and apart from Ray, the film director, and Janah, the photographer, had no great names. It had withdrawn from the Indian experiment, as area after area of India was withdrawing, individual after individual. The British, who had built Calcutta, had ever been withdrawn from their creation; and they survived. Their business houses still flourished in Chowringhee; and to the Indians, products of the dead Indian renaissance, who now sat in some of the air-conditioned offices, Independence had meant no more than this: the opportunity to withdraw, British-like, from India. What then was the India that was left, for which one felt

*

such concern? Was it no more than a word, an idea? From the train Durgapur, the new steel town, was a spreading pattern of lights. I went out to the corridor and watched them until they disappeared. Such a small hope, and it was easy to imagine the lights extinguished. Bomdi-la fell that night. Assam lay open; Mr Nehru offered the people of the state comfort which was already like helpless condolence. Tibetan refugees got off the train at Banaras. There was smiling bewilderment on their broad, ruddy faces; no one spoke their language and they stood uncertainly beside their boxes, outlandish in their bulky wrappings, grimed to khaki, their long hair, their boots and hats. The hotel was deserted: internal air services had been cancelled. The young dark-suited manager and the uniformed servants stood silent and idle in the verandah. Something of the bazaar spirit and the spirit of wartime opportunism stirred within me. I stood on the steps and haggled. Success went to my head. 'And that is to include morning coffee,' I said. 'Yes,' the manager said sadly. 'That is to include coffee.'

Here in the cantonment area Banaras felt abandoned, and it was easy to imagine oneself a squatter. But in the town nothing hinted at tragedy. Wood was piled high on the *ghats*. Brightly shrouded bodies lay on flower-strewn litters at the water's edge, unimportantly awaiting their pyres; and above occasional blazes, oddly casual and not too visible in the reflected glare of the Ganges, family groups smiled and chattered. The steep *ghats*, platformed and stepped, their names marked in large letters, were as thronged as a holiday beach. The pious stood in the water, relaxed below beach umbrellas or gathered round an expounding pundit; young men did exercises. Above, behind the high white river front, in the twisting alleys, dark between solid masonry and enchanting but for the cowdung, hawkers offered Banaras toys, silk and brass; and in the temples the guide-priests, young, washed and combed, chewed *pan* and cursed those who refused them alms.

I went to the Nepalese Temple, 'disfigured', Murray's *Handbook* said, 'by erotic carvings; they do not catch the eye, provided that the attendant can be discouraged from pointing them out.' The attendant was a youth with a long switch; I begged him to point them out. 'Here man and woman,' he began unexcitedly. 'Here other man. He Mr Hurry-up because he say, "Hurry up, hurry up".' Tourist lore: the gloss did not please me. The pleasures of erotic art are fragile; I wished I had followed Murray's advice.

At dinner I asked the sad young manager to put on the radio for the news. It was as bad as could be expected. The manager held his hands behind his back and looked down, correct even in his growing distress. Then a reference to 'Chinese Frontier Guards' alerted me.

'But we are listening to Peking, Mr Manager.'

'It is All-India Radio. It's the station I always listen to.'

'Only the Chinese and Radio Pakistan talk of the Chinese Frontier Guards.'

'But it is in English. And the accent . . . And it sounds so close.'

It did indeed; it was coming over loud and clear. We tried to get New Delhi; we got squawks and static and a feeble, disappearing voice.

And the next day it was all over. The Chinese declared a ceasefire and promised a withdrawal. And, as if by magic, the hotel began to fill up.

The fighting was over but the Emergency continued, and it was the duty of this Commissioner to make tours through his Division, keeping up morale and raising funds. He had just finished one tour and had been presented with an album of photographs, mainly of himself receiving and being received. I sat in the back of his station-wagon now with some junior officers and looked through the photographs. We were travelling along an Indian road: a thin metalled strip between two lanes of earth that had been ground to fine, thick dust by the wheels of bullock-carts. This was Indian dust: it disfigured the trees that lined the road, it discoloured the fields for a hundred yards on either side. And regularly, at stations in the dust, there were reception committees, garlands, displays of calisthenics and rough exhibitions of rough local manufactures.

The Commissioner was keen on soap and shoes, and

everywhere we stopped the bearded Muslim shoemakers stood beside their shoes and the soapmakers stood beside their heavy, imperfectly moulded cubes of soap. At dinner one evening the Commissioner, dressed in a dark suit, explained his interest in soap and shoes. His voice dropped to tenderness. His daughter, he said, was at school in England. Through television or some other educational medium her companions had learned that there were no towns in India, that no one wore shoes or lived in houses or washed. 'Is it true, Daddy?' the distressed child had asked. So now the craftsmen of the Division made soap and shoes. Sometimes, when he was being received, the Commissioner broke through the circle of local dignitaries to greet the children of the very poor who were on the other side of the road. Sometimes, exercising the Commissioner's prerogative, he took cakes of soap from the display and distributed them to these children, while the photographers, another album in mind, took pictures.

It was a swift tour. To me it was remarkable that an area so large and nondescript and comfortless should be capable of such organisation, and that behind the clouds of dust there should be people who, with so little encouragement and such poor materials, should yet be exercising craftsman's skills. I would have liked to linger, to draw hope. But there was no time. The displays were too many. I was sitting in the back of the station-wagon and was the last to get out whenever we stopped; and it frequently happened that before I had had time to inspect the first exhibit the Commissioner and his officials were back at the station-wagon and waiting for me: since I was the last to get out I was the first to get in.

We spent more time at the meetings. Here the thin-limbed boys in white shorts and vests had been assembled in the sun, ready to go through their gymnastic exercises. Here there were arches marked WELCOME in Hindi. Here the Commissioner was garlanded. The Indian politician, when garlanded, at once removes the garland and hands it to an attendant; this acceptance and instant rejection of dignity is the stylish Indian form. The Commissioner did not remove his garlands. Hoop after hoop of marigold was hung on his bowed head, until the marigolds rose to his ears and, from the back, he looked like an idol incongruously armed: in one hand he carried his lighted cigar, in the other his sun helmet. His attendant was not far away. He carried his master's cigar box and was dressed like a Mogul courtier: so the British had sought to degrade their predecessors.

In the decorated tent the peasants sat on mats. For the officials there were chairs and a table. Names were read out and peasants rose, came to the Commissioner, bowed and presented rupee notes for the National Defence Fund. (As the Fund rose in the area, an IAS man told me, National Savings dropped.) Some women shyly presented jewellery. Sometimes there was no response to a name, and then from all corners of the tent came explanations: a death, of man or beast, an illness, a sudden journey. The money rose in a shaky pile on the plate and was handled casually by all.

Then the Commissioner spoke. The Emergency was not over, not at all; the Chinese were still on India's sacred soil. The people of India had been preached at for too long about peace and nonviolence. Now they had to be roused. The Commissioner sought to do so first by appealing to the patriotism of the peasants and then by analysing the nature of the Chinese threat. By any Indian standard the Chinese were unclean. They ate beef: this was for the Hindus in the audience. They ate pork: this was for the Muslims. They ate dogs: this was for everyone. They ate cats, rats, snakes. The peasants remained passive, and were only roused when the Commissioner, playing his last card, invoked the Hindu goddesses of destruction.

The Commissioner had a cheer-leader, a tall elderly man in an old double-breasted grey suit. He wore spectacles and carried a sun-helmet which was the fellow of the Commissioner's. He chewed *pan* constantly; his mouth was large, with flapping red-stained lips. His face was without expression; he seemed to be doing sums in his head all the time. Clerk-like, adjusting his spectacles, he went to the microphone and stood silently before it. Suddenly he opened his enormous red mouth, revealing fillings and pieces of mangled betel-nut, and screamed: '*Kali Mata ki—*'

'*Jai!*' the peasants shouted, their eyes brightening, the smiles staying on their faces. 'Long live Mother Kali!'

'But what is this?' the Commissioner's assistant said. 'I heard nothing.' It was his line; at every meeting he used it. 'We will try again, and this time I want to hear you. *Kali Mata ki—*'

'*Jai! Jai! Jai!*'

Once, twice, three times the goddesses were invoked, to growing enthusiasm. Then abruptly the assistant turned, walked back to his seat, sat on it decisively, slapped his sun-helmet on his knees, stared straight ahead and, teeth and lips working over the *pan*, seemed immediately absorbed in mental arithmetic.

When the audience was too small, the Commissioner showed his displeasure by refusing to speak or to leave. Then officials and policemen bustled penitentially about; they summoned peasants from the fields and their homes and marched children out from the schools. But there was never any trouble in finding an audience for the evening concerts. Singers of local renown chewed *pan* and sang songs of their own about the Chinese invasion into microphones shrouded with cloth to protect them from *pan*-splutterings. There were sketches about the need to save, to grow more food, to contribute to the National Defence Fund, to give blood. Once or twice an ambitious play-wright showed a local hero dying in battle against the Chinese; and it was clear that no one in the village knew what the Chinese looked like.

From the railway train and from the dusty roads India appeared to require only pity. It was an easy emotion, and perhaps the Indians were right: it was compassion like mine, so strenuously maintained, that denied humanity to many. It separated; it permitted the surprise and emotion I felt at these concerts, simple exhibitions of humanity. Anger, compassion and contempt were aspects of the same emotion; they were without value because they could not endure. Achievement could begin only with acceptance.

We were now in a region which, though physically no different from the surrounding areas, was famous for its soldiers. Was this due to some ancient mixing of bloods preserved by caste rules? To some pertinacious Rajput strain? India was full of such puzzles. The crowd here was too large for the tent. Some had put on their uniforms and decorations. The cheer-leader picked them out and seated them on a bench at the edge of the tent. But one or two preferred to walk slowly up and down the road while the Commissioner spoke. So far the Commissioner had been speaking to people who were a little irritated and resentful at having to leave their fields or the idleness of their homes. But this crowd was attentive from the first. The old soldiers gazed steadily at the Commissioner and every point he made was registered on their faces. The Chinese ate pork. Brows puckered. The Chinese ate dogs. Brows puckered more deeply. The Chinese ate rats. Eyes popped, heads lifted as struck.

The Commissioner had scarcely finished speaking when a man ran out from the crowd and threw himself at his feet, weeping.

The crowd relaxed and smiled.

'Get up, get up,' the Commissioner said, 'and tell me what you have to say.'

'You ask me to fight, and I want to fight. But how can I fight when I have no food and my family has no food? How can I fight when I have lost my land?'

The crowd began to titter.

'You have lost your land?'

'In the resettlement.'

The Commissioner spoke to his cheer-leader.

'All my good land,' the man wept, 'they gave to somebody else. All the bad land they gave to me.'

There was laughter from the old soldiers.

'I will look into it,' the Commissioner said.

The crowd was breaking up. The weeping man disappeared; the jeers at his outburst died down; and we moved on to the tea which the headman, a man of few words, had prepared for us.

There was another concert that evening. It had been organised by the local teacher. He came on just before the end

and said that he had written a new poem which he would recite
to us if the Commissioner gave his permission. The Commissioner took his cigar out of his mouth and nodded. The teacher
bowed, then, with passionate intonations and tormented
gestures, he recited. The facile Hindi rhymes tumbled out as if
newly discovered, and the teacher worked himself into a frenzy
as he came to his climax, which was a plea for the settled reign
on earth of

. . . satya ahimsa.

He bowed again, anticipating applause.

'*Satya ahimsa!*' the Commissioner shouted, stilling hands
about to clap. 'Are you mad? Truth and nonviolence, indeed.
Is this what you are preaching with the Chinese about to rape
your wife? Have I been wasting my breath all afternoon? This
is a classical example of muddled thinking.'

The poet, holding his bow, cringed. The curtain fell un
ceremoniously on him.

Poor poet! He had devised a good evening's entertainment.
He had written the anti-Chinese pieces and the songs about
the Motherland; yet when it came to his own poem, the one
he wished to recite himself, he had lost his head. For years
he had recited, to official applause, poems about truth and
nonviolence. Habit had been too strong, and had led to his
public disgrace.

Some weeks later Mr Nehru went to Lucknow. Standing on
the airport tarmac, he bowed his head forty-six times to receive
forty-six garlands from the forty-six members of the State
cabinet. This at any rate was the story I had from an IAS man
in Lucknow, and he was a little peeved. The IAS, acting on
instructions from Delhi, had taken civil defence seriously in
Lucknow. They had practised blackouts and air-raid warnings,
they had dug trenches; they had much to show Mr Nehru
But Mr Nehru only lost his temper. All this digging of trenches,
ne said, was a waste of time.

In a way, the Emergency was over.

11. THE VILLAGE OF THE DUBES

The Emergency was over. And so was my year. The short winter was fading fast; it was no longer pleasant to sit out in the sun; the dust would not now be laid until the monsoon. One journey remained, and for this I had lost taste. India had not worked its magic on me. It remained the land of my childhood, an area of darkness; like the Himalayan passes, it was closing up again, as fast as I withdrew from it, into a land of myth; it seemed to exist in just the timelessness which I had imagined as a child, into which, for all that I walked on Indian earth, I knew I could not penetrate.

In a year I had not learned acceptance. I had learned my separateness from India, and was content to be a colonial, without a past, without ancestors. Duty alone had brought me to this town in eastern Uttar Pradesh, not even graced by a ruin, celebrated only for its connections with the Buddha and its backwardness. And it was duty that, after a few days of indecision, idleness and reading, was taking me along this country road, infested with peasants indifferent to wheeled vehicles, to the village which my mother's father had left as an indentured labourer more than sixty years before.

When you drive through parts of western and central India you wonder about the teeming millions; settlements are so few, and the brown land looks so unfruitful and abandoned. Here wonder was of another sort. The land was flat. The sky was high, blue and utterly without drama; below it everything was diminished. Wherever you looked there was a village, low, dust-blurred, part of the earth and barely rising out of it. Every

tiny turbulence of dust betrayed a peasant; and the land was
nowhere still.

At a junction we took on a volunteer guide and turned off
on to an embankment of pure dust. It was lined with tall old
trees. Below them my grandfather had doubtless walked at
the start of his journey. In spite of myself I was held. For us
this land had ceased to exist. Now it was so ordinary. I did
not really want to see more. I was afraid of what I might find,
and I had witnesses. Not that one, not that, cried the guide,
excited both by my mission and the unexpected jeep ride, as
village after village died in our dust. Presently he pointed: there,
on our right, was the village of the Dubes.

It was set far back from the embankment. It exceeded anything I had expected. A large mango grove gave it a pastoral
aspect, and two spires showed white and clean against the dark
green foliage. I knew about those spires and was glad to see
them. My grandfather had sought to re-establish the family he
had left behind in India. He had recovered their land; he had
given money for the building of a temple. No temple had been
built, only three shrines. Poverty, fecklessness, we had thought
in Trinidad. But now, from the road, how reassuring those
spires were!

We got out of the jeep and made our way over tne crumpling
earth. The tall, branching mango trees shaded an artificial
pond, and the floor of the grove was spotted with blurred
sunshine. A boy came out. His thin body was naked save for
his dhoti and sacred thread. He looked at me suspiciously—our
party was large and ferociously official—but when the IAS
officer who was with me explained who I was, the boy attempted first to embrace me and then to touch my feet. I
disengaged myself and he led us through the village, talking
of the complicated relationship that bound him to my grandfather and to me. He knew all about my grandfather. To this
village that old adventure remained important: my grandfather
had gone far beyond the sea and had made *barra paisa*, much
money.

A year before I might have been appalled by what I was
seeing. But my eye had changed. This village looked unusually

prosperous; it was even picturesque. Many of the houses were of brick, some raised off the earth, some with carved wooden doors and tiled roofs. The lanes were paved and clean; there was a concrete cattle-trough. 'Brahmin village, brahmin village,' the IAS man whispered. The women were unveiled and attractive, their saris white and plain. They regarded us frankly, and in their features I could recognise those of the women of my family. 'Brahmin women,' the IAS man whispered. 'Very fearless.'

It was a village of Dubes and Tiwaris, all brahmins, all more or less related. A man, clad in loincloth and sacred thread, was bathing, standing and pouring water over himself with a brass jar. How elegant his posture, how fine his slender body! How, in the midst of populousness and dereliction, had such beauty been preserved? There were brahmins; they rented land for less than those who could afford less. But the region, as the *Gazeteer* said, 'abounds in brahmins'; they formed twelve to fifteen percent of the Hindu population. Perhaps this was why, though they were all related in the village, there appeared to be no communal living. We left the brick houses behind and, to my disappointment, stopped in front of a small thatched hut. Here resided Ramachandra, the present head of my grand-father's branch of the Dubes.

He was away. Oh, exclaimed the men and boys who had joined us, why did he have to choose this day? But the shrines, they would show me the shrines. They would show me how well they had been kept; they would show me my grandfather's name carved on the shrines. They unlocked the grilled doors and showed me the images, freshly washed, freshly dressed, marked with fresh sandalwood paste, the morning's offerings of flowers not yet faded. My mind leapt years, my sense of distance and time was shaken: before me were the very replicas of the images in the prayer-room of my grandfather's house.

An old woman was crying.

'Which son? Which one?'

And it was seconds before I realised that the old woman's words were in English.

'Jussodra!' the men said, and opened a way for her. She was on her haunches and in this posture was advancing towards me, weeping, screeching out words in English and Hindi. Her pale face was cracked like drying mud; her grey eyes were dim.

'Jussodra will tell you all about your grandfather,' the men said.

Jussodra had also been to Trinidad; she knew my grandfather. We were both led from the shrine to the hut. I was made to sit on a blanket on a string bed; and Jussodra, squatting at my feet, recited my grandfather's genealogy and recounted his adventures, weeping while the IAS officer translated. For thirty-six years Jussodra had lived in this village, and in that time she had polished her story into a fluent Indian *khisa* or fairytale. It could not have been unknown, but everyone was solemn and attentive.

When he was a young man (Jussodra said) my grandfather left this village to go to Banaras to study, as brahmins had immemorially done. But my grandfather was poor, his family poor, and times were hard; there might even have been a famine. One day my grandfather met a man who told him of a country far away called Trinidad. There were Indians in Trinidad, labourers; they needed pundits and teachers. The wages were good, land was cheap and a free passage could be arranged. The man who spoke to my grandfather knew what he was talking about. He was an *arkatia*, a recruiter; when times were good he might be stoned out of a village, but now people were willing to listen to his stories. So my grandfather indentured himself for five years and went to Trinidad. He was not, of course, made a teacher; he worked in the sugar factory. He was given a room, he was given food; and in addition he received twelve annas, fourteenpence, a day. It was a lot of money, and even today it was a good wage in this part of India, twice as much as the government paid for relief work in distress areas. My grandfather added to this by doing his pundit's work in the evenings. Banaras-trained pundits were rare in Trinidad and my grandfather was in demand. Even the sahib at the factory respected him, and one day the sahib said, 'You are a pundit. Can you help me? I want a son.' 'All right,' my grandfather said. 'I'll see that you get a son.' And when the sahib's wife gave birth to a son, the sahib was so pleased he said to my grandfather, 'You see these thirty *bighas* of land? All the canes there are yours.' My grandfather had the canes cut and sold them for two thousand rupees, and with this he went into business. Success attracted success. A well-to-do man, long settled in Trinidad, came to my grandfather one day and said, 'I've been keeping my eye on you for some time. I can see that you are going to go far. Now I have a daughter and would like her to be married to you. I will give you three acres of land.' My grandfather was not interested. Then the man said, 'I will give you a buggy. You can hire out the buggy and make a little extra money.' So my grandfather married. He prospered. He built two houses. Soon he was wealthy enough to come back to this village and redeem twenty-five acres of his family's land. Then he went back to Trinidad. But he was a restless man. He decided to make another trip to India. 'Come back quick,' his family said to him. (Jussodra spoke these words in English; 'buggy' had also been in English.) But my grandfather didn't see Trinidad again. On the train from Calcutta he fell ill, and he wrote to his family: 'The sun is setting.'

Her story finished, Jussodra wept and wept, and no one moved.

'What do I do?' I asked the IAS officer. 'She is very old. Will I offend her if I offer her some money?'

'It will be most welcome,' he said. 'Give her some money and tell her to arrange a *kattha*, a reading of the scriptures.'

I did so.

Photographs were then brought out, as old to me and as forgotten as the images; and it was again disturbing to my sense of place and time to handle them, to see, in the middle of a vast land where I was anchored to no familiar points and could so easily be lost, the purple stamp of the Trinidad photographer—his address so clearly pictured—still bright against the fading sepia figure, in my reawakened memory forever faded, belonging to imagination and never to reality like this.

I had come to them reluctantly. I had expected little, and I had been afraid. The ugliness was all mine.

Someone else wanted to see me. It was Ramachandra's wife and she was waiting in one of the inner rooms. I went in. A white-clad figure was bowed before me; she seized my feet, in all their Veldtschoen, and began to weep. She wept and would not let go.

'What do I do now?' I asked the IAS officer.

'Nothing. Soon someone will come in and tell her that this is no way to receive a relation, that she should be offering him food instead. It is the form.'

So it happened.

But food. Though they had overwhelmed me, my colonial prudence remained. It had prevented me emptying my pocket into Jussodra's sad, wrinkled hands. Now it reminded me of the Commissioner's advice: 'Once it's cooked, you can risk it. But never touch the water.' He, however, was of the country. So: no food, I said. I was not very well and had been put on a diet.

'Water,' Ramachandra's wife said. 'At least have water.'

The IAS officer said, 'You see that field? It is a field of peas. Ask for some of those.'

We ate a pod of peas each. I promised to come back again; the boys and men walked with us to the jeep; and I drove back along a road that had been robbed of all its terror.

In the hotel in the town that evening I wrote a letter. The day had provided such an unlikely adventure. It distorted time; again and again I came back, with wonder, to my presence in that town, in that hotel, at that hour. There had been those images, those photographs, those scraps of Trinidad English in that Indian village. The letter did not exhaust my exaltation. The act of writing released not isolated memories but a whole forgotten mood. The letter finished, I went to sleep. Then there was a song, a duet, at first part of memory, it seemed, part of that recaptured mood. But I was not dreaming; I was lucid. The music was real.

Tumhin ne mujhko prem sikhaya,
Soté hué hirdaya ko jagaya.
*Tumhin ho roop singar balam.**

It was morning. The song came from a shop across the road. It was a song of the late thirties. I had ceased to hear it years before, and until this moment I had forgotten it. I did not even know the meaning of all the words; but then I never had. It was pure mood, and in that moment between waking and sleeping it had recreated a morning in another world, a recreation of this, which continued. And walking that day in the bazaar, I saw the harmoniums, one of which had lain broken and unused, part of the irrecoverable past, in my grandmother's house, the drums, the printing-blocks, the brass vessels. Again and again I had that sense of dissolving time, that alarming but exhilarating sense of wonder at my physical self.

At the barber shop, where I stopped for a shave and begged in vain for hot water, exaltation died. I became again an impatient traveller. The sun was high; the faint morning chill had been burnt away.

I returned to the hotel and found a beggar outside my door. '*Kya chahiye*?' I asked, in my poor Hindi. 'What do you want?'

He looked up. His head was shaved, except for the top-knot; his face was skeletal; his eyes blazed. My impatience momentarily turned to alarm. Monk, I thought, monk: I had been reading *Karamazov*.

'I am Ramachandra Dube,' he said. 'I did not see you yesterday.'

I had expected someone less ingratiating, less of a physical wreck. His effort at a smile did not make his expression warmer. Spittle, white and viscous, gathered at the corners of his mouth.

---

* "You gave love meaning.
    You awoke my sleeping heart.
    My beauty is you, my lover,
        my jewels are you."

The translation is by my friend Aley Hasan of the BBC Indian Section.

There were some IAS cadets in the hotel. Three of them came to act as interpreters.

'I have spent all day looking for you,' Ramachandra said.

'Tell him I thank him,' I said. 'But there was really no need. I told them at the village I was coming back. Ask him, though, how he found me. I left no address.'

He had walked for some miles; then he had taken a train to the town; then he had gone around the secretariat, asking for the IAS officer who had taken out a man from Trinidad.

While the cadets translated, Ramachandra smiled. His face, I now saw, was not the face of a monk but of someone grossly undernourished; his eyes were bright with illness; he was painfully thin. He was carrying a large white sack. This he now humped with difficulty on to my table.

'I have brought you some rice from your grandfather's land,' he said. 'I have also brought you *parsad*, offerings, from your grandfather's shrine.'

'What do I do?' I asked the cadets. 'I don't want thirty pounds of rice.'

'He doesn't want you to take it all. You just take a few grains. Take the *parsad*, though.'

I took a few grains of the poor rice, and took the *parsad*, grubby little grey beads of hard sugar, and placed them on the table.

'I have been looking for you all day,' Ramachandra said.

'I know.'

'I walked, then I took a train, then I walked around the town and asked for you.'

'It was good of you to take all that trouble.'

'I want to see you. I want to have you in my poor hut and to give you a meal.'

'I am coming back to the village in a few days.'

'I have been looking for you all day.'

'I know.'

'I want to have you in my hut. I want to talk to you.'

'We will talk when I come to the village.'

'I want to see you there. I want to talk to you. I have important things to say to you.'

'We will talk when the time comes.'

'Good. Now I will leave you. I have been looking for you all day. I have things to say to you. I want to have you in my hut.'

'I can't keep this up,' I said to the IAS cadets. 'Tell him to go away. Thank him and so on, but tell him to go.'

One of the cadets passed on my message, involving and extending it with expressions of courtesy.

'Now I must leave you,' Ramachandra replied. 'I must get back to the village before dark.'

'Yes, I can see that you must get back before dark.'

'But how can I talk to you in the village?'

'I will bring an interpreter.'

'I want to have you in my poor hut. I have spent all day looking for you. In the village there are too many people. How can I talk to you in the village?'

'Why can't you talk to me in the village? Can't we really get him out?'

They eased him towards the door.

'I have brought you rice from your grandfather's land.'

'Thank you. It will get dark soon.'

'I want to talk to you when you come.'

'We will talk.'

The door was closed. The cadets went away. I lay down on the bed below the fan. Then I had a shower. I was towelling myself when I heard a scratching on the barred window.

It was Ramachandra, in the verandah, attempting a smile. I summoned no interpreters. I needed none to understand what he was saying.

'I cannot talk in the village. There are too many people.'

'We will talk in the village,' I said in English. 'Now go home. You travel too much.' By signs I persuaded him to edge away from the window. Quickly, then, I drew the curtains.

Some days passed before I decided to go back to the village. The journey began badly. There was some trouble about transport and it was not until the middle of the afternoon that we were able to leave. Our progress was slow. It was market day at the junction settlement and the road was dangerous with carts, now occupying the right-hand lane, now changing without warning to the left, their manoeuvres obscured by clouds of dust. Dust was thick and constant; it obliterated trees, fields, villages. There were traffic jams, the carts inextricably snarled, the drivers then as passive as their bullocks.

At the junction it was simple chaos. I breathed dust. There was dust in my hair, dust down my shirt, dust, nauseatingly, on my fingernails. We halted and waited for the traffic to clear. Then our driver disappeared, taking the ignition key. It was useless to look for him: that would only have meant groping about in the dust. We sat in the jeep and occasionally sounded the horn. Half an hour later the driver returned. His eyelashes, moustache and oiled hair were blond with dust, but his smile was wet and triumphant: he had managed to buy some vegetables. It was late afternoon when we got on to the embankment; and the sun was setting, converting the dust into clouds of pure gold, so that each person walked in a golden aura, when we arrived at the village. No terror attached to the land now, no surprise. I felt I knew it well. Yet some anxiety remained: the village held Ramachandra.

He was waiting for me. He was without the cloak he had worn to the hotel. He wore only a dhoti and sacred thread, and I could scarcely bear to look at his emaciated, brittle body. As soon as he saw me he held himself in an attitude of ecstatic awe: shaved shining head thrown back, eyes staring, foam-flecked mouth resolutely closed, both sticks of arms raised. We already had an audience, and he was demonstrating his possession of me. It was seconds before he relaxed.

'He says God has sent you to him,' my IAS friend said.

'We'll see.'

The IAS man converted this into a formal greeting.

'Would you like something to eat in his poor hut?'

'No.'

'You must at least have some water.'

'I am not thirsty.'

'You are rejecting his hospitality because he is a poor man.'

'He can take it that way.'

'A mouthful of food.'

'Tell him it is late. Tell him you have to investigate that embezzlement of the National Defence Fund you were telling me about.'

'He says God has sent you to him today.'

'I don't think I can keep this up much longer. Ask him what he wanted to see me about.'

'He says he won't tell you until you eat something in his poor hut.'

'Tell him goodbye.'

'He believes you might appreciate a little privacy.'

He led us through his hut into a small paved courtyard, where his wife, she who had held on to my Veldtschoen and wept, squatted in one corner, her head decorously covered, and made a pretence of scouring some brass vessels

Ramachandra paced up and down. Then: wouldn't I eat?

The IAS man interpreted my silence.

It was really quite remarkable, Ramachandra said, that I had come to the village just at that time. He was, as it happened, in a little trouble. He was thinking of starting a little piece of litigation, but the litigation he had just concluded had cost him two hundred rupees and he was short of cash

'But that solves his problems. He can simply forget the new litigation.'

'How can he forget it? This new litigation concerns you.'

'Me?'

'It is about your grandfather's land, the land that produced the rice he gave you. That is why God sent you here. Your grandfather's land is now only nineteen acres, and some of that will be lost if he can't get this new litigation started. If that happens, who will look after your grandfather's shrines?'

I urged Ramachandra to forget litigation and the shrines and to concentrate on the nineteen acres. That was a lot of land, nineteen acres more than I had, and he could get much help from the government He knew, he knew, he said indulgently. But his body—he turned his long bony back to me, and the movement was not without pride—was wasted; he devoted himself to religious austerities; he spent four hours a day looking after the shrines. And there was this litigation he wanted to get started. Besides, what could be got out of nineteen acres?

Our discussion remained circular. The IAS man didn't help; he softened all my sharpness into courtesy. Outright refusal didn't release me: it only enabled Ramachandra to start afresh. Release would come only when I left. And this I at last did, suddenly, followed out to the grove by many men and all the boys of the village.

Ramachandra kept up with me, smiling, bidding me farewell, proclaiming his possession of me till the last. One man, clearly his rival, sturdier, handsomer, more dignified, presented me with a letter and withdrew; the ink on the envelope was still wet. A boy ran out to the jeep, tucking his shirt into his trousers, and asked for a lift into the town. While Ramachandra had been outlining his plans for litigation, while the letter was being written, this boy had hurriedly bathed, dressed and prepared his bundle: his clothes were fresh, his hair still wet. My visit had thrown the brahmins into a frenzy of activity. Too much had been assumed; I felt overwhelmed; I wished to extricate myself at once.

'Shall we take him on?' the IAS man asked, nodding towards the boy.

'No. Let the idler walk.'

We drove off. I did not wave. The headlamps of the jeep shot two separate beams into the day's slowly settling dust which, made turbulent again by our passage, blotted out the scattered lights of the village.

So it ended, in futility and impatience, a gratuitous act of cruelty, self-reproach and flight.

Flight

To be packed, after a year's journey, before dinner; to have dinner; to be at the airline office at ten, to see the decorative little fountain failed, the wing-shaped counter empty, the tiled turquoise basin of the fountain empty and wetly littered, the lights dim, the glossy magazines disarrayed and disregarded, the Punjabi emigrants sitting disconsolately with their bundles in a corner near the weighing machine; to be at the airport at eleven for an aircraft that leaves at midnight; and then to wait until after three in the morning, intermittently experiencing the horrors of an Indian public lavatory, is to know anxiety, exasperation and a creeping stupor. There comes a point at which the night is written off, and one waits for morning. The minutes lengthen; last night recedes far beyond last night. Lucidity grows intense but blinkered. The actions of minutes before are dim and isolated, and a cause of muted wonder when remembered. So even at the airport India faded; so during these hours its reality was wiped away, until more than space and time lay between it and me.

Paper fell into my lap in the aircraft. Long blond hair and a pair of big blue eyes appeared above the seat in front of me, and tiny feet pattered against the small of my back. 'Children!' cried the American next to me, awakening from middle-aged, safety-belted sleep. 'Where do they take on all these children? Why are all these children *travelling*? What's my crazy luck that every time I go to sleep on a plane and wake up I see children? Shall I tell you a funny thing a friend of mine said to a child on a plane? He said, "Sonny, why don't you go outside and play?" Little girl, why don't you take your pretty paper and

278

go outside and play?' Eyes and hair sank below the dark blue
seat. 'That child behind me is going to get hurt. The little
bastard is kicking my kidneys in. Sir! Madam! Will you please
control your child? *It* . . . is . . . annoying my *wife*.' She, the
wife, lay relaxed beside him, her skirt riding up above a middle-
aged slackly-stockinged knee. There was a smile on her face;
she was asleep.

No sleep for me. Only a continuing stupor, heightened by
the roar of the engines. I made frequent trips to the lavatory
to refresh myself with the airline's eau-de-cologne. The
Punjabis at the rear were wakeful, in a ripe smell: one or two
had already been sick on the blue carpet. Lights were low. The
night was long. We were flying against time, into a receding
morning. Yet light was coming; and when at daybreak we
reached Beirut it was like arriving, after a magical journey, with
all its attendant torment, in a fresh, glittering world. Rain had
fallen; the tarmac was glazed and cool. Beyond it was a city
which one knew to be a city, full of men as whole as these who,
in airport dungarees, now wheeled gangways and drove up in
electric lorries to unload luggage: labourers, menials, yet
arrogant in their gait, their big bodies and their skills. India
was part of the night: a dead world, a long journey.

Rome, the airport, morning still. The Boeings and Caravelles
lying this way and that, like toys. And within the airport
building a uniformed girl paced up and down the concourse
She wore a jockey-cap hat, to me a new fashion; she wore
boots, also new to me. She was extravagantly made up: she
required to be noticed. How could I explain, how could I
admit as reasonable, even to myself, my distaste, my sense of
the insubstantiality and wrongness of the new world to which
I had been so swiftly transported. This life confirmed that other
death; yet that death rendered this fraudulent.

In the late afternoon I was in Madrid, most elegant of cities.
Here I was to spend two or three days. I had been last in this
city as a student, ten years before. Here I might have taken up
my old life. I was a tourist, free, with money. But a whole
experience had just occurred; India had ended only twenty-four
hours before. It was a journey that ought not to have been

made; it had broken my life in two. 'Write me as soon as you get to Europe,' an Indian friend had said. 'I want your freshest impressions.' I forget now what I wrote. It was violent and incoherent; but, like everything I wrote about India, it exorcised nothing.

In my last week in Delhi I had spent some time in the cloth shops, and I had arrived in Madrid with a jacket-length of material in an untied brown parcel printed with Hindi characters. This was the gift of an architect I had known for a short time. Two or three days after we met he had made a declaration of his affection and loyalty, and I had reciprocated. This was part of the sweetness of India; it went with everything else. He had driven me to the airport and had put up with my outbursts at news of the aircraft's delay. We had coffee; then, before he left, he gave me the parcel. 'Promise me you will have it stitched into a jacket as soon as you get to Europe,' he said.

I did so now; and above all the confused impressions of a year, then, was this fresh memory of a friend and his gift of Indian cloth.

Some days later in London, facing as for the first time a culture whose point, going by the advertisements and shop-windows, appeared to be homemaking, the creation of separate warm cells; walking down streets of such cells past gardens left derelict by the hard winter and trying, in vain, to summon up a positive response to this city where I had lived and worked; facing my own emptiness, my feeling of being physically lost, I had a dream.

An oblong of stiff new cloth lay before me, and I had the knowledge that if only out of this I could cut a smaller oblong of specific measurements, a specific section of this cloth, then the cloth would begin to unravel of itself, and the unravelling would spread from the cloth to the table to the house to all matter, *until the whole trick was undone*. Those were the words that were with me as I flattened the cloth and studied it for the clues which I knew existed, which I desired above everything else to find, but which I knew I never would.

The world is illusion, the Hindus say. We talk of despair,

but true despair lies too deep for formulation. It was only now, as my experience of India defined itself more properly against my own homelessness, that I saw how close in the past year I had been to the total Indian negation, how much it had become the basis of thought and feeling. And already, with this awareness, in a world where illusion could only be a concept and not something felt in the bones, it was slipping away from me. I felt it as something true which I could never adequately express and never seize again.

February 1962—*February* 1964

VINTAGE BELLES—LETTRES

VINTAGE CRITICISM: LITERATURE, MUSIC, AND ART